Bizarre Ships of the Nineteenth Century

THE HUTCHINSON LIBRARY OF SHIPS AND SHIPPING

General Editor: A. Silverleaf
National Physical Laboratory,
Teddington, England

ALREADY PUBLISHED
Basic Naval Architecture   K. C. Barnaby
Some Ship Disasters and their Causes   K. C. Barnaby
Design of Marine Screw Propellers   T. P. O'Brien
Merchant Ship Design   R. Munro-Smith
Merchant Ships and Shipping   R. Munro-Smith
Screw Tug Design   J. B. Caldwell and Jeffrey N. Wood
Bizarre Ships of the Nineteenth Century   John Guthrie

IN PREPARATION
Marine Propeller Design Manual   T. P. O'Brien

John Guthrie

Bizarre Ships
of the
Nineteenth Century

 Hutchinson Scientific and Technical

HUTCHINSON & CO (Publishers) LTD
178–202 Great Portland Street, London W1
London Melbourne Sydney Auckland
Bombay Toronto Johannesburg New York
First published 1970

This book, designed by Yvonne Dedman,
has been set in Garamond, printed in Great Britain
on cartridge paper by Anchor Press, and
bound by Wm. Brendon, both of Tiptree, Essex

09 100010 6

Contents

Illustrations

N.M.M. National Maritime Museum
I.L.N. Illustrated London News
A. & N. Gazette Army & Navy Gazette
R.I.N.A. Royal Institution Naval Architects
H.L. Hawthorn, Leslie & Co. Ltd.
M.d.M. Museu da Marinha

Acknowledgements

A book of this nature cannot be written without first hand-references, and these are amply provided by the contemporary periodicals, both technical and lay, also by the proceedings of learned institutions. I am therefore deeply grateful to the Editors of *The Engineer*, *Engineering* and the *Illustrated London News*, and to the Secretary of the Royal Institution of Naval Architects, for permission to use material from their magazines and transactions published in the last century. I am also indebted to the National Maritime Museum, Greenwich, for many of the illustrations, and to Messrs. Hawthorn Leslie (Shipbuilders) Ltd., and The Doxford and Sunderland Shipbuilding and Engineering Co. Ltd., for their help and permission to use the plates for *Calais Douvres* and *Sagamore* respectively.

I would like to acknowledge the kindness of the director of the Museu da Marinha, Lisbon, for supplying photographs of the Portuguese inshore craft, also of the Controller of H.M. Stationery Office for his permission to use sketches from the Patent Specification for an articulated ship.

Mr R. R. Le Maistre, of South Australia, has been very generous with his help in connection with the Australian vessels and the photograph of *Gemini*.

Finally, I am indebted to many of my friends and colleagues for their help in either producing material for the book or drawing my attention to peculiar-looking vessels over the last thirty years and who are far too numerous to name but who are now thanked collectively.

John Guthrie

Editor's note

This series of books is primarily intended to be of interest to those professionally concerned with the design, construction and operation of ships and other marine vehicles. Many remarkable changes are now taking place in the size, shape, speed and capability of conventional ships of all types, while hovercraft, hydrofoil ships and other unusual vessels are beginning to have a striking effect on the maritime scene. Technical staff and management increasingly need up-to-date design data and specialist information on a wide range of topics, and it is hoped that most books in the series will be of direct value to them, and to many students at universities and technical colleges.

In addition to specialist monographs and student textbooks, the series also includes books having a broad appeal to all those who want to know more about the fascinating variety of craft which can be seen in ports, on rivers, and at sea: this book is one of that group. Its principal purpose is to remind us of some of the odd and highly unorthodox vessels which have played a minor but not inglorious role in the development of the modern ship. This chapter of nautical history is easily overlooked and often decried, but many of the freak ships built a century ago taught a technical lesson which had to be learnt the hard way and which is not always fully understood even to-day. Quite apart from its professional value, this story of the mostly unsuccessful, but always brave, attempts of bold inventors and enthusiastic cranks has a personal appeal which is difficult to resist. It is written simply and directly by a ship surveyor with a lifelong experience of all types of craft and an enduring passion for the telling details which are essential to a real understanding of the way in which ships, large or small, successes or failures, matter to the men who design and build them and then risk their lives to test their belief in something different.

Introduction

Modern naval architecture, the scientific approach to ship design, is little more than a hundred years old. It came into being with the iron steamers and developed from the intuitive craft of wooden ship design, where in most cases the designer was the builder, sometimes the owner, and occasionally the captain. Ship design in the days of wooden sailing ships was concerned not only with the economics of maximum carrying capacity with a minimum crew; it was also conditioned by the inherent weakness of wooden joints in a very highly stressed structure and by the limits set by Nature herself. After all, a lot of the timbers used in a ship's framework were sawn 'as grown' from the tree, and even to this day in the smaller Mediterranean boatyards the size and tonnage of a boat will depend entirely on the number and size of naturally grown timbers available at the time.

The design of wooden sailing ships had changed but little in the thousand years before the mid-nineteenth century. The vessels were very much bigger, of course, much more sophisticated, and they could sail around the world with a reasonable certainty of returning intact to their home port; but basically they were similar, just as a pre-Conquest ox cart was in principle similar to a stage coach. The arrival of the steamboat on the scene changed the whole concept of ship design, just as the modern automobile changed the pattern of road transport.

The steamship was essentially a product of the eighteen hundreds, and by the end of the century it had achieved a respectable middle age. During its adolescence, however, the central idea of the steam-propelled ship developed in many different directions. Before finally coalescing into the type of steamer with which we are all familiar it left in its wake a vast number of bizarre vessels of which very little is known—the world does not admire failures, and the Press has no time for a wonder after the ninth day. A more recent parallel can be drawn with the marine diesel engine in the nineteen twenties, when some fearful and wonderful engines were produced, to the bewilderment of that long-suffering person the marine engineer, engines in which, as one of them caustically remarked, 'everything moved except the propeller'.

In the early period of the steamboat the engine and boiler were simply installed in a normal wooden sailing vessel, but after a while it was realised that a special type of ship might be needed. While this new design was being worked out the use of iron for the ship's framework, and later for her entire structure, completely revolutionised the art of shipbuilding; and it is at this point that the naval architect appeared on the scene and took over responsibility for ship design, not only in the industry itself but in the various governing bodies which ensured safety and efficiency for cargo and crew. The naval architect crystallised the experience of centuries of shipbuilders into a scientific study; he evolved a type of iron ship suitable first for paddle propulsion, subsequently for screws, and which to us has become the conventional ship. Hence, to ship designers, builders, owners and sailors alike there is one basic type of ship only and that is the conventional one, the ship we all know and recognise.

This view, however, was not necessarily accepted by the laity. There were plenty of people about who did not believe in the old professional dictum that if you want someone who knows more about sailing than a sailor, find another sailor. There were still many who could not realise that in any art or craft which has freely developed over the centuries there is an instinct which guides the various craftsmen to produce the optimum design. During the nineteenth century, when the steamboat was slowly moving towards a set pattern, there was a long succession of intelligent laymen, experimenters and enthusiastic cranks who were quite happy to spend a fortune, sometimes their own but preferably somebody else's, in attempting to find a better, cheaper, simpler or just a different type of ship from the orthodox, accepted type. Most of them failed, but not all, and the science of naval architecture has benefited considerably from their efforts, both successes and failures.

Nautical history has been very reticent about these unorthodox ships, and very little mention of them is ever made in the host of books written about ships and shipping matters. Their designers, having strutted across the stage for one brief moment of glory, return to obscurity; their builders, apprehensive of their reputations, prefer to avoid the limelight; and their owners, having lost a fortune, see no point in drawing the public's attention to the fact.

Most of the freak ships built in the nineteenth century are discussed in the following chapters, most types that is, not every individual freak, as this would be an impossible task. After all, that which might appear odd in a ship to one person could be perfectly natural to another; it is difficult to draw a line anywhere and say—everything beyond this line is a freak. Such ships as stern trawlers, bucket dredgers, hopper barges, oil rigs, heavy lift craft, etc., may look pure freaks to a layman yet be standard type utility vessels to the sailor. It is difficult to define what is bizarre; there are no terms of reference.

Possibly the best definition is the one which simply states that a bizarre vessel looks just as freakish to the professional shipbuilder as to the man in the street.

These odd ships fall naturally into a number of genera: some of them, the successful ones, expanded into large fleets (American River Steamers and Monitors) while others remained uniquely *sui generis*. All the vessels described were built as full-scale commercial ventures, duly registered with the authorities, and, with the exception of the *Cleopatra* and the submarines, they all had the same underlying idea or common denominator: stability.

An interest in odd-looking ships is not peculiar to the humble sailor or shipbuilder. It can be found in most exalted circles, and both Henry VIII and Charles II were concerned in developing shipbuilding along extreme lines. But the honours must surely go to a ruler of antiquity, Ptolemy Philopator, who was indirectly far more important to posterity than either Henry or Charles inasmuch as his son Ptolemy Epiphanes recorded his accession to the throne of Egypt on the Rosetta Stone and thus bequeathed the key to 3,000 years of pre-history. As a result we know that Philopator not only collected existing freak ships; he is credited with ordering other peculiar ships built to his own design, being in the fortunate position of getting them financed by the local peasantry!

Finally, although my concern is to describe and illustrate the odd ships which came into being in the middle of the nineteenth century, I just cannot ignore the people who designed and tested them; the men who were prepared to risk reputation, fortune and even life itself for an idea. These men lived in a spacious age, that Golden Age of engineers brought about by the Industrial Revolution early in the century. Every inventor was given a hearing, and the credulity of financiers had to be seen to be believed. There was never any suggestion of a pilot scheme to try out an experiment on the cheap. Having tested a basic idea in the bathtub and found it workable the inventor immediately rushed into building a full-scale vessel at enormous expense, complete with gilt, mirrors and all the other Victorian trappings.

These same men, however, also had the courage of their convictions, and took hideous risks to prove their cases. This was especially so with the designers and crews of the earlier (and not so early) submarines, 'a type of ship which brings about the disasters of war in a time of peace'.

These men allowed themselves to be boxed up inside a tank and submerged in deep water, confident in their ability to extricate themselves somehow,

B

sometime, by their own resources, before the supply of air ran out—a sort of Houdini act by untrained men.

So much then for the nineteenth century freak ships. But the picture is somewhat different when we consider the Portuguese *Saveiro* and *Meia Lua*; these vessel types are still in existence and their crews go down to the sea in them, as they did hundreds of years ago, daily risking their lives, not for glory or an ideal but simply to earn their bread and butter, their *pão para a bôca*. These men are the true heroes of the sea.

I   American river steamers

With the possible exception of the China Clippers, no other type of ship has made such an impact on the public as the Western River steamboat in the mid-nineteenth century. Through stage, screen and story it became known as the symbol of American plantation culture, of glamour in the deep South, of adventure in the West, and of the wild and reckless life of the Big River itself, with as background music the delightful Indian names of the states through which it sailed—Mississippi, Arkansas, Kentucky, Tennessee. Yet, while many laymen of the time could give a very fair description of a Clipper Ship and of her sails and rigging, and even understand the various sailing terms, how many nowadays could describe an American River Steamer of the 1850's or interpret such orders as: 'Ease the hog chains', 'Starboard the ballast' or 'Start the doctor'?

Now if we accept the narrow dictionary definition of a freak as 'a monstrosity of any species' then obviously these river steamers were not freaks; they formed a whole species on their own, and one could hardly expect them to figure on our list of freak ships on the score of glamour alone. However they had two peculiarities which place them among the unorthodox ships of their age: their 'wooden' engines and their exoskeletal structure.

In the 1850's Britain had plenty of iron and knew how to use it in ships and engines. The marine steam engine was still only a few decades old and its design had not yet crystallised. It was still something of a mystery even to its builders, and while they recognised the strength of cast and wrought iron they believed in being sure rather than sorry. Consequently even low power engines were huge, ponderous affairs placed deep down on the vessel's keelson and seldom seen by the passengers. By contrast the Americans had very little iron, and any obtainable was most expensive. Their staple building material was timber and they certainly knew how to use that. Wood was used for engine frames and bedplates, for cylinder entablatures, paddle-shaft bearing frames, guide supports and even for the connecting rod itself. The engines were placed on the main working deck in full view of the passengers and crew with, as far as one can ascertain, precious little regard for safety of life or limb.

Most of the American rivers were, and are, extremely wide and shallow, especially in summer, and the steamboats were accordingly built for very shallow draught, not only to negotiate the shoals but also to come alongside the landing stages. These landing stages, often mere planks on to the river bank, offered no provision for loading cargo other than normal labour. And so were determined the main characteristics of the hull: very shallow draught, and low working deck to enable cargo to be wheeled onboard and stowed upon the deck or placed in the shallow hold by hand without the use of a crane or derrick.

When designing a ship the naval architect considers the hull as a box beam, and the strength of a beam is a function of its width and of the square of its depth. In a conventional steel ship with a reasonable depth of hold the strongest single member is the shipside plating and framework, and it is precisely this part which varies as the square of the depth: the deeper the ship, so very much the stronger. But, with her shallow, wooden hull, the American River Steamer had very little inherent strength and the designers had to think up special systems of external strengthening for different types of steamers; these will be described under their relevant headings.

There were two distinctive types of river steamboats in the U.S.A. in the nineteenth century, the Eastern and the Western. Both were unique in their own style, and both lingered on into the twentieth century.

Eastern River steamboats

These vessels plied on the Hudson between New York and Albany, which in those days was connected by rail and canal with Canada, the Great Lakes and the great North-West. This service, incidentally, was originated by Robert Fulton with his *Clermont* in 1807, the first successful paddle steamer built in the American continent. Another line ran between New York and the ports in Long Island Sound, which in turn were connected by rail with the New England States.

The Hudson, though normally a deep water river, was very shallow near Albany, with a limiting draught of eight feet. On the Long Island Sound run, although the steamers were actually at sea, the water was extremely shallow in parts and limited the draught to nine feet. The same type of vessel covered both services: up to 350 feet long, built with very fine lines, several passenger decks high and with accommodation in two classes to feed and sleep some 1,000 people on the overnight passage. It was on a scale unknown in England at that time.

The hull was of necessity very lightly built, with one long hold extending from end to end, unobstructed by bulkheads, boilers or cargo. This hold was the second class saloon-cum-dormitory and slept 500 passengers in three tiers of bunks around the shipsides at three dollars a head. In this saloon notices were prominently displayed requesting gentlemen to refrain from turning in with their boots on!

The main deck extended on each side well beyond the moulded breadth, the overhang being termed the guards; the superstructure was built up from the overall width across the guards, thus giving an extremely broad deck on a comparatively narrow hull. The guards were supported by a row of struts extending up from the shipsides above the waterline, and in the Long Island Sound vessels these struts were planked over to offer less resistance to the seas.

This main deck was the working deck. Here the engines were worked, the passengers embarked and bought their tickets, and the cargo was loaded and stowed at the vessel's ends. The boilers were installed on the guards, outside of the line of the hull, with the fuel stacked all round, as being most conveniently placed for removal when they were worn out. In these crack ferry boats boilers were not made to be repaired: they were simply lifted off and replaced after four or five years life.

Above this main working deck, and reached by the main staircase, was the passenger deck, just as wide as the main deck and supported on pillars. The central feature of this deck was the main saloon, some 250 feet long, with double-berth passenger cabins at the sides and a promenade deck all round. Another deck on top of this carried still more passenger cabins, with the pilot house at the forward end.

These ships were propelled by huge side paddles up to 40 feet in diameter driven by a single cylinder beam engine, the characteristic feature here being the lozenge-shaped walking beam, placed high above the uppermost cabins, which see-sawed to the beat of the gigantic 14-foot stroke piston. The whole of this massive machinery was supported on a triangular wooden trestle resting on the vessel's keelsons. This trestle supported the wrought iron walking beam trunnions on its apex and the main paddle shaft about half-way down the after leg, with the vertical steam cylinder and its jet condenser sitting on the keelson at its forward foot.

Now timber, properly applied, makes a most effective support but a poor tie, and as an engine frame has to do work all round the circle it must be prepared to withstand both push and pull. Wood alone would tear itself apart and the American designers neatly solved the problem by fitting an iron stay to each wooden strut, the stay having a bottle or stretching screw to allow it to be tightened or eased to compensate for wear in the bearings or for uneven working of the shaft.

A ship as described above, consisting of a very narrow, shallow hull, with several layers of decks supported only on a series of pillars—with, moreover, heavy concentrated loads in the form of engine, paddle bearings, boilers, etc., situated in extremely awkward positions—would be in a very stressed condition even at rest in still water. Sailing at fifteen knots she would probably fall apart like a house of cards. Here again the American genius worked out the answer in the form of external stiffening by means of the hogframe for general strength, and local stiffening with masts and guys.

The hogframe consisted of an arched truss extending on each side for almost the full length of the vessel. Vertical posts some 15 inches square

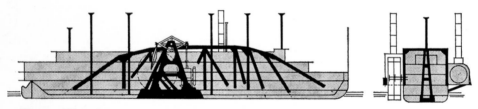

1 Eastern River boat

were built up from the shipsides and connected at their tops by horizontal and diagonal beams reaching down to the forward and after ends. The hogframes stretched well above the vessel's outline and were connected to each other across the accommodation.

This massive wooden framework acted as the arch to the deck of a bridge, and served as an external skeleton to bind the ship together.

These vessels also had several masts, some stepped on the centre keelson, some on the side keelsons. The masts carried neither sails, rigging nor spars but served merely to distribute the load by keeping down those parts with excessive buoyancy and lifting others carrying excessive weight, such as engine, boilers, paddle shaft bearings, bow and stern, etc.

Each mast carried a pair, or several pairs, of guys. These were iron rods fitted with stretching screws, and they extended to such parts of the ship as were deemed by the designer to require extra support. The exact amount of support was decided by the captain, whose duties covered a wider field in those days.

Because of their immense superstructures on narrow, shallow hulls, their high centres of gravity due to their immensely tall engines and their heavy hogframes, these vessels were not very stable, and the mate's principal duty on watch was to stand with a gang of sailors by a heavy ballast box, which was run over to either side of the vessel when steaming at speed round a sharp bend in the river.

Now let us see what an English passenger had to say about one of these steamboats:

With black funnels and painted pure white, she rose like an iceberg on the water. On either side of the entrance were broad staircases descending to an immense lower cabin, along the sides of which were more than 500 berths. The supper tables were set with a degree of splendour for which an English traveller would be altogether unprepared. Nearly amidships, on the main deck, a grand staircase sweeping both to right and left, conducted to the great saloon nearly 300 feet in length, several yards in width and having an upper gallery with a second storey of staterooms, a lofty arched ceiling glazed with ground and coloured glass and supported by richly carved columns covering the whole.

And all this on a river steamer!

A similar type of strengthening was used in the British-built paddle steamers sailing on the lower reaches of the Indus. These vessels were up to 370 feet in length and 46 feet beam, yet drew only two feet of water. Their stiffening consisted of four longitudinal arched hogframes, two in way of the ship's sides and two on the outboard members of the paddle sponsons. These frames were joined together at intervals by transverse arched frames, and, as will be seen from the deckplan, the hogframe structure was in effect an inverted ship's framework fitted above the deck.

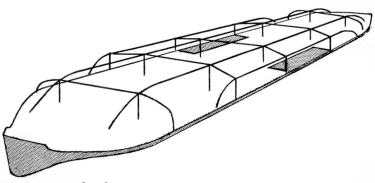

2 Indus River steamer framing

Western River steamboats

While the Eastern River steamboat was essentially a well defined type of high speed passenger ferry on a limited run the Western River steamer was of a type varying considerably in shape, though adhering to a common general design. This vessel was, and still is, peculiar to the Mississippi-Missouri-Arkansas-Ohio-Red River basin extending from Pennsylvania in the east and Montana in the west down to the Gulf, draining half the total area of present-day U.S.A. In the 1850's there were few roads and fewer railways in the Middle West, and all passenger and goods traffic was by river.

The rivers were usually broad and shallow, with occasional rapids, many sandbanks, and a strong tendency to burst their banks and change their course with little warning.

In addition to these 'normal' navigational hazards, there were others much more dangerous and which no amount of caution could guard against: trees falling into the water through washing away of the banks. These impediments assumed such importance with the river people that they were given names in accordance with their position in the water. Thus, apart from the danger of a floating tree becoming entangled in the paddle wheels, a waterlogged tree could sink and become lodged in the river bottom in an upright position, with the branches breaking the surface. This was called a 'Planter'. A 'Sawyer' was a floating tree entangled by its roots and alternately raised and depressed by the force of the current; it usually gave warning of its presence. But the most dangerous of all, the dreaded 'Snag', was a tree stump firmly embedded in the mud at an angle and below the surface. It could rip the bottom out of a steamer's wooden hull in seconds, and no care on the part of the pilot could prevent this disaster. For this reason lavish expenditure on the construction of the vessels would have been a folly, and accordingly, with the exception of the saloon and the first class passenger accommodation, they were cheap and flimsy structures with light-weight high-pressure engines, lasting little more than five years.

The earliest navigation on these rivers consisted of one-way traffic timber cargo rafts, which were broken up and sold with the cargo, the crew returning home on foot. Subsequently the river keelboats came into use for both passenger and cargo, floating down on the current and being poled back upstream. With the advent of the steam engine the steamboat gradually took over, and, with the increase in passenger demand due to the opening of the Middle West, the number and the size of the steamers had to increase. However the increase in size as far as the hull was concerned was in two dimensions only, length and breadth, as the draught had to remain at a minimum. Hence the specialised type of river steamer in these waters: an evolution rather than a revolution.

The draught was measured in inches rather than in feet, and one side-wheeler, the *Daisy*, some 100 feet long, drew only 16 inches of water. In fact some old steamboat skippers used to boast that they could float their vessels over a heavy dew.

These steamers ranged from the crack passenger side-wheel steamers on the main rivers, through general purpose or tramp steamers—either side- or sternwheelers—on the upper reaches, to the modest, medium-sized sternwheelers on the tributaries, where side paddles were too vulnerable. They also included the showboats, floating theatres towed from landing stage to landing stage, which served the entertainment-starved plantation hands in much the same fashion as our present-day travelling circus.

The steamboats had various shapes but they were all built on the same basic principles, with an apparent nakedness in the display of their engines and boilers, and their open cargo spaces. The earlier boats were functional and rather severe in line, but after the Civil War they broke out in a rash of elaborate carving and fretwork, the gingerbread around the accommodation which inevitably gave rise to the expression 'Steamboat Gothic'.

The hull was generally of very blunt form, with little depth of hold and, as in the Eastern steamboat, with the main deck extending well beyond the moulded beam to form the guards. These guards were supported by hog braces, iron rods with stretching screws, extending from one side to the other over the top of the upper deck pillars. Here again this main deck was the working deck upon which were fitted the engine(s) and boilers, all the cargo, fuel and stores. The upper deck, supported on wooden pillars, stood some 20 feet above the main deck and thus formed a large warehouse open at the sides, front and back, a sort of Dutch barn in fact. Above the upper deck, another deck of one-inch planks on $5'' \, 1''$ beams, contained the main saloon and the passenger cabins. The deck was reached by a double winding staircase right in the bows of the ship. A further deck, sometimes more than one, was situated above this with the pilot house placed right on top of the accommodation.

As the pilot could not see the vessel's stem from the wheelhouse, and therefore would not be able to gauge the amount of helm required for turning, a tall post with a coloured ball was fitted to the stem post, forming an extension of the latter and rising above the level of the accommodation deck.

The magnificence of the Mississippi steamer saloons was far famed, and they formed a strange contrast to the rest of the ship. They were unbroken by columns, tie rods or engine frames, as in the Eastern steamers, and there was very little colour used in their decoration, except in the carpets and furniture, the panelling being mainly white. From each beam fretwork and open latticework hung down, and the constant repetition of this

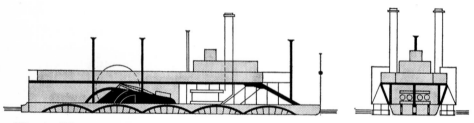

3 Western River steamer

carving, illuminated by coloured light from the painted glass skylights on each side, in a saloon over 200 feet long, produced a most agreeable effect of light and shade.

The paddle wheels were usually placed slightly aft of midships, each wheel about 30 to 35 feet diameter being driven by its own single-cylinder diagonal engine. The engine was mounted on a wooden frame attached to the side keelsons, which supported the cylinder, guides and paddle-shaft bearings. Even the connecting rod, the 'pitman', was made of timber, reinforced by iron rods, and with the bearing blocks held by iron strapheads.

These engines worked at high pressure (120 lb. sq. in.) for the sake of lightness, and used a standard type of locomotive boiler, the number of boilers being in proportion to the power of the engines. They were fed by a general service pump called the 'doctor' which acted as feed pump, fire pump or bilge pump as the occasion required.

The hull was strengthened by deep centre and side keelsons, but as these could not extend above the main deck additional strength was supplied by the hog chains, the counterpart of the hogframe, but in reverse. A series of queen posts were set up along the ship's sides, and iron rods were extended from forward to aft along the tops of these posts, with stretching screws at intervals; these 'chains' prevented the hull from hogging, i.e. bending upwards in the middle when loaded.

A good captain knew how to handle his hog chains, and they used to be hardened up or eased, as experience dictated, when the vessel was sailing at speed, to allow her to 'wring and twist' and so obtain another half knot. Minor leakage was of no account.

Some of these vessels also had masts and guys, as in the Eastern River steamers, though possibly not to such a great extent as they were placed mainly at the ends.

The Western River steamboats were exceedingly vulnerable to fire, explosion and snagging, and their losses for 1859 and 1860 are tabulated below. The figures have no statistical significance as we do not know how many ships were in service during these years.

	1859	*1860*
Destroyed by snags	44	44
Destroyed by boiler explosion	8	19
Destroyed by fire	52	31
Destroyed by other causes	44	26
TOTAL	148	120

We can understand the sinkings due to snags and other causes (collision, stranding, ice, engine breakdown or plain old age) but the very high percentage of losses due to boiler explosion and fire requires some explanation.

As already mentioned these engines and boilers were worked at pressures of up to 120 pounds per square inch when we in Britain were still cautiously feeling our way with boilers built to work at 20 lb. We designed with a factor of safety of 4 or 5, i.e. we utilised only a quarter or a fifth of the ultimate strength of the material, while the Americans, with their reckless Frontier philosophy of living dangerously, pushed their materials to the utmost.

These small, rapid-steaming boilers burnt wood, which requires a large grate area for complete combustion; as these conditions were not obtainable in the locomotive boilers combustion was either incomplete in the form of dense black smoke, or completed in the smoke stacks, producing sparks, flames or glowing embers. The close proximity of all the sun-dried fretwork on the hurrican deck did the rest.

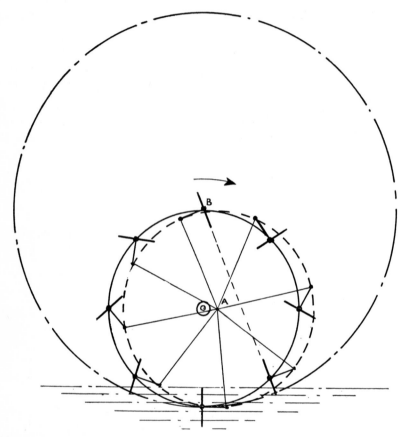

4 Paddle wheel with feathering floats

In both Eastern and Western River side-wheelers it was universal practice to use long-stroke, slow-running steam engines driving large diameter paddle wheels with fixed wooden floats, whereas in Britain small, high speed iron wheels with iron feathering floats were invariably fitted as being much more efficient. In relatively smooth water, such as large rivers, these smaller wheels were just as efficient as screw propellers, and one might wonder why American designers, who in the 1860's led the world in naval architecture, persisted in fitting those big radial wheels with their fixed floats.

A glance at the feathering paddle wheels in Figure 4 will show that each iron feathered float is pivoted about the wheel rim and has a short lever on its back connected by a rod to a disc revolving on a pin fitted to the paddle sponson at A. This disc is situated some 12 inches forward of the paddle-shaft centre, and by reason of this eccentricity the floats are made to feather into and out of the water, i.e. their position in the water is more vertical and the energy of the wheel is expended in pushing the water aft rather than splashing it about inside the paddle box. It will be seen from the position of the feathering float about to enter the water that it corresponds to the position of a fixed float on a radial wheel exactly twice the diameter, with its centre at B. In short, by fitting feathering floats it is possible to fit a very much smaller, faster wheel with lighter, cheaper engines.

The Americans recognised this, of course, but in their rivers, with so many navigational hazards, their wheels were extremely vulnerable. They could foul the bank when approaching the landing, hit a snag, entangle tree branches in their wheels or bump into another vessel while man-œuvring. With fixed wooden floats a repair could be carried out by the crew in a couple of hours; with iron feathering floats it took a dockyard to repair them, and there were very few dockyards available on the rivers.

Most people picture the Mississippi steamboat as a sternwheeler, but this was true only of the vessels plying in the smaller rivers and in narrow channels where side wheels and wide sponsons would be an encumbrance. The stern wheel was excellent for towing as it gave a good grip of the water with its wide floats. However, in this type of steamer with very full form, it had one great disadvantage if fitted too close to the stern: when reversing the engine, it could never be certain that the vessel would go astern. In some cases, where the water was very shallow and gave little bite to the floats, the surface water would be carried right round the top of the wheel and thrown astern, thus propelling the steamer ahead.

Altogether the American River Steamers were excellent specimens of practical engineering and adaptation of machinery to the circumstances of shallow and rapid rivers, and the fact that they lasted for over 100 years is eloquent testimony to the soundness of their design.

The concept of armour applied to a ship for the protection of the hull structure, machinery, steering gear and guns, as opposed merely to shielding personnel, became widespread about the middle of the nineteenth century with the general adoption of iron shipbuilding and steam propulsion. The form of attack, however, remained the same as before: sailing as close as possible to one's adversary on a parallel course and firing a broadside into her from a row of fixed guns in the hope that some at least of the shots would take effect, and presenting at the same time a target which the enemy could hardly miss.

In 1855 the French Government built several battery ships to a novel plan in order to protect their ports. These were low-lying dumb vessels, i.e. without engines, with a central citadel or casemate armoured with 4-inch plates, and pierced all round for heavy guns on gun carriages. The vessels were intended to be towed to their destination and anchored at strategic points to serve as floating forts.

The battery ships were copied by several nations, and in due course we hear of the construction of heavily armed and armoured gunboats at St. Louis and other towns on the Missouri. These were, as before, vessels with very little freeboard, the superstructure consisting simply of a huge, sloping gun housing with several guns pointing in all directions. The vessels, being shallow-draught river steamers, were driven by an exposed sternwheel and were vulnerable to heavy return fire.

They were used by the Federal Army at the beginning of the Civil War, towards the end of 1861, but they were still essentially river boats, and they were very awkward to manœuvre in narrow waters.

Probably the most famous of these batteries was the American ship *Merrimack*, better known as the *Merrimac*, a large steam frigate of some 5,000 tons with a wooden hull and disconnecting screw, which visited Southampton in 1856. When the Civil War broke out in the States she happened to be visiting Chesapeake Bay and to avoid capture she was scuttled at her moorings in early 1861. Salvaged by the Confederate Government, she was stripped down to the water line and given a long casemate with sloping sides and ends, armoured with 4-inch iron plates laid on wood, and provided with a number of fixed guns facing both port and starboard, forward and aft. There being very little of her hull showing above water, and with an iron-bound sloping casing which was proof to any shot fired at her from an enemy ship, the *Merrimac* turned out to be a serious menace to the Northern Navy and kept the bay effectively sealed after sinking a number of Federal ships. Incidentally, although rechristened *Virginia*, she was always known as *Merrimac*.

The secret of her success was simply that there was nothing about her to fire at, for while the conventional ship of the day could be put out of action by a lucky shot in the paddle wheel, steering gear, casings or rigging the *Merrimac* offered to the enemy nothing but a formidable iron fort with heavy guns.

But sometimes when a country is in serious difficulties the right man appears with the right solution like a god from the machine, and this man was John Ericsson. A Swede by birth, but living in North America, he was a prolific inventor in the military, civil, naval and mechanical engineering fields. He submitted to the government designs for his turret ship and, in view of the urgency, offered to build one in record time.

The idea was not new. In 1854 he had presented Napoleon III with his plan for a partially submerged armoured ship with no superstructure other than a shot-proof revolving cupola containing a number of guns. The Emperor rejected the offer, building the dumb battery barges instead. But Ericsson had such faith in his idea that he convinced the Northerners that his ship would provide the answer to *Merrimac*'s seeming invincibility. The Navy Board accordingly instructed him to build his turret vessel, the *Monitor*, and the contract required him to furnish the vessel with masts, spars, sails and rigging. This part of the order was wisely ignored. The building was commenced in late 1861, and she was launched within 101 days of signing the contract.

To expedite delivery no curved plates or frames were used, the flat plates being bent or faired round the frame work and drawn up by bolts before riveting, while the frames themselves were all straight, the vessel being slab sided with hard chines at the bilge. Rather aptly compared to a cheese box on a raft, the *Monitor* consisted of an armoured hull some 173 feet long by 41 feet beam sitting upon a much smaller, unarmoured vessel of similar shape containing the machinery, steering gear and magazine. This hull was shipshaped with very coarse lines and there was a parallel body for half the length tapering to a point at each end. The upper hull was armoured with layers of 1-inch plate to a depth of 5 inches on the sides and 2 inches on the deck, and, in accordance with already accepted practice for battery ships, there was very little freeboard, the deck being a bare eighteen inches above the surface of the water.

The lower hull, being completely submerged, Figure 7, was considered immune from surface attack, but was protected by the wide ledge formed by the upper hull, and by virtue of the shell plates being sloped outward from the chine. This slope was fixed at 52° to the vertical, and whether by chance or by design this angle happens to be the critical angle of a horizontal beam of light in salt water. The bow, and especially the stern with its vital propulsion and steering apparatus, were similarly shielded by the projecting upper hull.

The essential part of this *Monitor* was the revolving gun turret situated amidships. This was a steel tower 20 feet in diameter, 9 feet high, with 8-inch armour all round, and carrying two 11-inch Dahlgren smooth-bore muzzle loading guns. These guns were mounted on spring loaded carriages running on short rails within the tower to take the recoil, while the turret could revolve around a fixed king post firmly stepped upon the main keelson, the rotation being by means of a small steam engine below deck driving a large toothed wheel.

This characteristic feature of the rotatable gun turret was a huge step forward in naval warfare, as the two guns could be aimed at the enemy at all stages of the battle and firing was not dependent upon navigation as it would be with fixed guns.

The guns fired through oval ports in the turret and during reloading, to protect the gun crew, hinged shutters were dropped down into the scuttles. After loading, the shutters were hoisted back into the open position by means of chains, and the guns were run out for action. The turret normally rested on a bronze deck ring to form a reasonably watertight joint with the hull and turning mechanism, and to prevent water from leaking below deck. In action this tower was jacked clear of the ring to allow freedom of rotation.

In the original design the wheel house was placed on deck well forward of the turret, which was about the size of a sentry box and heavily armoured, but the pilot was found to be very much in the line of fire from his own guns during attack. The pilot house was subsequently placed above the turret and fastened directly to the king post, i.e. it remained stationary when the turret rotated.

The only other projections on deck were two stumpy funnels abaft the turret, which could be removed in action. The only way to get into the ship, and, of course, the only means of escape in an emergency, was through the top of the turret. Also there were no skylights, no side-scuttles, no ventilators or other means of getting light and air into the accommodation, for the forced draught fan drawing air through the gun turret was intended for the boiler furnaces alone.

The propelling engine, designed by Ericsson, was of the diaphragm

type common to most of the Monitor class, and consisted of two horizontal steam cylinders placed back to back; each piston was fitted with a
trunk and connecting rod laying on to a bell crank, the other arm of the
crank being connected by a connecting rod to the propeller shaft. As the
line of effort of the bell cranks lay at 90°to each other it was impossible for
the engine to stick on dead centre.

Regarding the actual encounter between *Merrimac* and *Monitor* on 9th
March 1862, it would appear that they were pretty evenly matched and,
while the Northerners claimed a victory for their revolving turret ship,
one feels that the battle was inconclusive and proved nothing. This seems
to have been the way the Confederates looked at it, for they converted
another wooden ship in much the same fashion as the *Merrimac* to succeed
her.

The publicity given to the *Monitor* after this brief battle at the mouth of
the James River, and the comparatively small amount of damage suffered
in the face of such severe bombardment from the enemy ship, caused the
Federal Government to order a number of additional vessels of this type.
They were of different classes for various duties, and some 45 in all were
eventually built in succeeding years. There were harbour and river
monitors, shallow draught and deep sea Monitors, and the type was soon
adopted in Europe and the Near East.

It is ironic that the original *Monitor*, built to withstand the heaviest
punishment that could be inflicted by any naval ship of her day, was a
victim of her own design. Those features which made her so unassailable
in warfare: the low funnels, the projecting upper deck shelf, and above all
the rotating turret, were no proof against the sea, and, as a Scottish
shipbuilder of old lucidly remarked, 'Ye canna cheat wa'er.' The funnels,
being easily removable, could also wash away. The blowpipes, fitted low
on the deck, could be flooded, extinguishing the boiler fires and flooding
the stokehold. That projecting upper shelf, so useful against attack by
enemy shells, could not withstand the slamming occasioned by such a
ponderous vessel pitching in a seaway.

Possibly the weakest point in her structure was the hatch in the low
deck, opening into the turret, and protected from the sea only by the
bronze deck ring. With a freeboard of 18 inches this deck would be constantly awash even in the mildest weather.

Whatever the actual cause of the leakage, *Monitor* foundered in a gale
off Cape Hatteras on the last day of 1862, with most of her crew on board.

In spite of this disaster, however, the government went ahead with

C

1.Sewalls Point Battery 30 Guns..2.Craney Island Battery 42 Guns..3.Yorktown..4.Jamestown...5.Monitor.. 6.Merrimac..7.Norfolk..8.Portsmouth..9.Suffolk...10.Minnesota..11.Pig Point Battery..12.Barre Point Battery.. 13.Burning of the Congress..14.The Cumberland sunk..15.Newport News Point 9.Camp..16.St Lawrences..17. Rip Raps..18.French Man-of-War...

THE NAVAL ENGAGEMENT BETWEEN THE MERRIMAC AND THE MONITOR AT HAMPTON ROADS
ON THE 9TH OF MARCH 1862.

5 Naval battle between *Monitor* and *Merrimac*

6 *Monitor* and *Cupola*

their plans for rebuilding the navy in terms of turret vessels, successive vessels becoming more sea-worthy and shipshape, having better closing appliances on deck and softer lines below. They still retained the original idea of a low deck and a revolving gun turret with the two heavy guns, although in some cases the turrets were duplicated, there being one forward and one aft of midships, and in some cases shaped like cupolas. The guns themselves were altered, of course; sometimes two 11-inch guns were fitted, at other times one 11-inch and one 15-inch, or a Parrott gun together with an 11-inch gun. In the event, the 'turrets' became almost as good sea-keeping ships as the old-time wooden vessels they replaced, and were quite happy in the Atlantic.

In 1866 we hear of the vessel *Miantonomah*, an iron clad turret ship of the Monitor class built in 1865, arriving at Cork with two escort vessels and attracting considerable attention at that port. She was an improvement on Ericsson's original idea and was described in the local Press as a monstrous iron raft with a hull shaped like an ordinary vessel but scarcely showing above water. She had two turrets, one at each end, with the navigating bridge amidships, there being a catwalk connecting all three superstructures. This vessel had twin screws and was reputed to make 10½ knots at sea. She had seventeen separate engines to work the screws, turrets, steering engines, capstans, and fans, one of which was to provide ventilation below decks.

What were the conditions below decks in one of the original Monitors? We must remember that the only supply of air available to the crew came through the turret hatch by natural circulation, and this had to contend with the foul air from inside the hull trying to get out. This meant that sailors at stations remote from the turret got precious little fresh air at all. The same, of course, for light. In the days before electric lighting came into general use at sea sailors and firemen were accustomed to grope their way along dark alleyways lit only by a paraffin lamp or not at all, while engineers were quite happy to pass the watch walking between wildly moving masses of unfenced ironmongery with nothing but the smoky yellow flame from a duck lamp to show the way. These conditions were taken for granted in the 1860's.

Here is a vivid description of living conditions inside the Monitor *Lehigh* on passage Brooklyn to Charleston in an Atlantic gale, written by one of her officers:

Vessel very sluggish in the heavy sea, slow to rise over the waves, extremely heavy

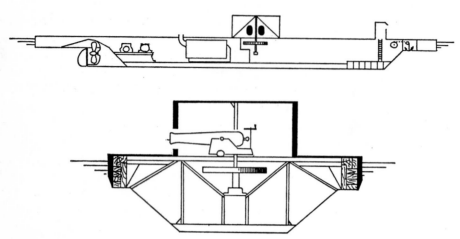

7 *Monitor*—longitudinal and transverse sections

and uncouth. Innumerable little streams of sea water, red with rust, poured down into every cabin, and the (tween) deck was running with water. All clothing in the accommodation soaked and rooms flooded. It was necessary to wear sea boots below decks. Hatch closed, vents shut, no daylight and the only lighting was by candle. Air foul, and with 70° on deck, it was 101° below decks.

Obviously not a pleasure cruise, and this was on one of the *Passaic* class Monitors, somewhat larger than her prototype and assumed to have been built to a more sophisticated design.

But what about the original *Monitor*'s value as a warship? Some critics maintained that, while she may have been unbeatable by enemy fighting ships, she could have been captured by a determined boarding party from a small boat. They claimed that the immense 11-inch guns would be useless against such a small moving target as a rowboat, and apart from rifle fire from the turret or pilot house there was no other deterrent. All the boarding party had to do was to drive a couple of wedges between the turret base and the deck, thus jamming the turning mechanism and rendering the guns useless. After that it would be a simple matter to drop a grenade or two down the smoke stack or blowpipe to put the vessel completely out of action.

This may have been armchair criticism, but it is borne out by the experience of some of the men who sailed in the Monitors and took part in the engagement against Fort Sumter. The captain of *Passaic* reported that the lower part of his turret was hit by an 11-inch shell from the fort, the turret floor was set up and his gun-carriage rails were bent, putting his guns out of commission for several hours. After that the bronze deck ring under the turret was found to be broken and jamming the turning rack, and had to be cleared by the crew exposed to heavy shell fire.

The captain of a sister Monitor reported several shots hitting his deck armour in the same position, starting heavy leakage. He also reported difficulty in turning his turret.

A third captain complained that the armour round the pilot house was so effective that his view was severely restricted, while yet another reported that a lucky shot from the fort shattered the chain holding up the gun port shutter, which promptly dropped down and sealed the openings, rendering the gun harmless until the unlucky gun crew braved the fire from a hostile battery and locked the shutter back into the open position.

Another defect generally reported upon by the gunners was the impossibility of laying the guns correctly or checking the results of a shot from the turret owing to the very restricted view from the gun ports. All information had to be relayed from the pilot house to the turret by messenger, losing precious time in the process.

In spite of these drawbacks, however, the Monitors showed themselves immeasurably superior to the existing conventional battleships and, though possibly at a disadvantage when attacking a fort with stationary guns, they were a match for anything afloat. The design was adopted in Britain by Captain Coles, who persuaded the Admiralty to construct a twin turret Monitor in 1869 to a design based on that of Ericsson's. This vessel, H.M.S. *Captain*, was a three island type of vessel: poop, bridge casing and topgallant forecastle, with a very low weather deck and a freeboard of only a few feet. Her turrets were sited between the bridge and the end castles, the latter being wedge shaped to give the guns as much fire range forward and aft as possible.

The gun turrets were rotating, as in the original *Monitor*, but were mounted on the tween deck, protruding through the weather deck and with the gun barrels almost at deck level. A hurricane deck connected the three islands and formed the working deck for the crew.

The *Captain* was ship-rigged with an auxiliary steam-driven screw, and the masts were tripod-type, dispensing with shrouds. There is no doubt that she would have been a success had she been fitted out purely as a steam-driven warship, but the mentality of the times was still in favour of sails, and the effect of such a high centre of wind pressure on a vessel with very little freeboard can be imagined. She overturned in the Bay of Biscay in a storm in 1870, drowning most of her crew.

Another unlucky turret ship was H.M.S. *Royal Sovereign*, which was converted from an ordinary three-decker in 1864. After conversion the vessel put to sea to test the machinery and guns, and during these trials the captain sent a brief signal advising his return to the dockyard for re-positioning one of the boilers. Upon arrival it was shown that a boiler had worked loose on its cradle and had severed its stopvalve from the main steam pipe, allowing the steam to discharge directly into the stoke-hold. Only an engineer can appreciate the horror of such an accident.

Ericsson's *Monitor* may not have revolutionised naval warfare, but she did set the design for several generations of naval vessels, not only in their structure but also in their manning. The *Merrimac* in her heyday as a 44-gun frigate required a crew of 570, reduced to 320 as a battery ship; the *Monitor* needed only 75 men.

3 Cigar ships

The spectator, they say, sees most of the game, not only because of his vantage point above the players but also because he can take a detached view of the play as a whole without having to concentrate too hard on one particular manœuvre. Thus it is with the amateur and the expert: the one, in his ignorance of traditional methods, can bring fresh ideas to a calling, whereas the other, hidebound by his training, can see progress only as an extension of his present experience.

A ship designed and constructed by a professional shipbuilder may be a most efficient, pleasing and modern vessel, but it will still conform to a traditional type. If, on the other hand, you engage someone with considerable mechanical knowledge but no previous naval experience to draw up the design, the finished vessel may or may not float upright and earn her keep, and she may look odd to the seaman, but there is a strong probability that some of the features wrought into her will be found useful and may eventually be adopted in other vessels.

This point is illustrated in the cigar ships, the American railwayman's approach to naval architecture. The cigar in this context refers of course to the vessel's shape, not her cargo.

The Winans brothers were successful and wealthy railroad engineers and in 1858 they launched their first cigar ship at Baltimore. Such was their novel approach to ship design that they broke away entirely from the then prevailing concept that steam propulsion was merely an auxiliary to sail. Seamen of the day had a fixation about sail, and it took several generations of sailors to realise that sails were no longer necessary on a mechanically propelled ship.

The theory of the cigar ships was that the designers would discard all masts, sails and rigging, do away with casings on deck, in fact even discard the deck itself. There would be no keel and no cutwater or blunt bow to take the shock of heavy seas. There would be no flat deck to hold the water and no flimsy superstructures to present a front to the waves and a way of ingress into the accommodation. The hull would be shaped the same above water as below and would thus move easily through the waves, not over them. The waves would slide over the rounded hull like the sea over a half-tide rock, and therefore could not make the vessel roll. With all these advantages i.e. no appreciable appendages for wind or water, and no pitching or rolling, the cigar ship should attain a high speed on very little coal consumption. That, at least, was the specification.

The ship, when completed, fulfilled her designers' wish for novelty to such an extent that it is difficult to pinpoint any traditional element in her structure. The hull, about 180 feet long, was shaped like a narrow spindle 16 feet in diameter at its widest. It consisted of a pair of paraboloids placed base to base, some 4 feet apart. These two half-hulls were joined together by a circular iron shroud ring 25 feet in diameter, bracketed to the side plating. A transverse annular propeller was fitted between the two hulls and worked inside the shroud ring. This propeller consisted of a drum roughly the same diameter as the hull, fitted with a series of projecting diagonal blades or vanes, and could be compared in action with a modern turbine in its casing. In fact, the propeller was simply a paddle wheel with skew blades fitted athwartships.

The cigar ship was in reality a pair of steamships joined together in tandem by a common propeller. There was no communication between the two hulls other than by a catwalk along the upper plating. The propeller was driven by a central shaft passing through the base of each half-hull, with an engine and boilers at each end, while the shaft had the usual watertight sterngland at each bulk-head.

Two rudders were fitted, one at each end, but although the ship appeared double-ended her normal direction was ahead only.

However she justified her designers' claims inasmuch as she had no flat deck and no superstructures other than the four slender funnels. Access along the outside of the hull was by means of a narrow grating for the greater part of her length, with a gangway over the propeller structure. The navigating bridge was in the form of a scaffolding tower, and the pilot was exposed not only to the occupational hazards of wind and sea but also to the spray shot up by the propeller wheel, with the smoke from the forward funnels in his eyes for good measure.

In spite of her form, which appeared very shipshape to a landsman, she was not a success. The huge rotating propeller wheel threw so much spray from amidships aft that it was almost impossible to stay on deck. And apart from this discomfort, the shroud ring with its heavy brackets offered considerable resistance to motion in the sea, and the working of the two half hulls about their junction caused cracking and consequent leakage. In addition, the screwshaft glands were difficult to keep tight.

Another problem was the difficulty of coordinating the orders to the two engine rooms. In the days before the invention of the engine room telegraph orders from the bridge were transmitted either by bell or by voice pipe, but in the case of one propeller shaft worked from two engine rooms, it would be almost impossible to start up one end of the shaft with its opposite end in neutral position.

8 Winans' cigar ship

9 Launching of *Ross Winans*

I believe this ship was redesigned in an attempt to reduce the working about the central shroud which formed a nodal point, by introducing two transverse propellers situated at about a quarter hull length, one forward and aft. These two positions, called the airey points and situated 0·554 of the hull length apart, are those where minimum working would be expected to occur in a seaway. However, this ship was never built.

The success of this first of the cigar ships is debatable and we hear no more about them until 1865, when another vessel was launched at St. Petersburg. This one was quite small, about 70 feet long by 9 feet in diameter, and we gather that she was built in the hopes that the Czar would be interested and place an order for an imperial yacht on similar lines. The propeller in this case was of the orthodox pattern, but as it stuck out considerably below the hull outline it was found to be too vulnerable in shallow water.

A third vessel, *Walter S. Winans*, was built at Le Havre by Nilus & Son, also in 1865, oddly enough of similar dimensions to that built in Russia. She was equipped with four propeller shafts, two at each end, all driven by a centrally placed 25 nominal h.p. steam engine. The ship could thus be powered by a combination of screws to determine the most efficient and economical drive.

Ross Winans

The fourth and largest of the Winans brothers' ships was the steam yacht *Ross Winans*, which was launched at Hepworth's Yard on the Isle of Dogs in the Thames in London, in 1866, and, as will be seen from the illustration, she was lowered into the water on a wedge-shaped cradle. Obviously the owners still had hopes of impressing the Czar as she wore, among other flags, the ensign of the Imperial Yacht Club of St. Petersburg.

The new vessel was built to the same spindle shape as the previous ones, with a maximum diameter of 16 feet amidships, but was some 256 feet long overall. The centrally placed propeller wheel had now been discarded in favour of a large propeller at each end driven by a central shaft extending the full length of the hull.

The iron grating over the top of the hull had been replaced by a low superstructure some 130 feet long by slightly over 10 feet wide, tapering to a point at the ends. This short deck had a companionway at each end leading to the accommodation, machinery spaces and crew's quarters, and two fairly sturdy funnels were placed slightly forward of amidships.

The general appearance showed a tendency for the superstructure to revert to the orthodox, while still retaining the characteristics of a cigar ship body.

The hull was subdivided into reasonably watertight compartments by 13 transverse bulkheads, and further sub-compartmented by a tween deck, set 2 feet below the shaft centre line, for most of the length except in the machinery spaces and stores forward and aft. Passenger and crew accommodation was above tween deck level, with 10 feet headroom at centre, and below this deck were the coal bunkers, both forward and aft, store rooms, etc.

The main saloon, semi-circular in section, and 25 feet long was decorated in white and gold with royal blue furnishings and had seats along the shipsides. Access to this saloon was from the after companion, which finished on a platform deck built over the shaft, with short steps leading forward to the saloon and aft to staterooms.

The forward companion led down in similar fashion to a vestibule, and thence to the smokeroom and more staterooms, also to the crew's quarters. The propeller shafting was boxed in by a continuous casing which did duty as a table in the saloons, but which had the inconvenience of dividing the cabins longitudinally.

Access through the iron bulkheads was by hinged doors closing on rubber gaskets, and natural light was admitted through bullseyes let into the hull plating clear of the hurricane deck.

Ventilation was by means of forced draught fans in the boiler room drawing air from outside down through the companionways and passenger rooms, and realising in one operation the modern ideas of pressurised stokehold and mechanical ventilation. This method of ventilation, incidentally, was in common use for passenger vessels on the Western Ocean in the 1880's.

The 3-cylinder engine was situated amidships. The propellers were 4-foot diameter hubs, each with nine blades bolted on, forming wheels 22 feet in diameter, turning at about 50 revolutions per minute. The hubs continued into 10 feet long hollow bossings tapering to a sharp point, which formed the extremities of the vessel.

Steering was by direct hand control on to two spade rudders, one at each end, which could be used either coupled together or worked independently.

A peculiar feature of this vessel was its ballast donkey engine which played a very different role from that which its name usually suggests.

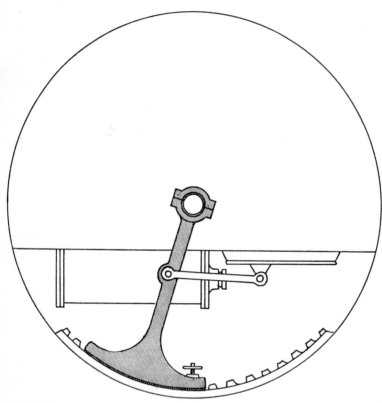

10 Steam yacht *Ross Winans*—ballast donkey engine

The hull of the vessel being completely circular, with no central or bilge keels and consequently no inherent stability, it was necessary to devise some means to counter the hull reaction to the rotating screws. This was achieved by means of 12 tons of lead ballast fitted at the end of a pendulum hung from the main shaft on a free bearing, the arm of the pendulum being connected to the piston of a steam servo cylinder 24 inches in diameter with a stroke of 5 feet. Movement of this piston, and hence of the balance weight, to port or starboard was controlled by a valve worked through linkage from the main engine reversing gear. Thus, with the screw revolving clockwise, the hull would tend to rotate anti-clockwise, and the balance weight would automatically swing over to counteract this rotation. The amount of swing was governed by the travel of the servo-piston, and this travel was directly proportional to the steam pressure in the main engine: the higher the speed, the greater the swing.

11 Steam yacht *Ross Winans*—after end showing anchors and windlass

The illustration shows how this pendulum was installed in the engine room. A manual locking device engaging in a circular rack attached to the ship's framework enabled the crew to fix the weight in any desired position. This locking device came in handy when in port, as, by jacking the balance weight over with the engines at rest, it was possible to careen the vessel and scrape and paint the bottom without entering dry-dock.

Like everything else, the mooring arrangements were most unusual. The two anchors consisted each of a 30 cwt. conical iron weight raised by a hand capstan in the crew's quarters aft. Each hawsepipe consisted of an 18 inch diameter open iron pipe fitted to the ship's bottom and rising to within a few inches of the weather deckhead, the cable being led through this pipe over a pulley at the top.

The hawsepipes were flared at their bottom ends, where they were riveted to the ship's hull, and when the anchors were secured home the conical iron plugs were intended to fit neatly into the flared ends and thus seal the pipes; in fact, they formed a couple of Kingston valves and, just as surely, a direct invitation to Davy Jones. It is possible that the Winans brothers were proud of this unusual design of hawsepipes, with no mooring appliances visible above water, but probably they slept in the saloon. As for the poor crew, we can have no doubt whatever that when the order was given to let go the anchor the forecastle would be vacated with indecent haste, and the coveted bunk would be that nearest the door. Incidentally, the sound of an anchor dropping, when heard from the deck, is enough to startle the casual onlooker; but the roar of anchor cable thundering out of the chain locker, up through the spurling pipe, whipping over the windlass gipsy and down the hawsepipe, when heard from the chain locker, is terrifying indeed.

Other novel features were derricks for the lifeboats, instead of davits with their limited reach, funnels as integral parts of the hull instead of the usual flimsy sheet iron affairs, a flexible propeller shaft with self adjusting couplings and a thrust block on spring mountings, controllable super-heated steam, rocking bars in the furnaces, and several other innovations which came into general use only in the twentieth century.

As the Winans' cigar ships embodied so many useful ideas and appeared to be such efficient, economical vessels it is pertinent to ask why they never became popular and set the trend for future passenger vessels.

Actually, apart from one or two coastal voyages and some protracted trials on the Solent, the *Ross Winans* never put to sea in earnest and was eventually written off as a failure. One of the reasons was the amount of spray thrown over the deck by the forward propeller. This made the exposed deck untenable and obscured the view forward by the look-out and the quartermaster. Another reason was the extremely narrow beam, which reduced living conditions to their lowest common denominator, with passengers, officers and crew all pigging it together and in the 1860's the social gap between officers and crew was very much wider than it is today. With a maximum beam of 16 feet, there was only slightly more than 10 feet average beam, which gave little room for moving about below deck while at sea. With the impossibility of staying on deck, who can blame the passenger for preferring the comfort of a conventional ship?

From the point of view of design there was no need for the Winans brothers to keep to 16 feet diameter, as the beam could have been considerably increased without adversely affecting either speed or consumption. The spindle shape is an ideal shape for a hull to slip through water as there is practically no wave-making, the phenomenon which accounts for a large part of the horsepower expended. By increasing the diameter one increases the wetted surface and consequently the skin friction, but in the cigar ship the very fine entrance and run, even with a fatter model, would still show an advantage over a conventional type ship.

A further disadvantage was the method of shovelling coal, which had to be hoisted from bunkers below the tween deck, wheeled across the exposed weather deck and tipped down the shute into the boiler room. As this operation had to be performed when the 'vessel was cleaving her way through the waves' there would quite naturally be occasions when a green sea would follow the coal down the shute.

Possibly even in mid-nineteenth century, when poverty and insecurity at home drove men to sail in almost any type of vessel, Dr. Johnson's description of a ship might have been a shade too near the mark in the cigar types, and have discouraged even desperate men from sailing in them.

Both the *Walter S. Winans* and the *Ross Winans* lingered on at their moorings near Southampton for nearly 30 years. They were well maintained, both as regards hull and machinery, and were considered as items of interest to holiday sightseers. When the owners died, the ships were put up for sale and bought by a Bristol ship-breaker, the smaller vessel fetching £190 and the larger one £210.

The original cost of *Ross Winans* was £60,000, and the other cigar ships cost in proportion to their size. One might regret the brothers' perseverance in a lost cause, but one cannot but admire their tenacity and courage in staking their fortune on an idea.

Let us now investigate the claims put forward by the Winans brothers regarding the stability and sea-kindliness of their cigar ships. We know by experiment that a light wooden plank with a width rather more than its thickness will float freely with either face up, but not edge up. On the other hand if the same plank is trimmed until it has a square section it will only float with the edges up. However a heavier plank of the same shape will now float only with a side facing up, and any log of circular section will float in any horizontal position.

We thus see that the stability of any floating body depends (1) upon its weight in relation to its displacement and (2) upon the shape of its immersed cross-section. As most ships are symmetrical about a vertical, longitudinal plane, the question of how they will float resolves itself into a simple relationship between the centre of gravity and the centre of buoyancy of the displaced water.

Figure 12 *a* shows the cross section of a conventional ship in smooth water, the points G and B denoting respectively the centre of gravity of the section and the centre of buoyancy of that portion of hull below the waterline. In *b* the same vessel is inclined to port, and, while the centre of gravity remains in its same position in the hull, the centre of buoyancy has shifted to port. Now gravity acts vertically downwards, and buoyancy vertically upwards, and the couple so formed constitutes the righting arm

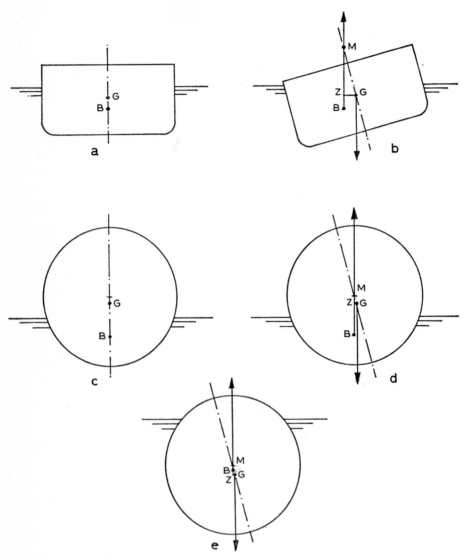

12 Stability—the orthodox and the cigar ships compared

GZ. The perpendicular through B crosses the ship's centreline at M, the metacentre. The distance GM, the metacentric height, controls stability, and in any normal ship it must be positive, i.e. M must be above G. If the GM is too great the vessel will be very stiff and will roll jerkily, whereas if it is too small the roll will be smooth, but possibly to a greater angle.

Item *c* represents a cross section of the cigar ship at her loaded draught, and it will be noted in *d* that as the immersed portion of the hull is segmental the centre of buoyancy does not shift when the vessel is inclined; consequently the metacentre is at the geometrical centre. Now in a vessel of this section, with most of its machinery built either around the centre-line shaft or alongside it, with accommodation and stores, etc., in the upper

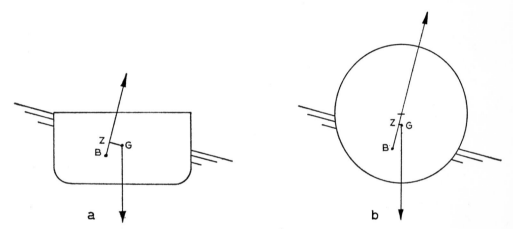

13 Rolling—the orthodox and the cigar ships compared

section and a diminishing supply of coal in the lower section, the centre of gravity must inevitably be very near to the geometrical centre of the hull, i.e. G is getting very close to M. This is brought out in *d*, where, due to the inclination, G moves out very little to starboard, but B, instead of moving over to port and thus providing a good righting arm, remains stationary, and the righting arm is consequently very small indeed.

If the centre of gravity ever approached the geometrical centre M, by, say, using up all the coal in the bunkers, the GM would become nil and the vessel could capsize. We see, therefore, that a ship with a circular section has no inherent stability, and must have permanent ballast to keep the centre of gravity under control. Incidentally, *e* shows that the stability of a cigar ship is not influenced by draught.

Investigation of stability starts with a ship floating upright in smooth water, which is then inclined by an external force. Rolling deals with a ship which is inclined by the action of waves, and by no other action, the force of wind being ignored in the calculations. In Figure 13, *a*, we have a conventional vessel floating upright in a long, smooth wave, and the centre of buoyancy moves over to B. In this case, owing to the energy contained within the wave, the force acting upon B is not vertically upwards but normal to the wave surface, and we now have a heeling arm =GZ tending to incline the ship until her deck assumed the same slope as the wave surface.

In *b* the same conditions apply to the cigar ship, and we see that the line of thrust from B, passing through the centre is very close indeed to G, and there is therefore very little heeling arm. In short this ship will have a slow, easy roll in heavy seas, but the small GM, while ensuring comfort for passengers and crew, requires a large range of stability, as the ship will eventually roll *against* the waves when her virtual angle of heel will be much greater than the inclination from the vertical.

By and large I feel that the Winans brothers' cigar ship justified their claim for comfort and sea kindliness, but certainly not for stability and safety.

H.M.S. *Polyphemus*

Although the Winans' cigar ships were discredited the concept of a spindle-shaped vessel remained in the nautical mind, and in the 1870's Admiral Sartorius revived the idea and produced plans for an armoured steam ram with a rounded midship section and a pointed fore end. H.M.S. *Polyphemus* was the only ram ship in the British Navy, and her design was copied on both sides of the Atlantic. She was built in 1880, of 240 feet b.p. by 40 feet major diameter, displaced 2,610 tons and her twin screw engines developed 5,500 h.p. at 17 knots, quite a performance for those days.

Her section was oval with the major axis horizontal, and the fore end, which protruded well beyond the hull proper, ended in a combined ram-torpedo tube arrangement. A marked feature of her type was the very small portion of her main shell showing above water and vulnerable to gunfire. The rounded deck was armoured with 3-inch plate down to 6 feet below water level, and the top shell itself was equipped with the minimum number of openings, each fitted with glacis. A light super-structure was placed on top of the rounded hull, generally shipshape, containing the navigating platform and supporting the only armament (originally six Nordenfeldt guns, each in a cocoa tin turret) against light surface attack.

As a ram she had to be exceptionally strong forward, highly manoeuv-rable and very fast, and it would appear that she fulfilled all these require-

14 H.M.S. *Polyphemus* on speed trials

15 H.M.S. *Polyphemus* in dry dock

ments. She was fitted with twin retractable bow rudders which could be lowered and controlled from a position at the fore end or coupled to the normal power steering gear, as required. They were not used in cruising, only in attack.

She had twin engine rooms and four stokeholds and came out originally with 12 locomotive type boilers steaming at 110 p.s.i., although these were later reduced to eight circular boilers with slightly higher pressure.

Her bunker capacity of 240 tons was sufficient only for a day and a half at full speed, and she was unusual inasmuch as her black gang considerably outnumbered her deck crew.

She had 5 torpedo tubes, one fitted right in the nose of the ram and all of them below the waterline. When not in use the central torpedo tube was covered by a removable cast steel cap which formed the ram. This could be rotated clear of the tube, the torpedo fired and the cap replaced ready for ramming.

This bow torpedo tube which doubled as a ram must have troubled the designers somewhat, for they included provision in the lower part of the bow for some 300 tons of loose ballast which could be quickly released in the event of serious bow damage.

As with the cigar ships all accommodation was within the strength hull which, naturally, was pierced with the minimum of openings for ventilation, resulting in exceedingly hot and oppressive conditions below deck. In the Mediterranean where the ship was stationed her engine room temperature sometimes reached 140°F and one wonders what it would have reached in the Persian Gulf.

Having a roughly circular shape (although with a conventional stern) she would have little inherent stability, and we are not surprised to learn that her behaviour at sea was unpredictable. Although not prone to excessive rolling she sometimes 'flopped over' and stayed like that for some time before righting herself. This may have been caused by her unusual bunker lay-out, whereby the lower bunkers had to be emptied before starting on the upper ones.

It is difficult to assess the value of *Polyphemus*, whether she could be called a success or a failure, as she never had the opportunity to ram a vessel. Just as well, perhaps. In the 1880's naval vessels were fitting heavier and tougher armour and their displacement was increasing every year. A steam ram ship sailing at 17 knots against a heavily armoured battleship could do an enormous amount of damage, but the probability is that the greater damage would be sustained by the steam ram herself. Being brought

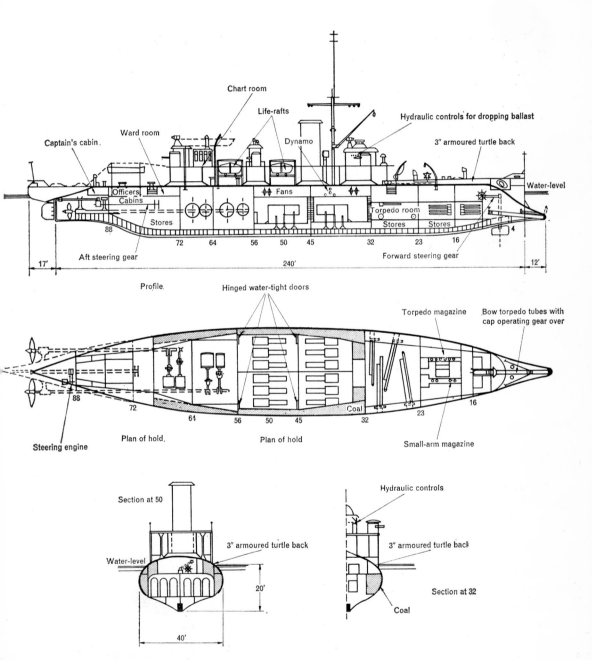

Chart room

Life-rafts

Hydraulic controls for dropping ballast

3" armoured turtle back

Ward room

Dynamo

Captain's cabin.

Water-level

Officers
Cabins

Fans

Torpedo room

Stores

Stores

Stores

88

72   64   56   50   45   32   23   16   4

Aft steering gear

Forward steering gear

17'   240'   12'

Profile.

Hinged water-tight doors

Torpedo magazine

Bow torpedo tubes with
cap operating gear over

88

72   64   56   50   45   32   23   16

Coal

Steering engine

Plan of hold.   Plan of hold

Small-arm magazine

Section at 50

Hydraulic controls

3" armoured turtle back

Water-level

3" armoured turtle back

Section at 32

20'

Coal

40'

6 H.M.S. *Polyphemus* general arrangement

up all standing from that speed there would be an appalling strain on the holding down bolts for the engines and boilers, with serious risk of steam pipe failure and buckling of some of the delicately balanced machinery parts. With the propelling machinery out of commission the ram would have no chance at all against an enemy ship's heavy guns.

H.M.S. *Polyphemus'* resemblance to the Winans' ships was purely fortuitous and her shape was the best compromise of a conventional fighting ship with a sharp instrument for stabbing. She can, however, be included in the cigar ship category, although by now the hull shape was tending towards the orthodox.

Back across the Atlantic the Americans carried on the tradition of the 'spindle' ships in their whaleback steamers, designed towards the end of the 1880's by Capt. McDougall, which remained peculiar to the Great Lakes. By this time the cigar ship had attained respectability—the design had matured into a quasi-conventional type and came to be accepted by the sailors of the day; this acceptance was possibly tempered by the fact that the new steamers had been designed by a professional sailor.

The whaleback steamer was an early form of the bulk carrier, basically a huge self-propelled barge with one, long, continuous hold and with engines aft. The hull was conventional in respect of the underwater body, having square bilges, but the deck had an exaggerated camber for its full length and it was this curvature which gave rise to the popular name. The midship section shows a semi-elliptical deck merging smoothly into the straight sides and the elevation shows a spoon stem and stern, ending in flat capping plates and a complete absence of sheer.

All deck housings and casings were formed as turrets, either circular or oval in section, to present as little flat surface to the seas as possible, and had conventional accommodation on top. The various casings, engine, bridge and winch platforms were connected by a catwalk or gangway, the deck normally being awash when the ship was at sea in loaded conditions. The hatches were mounted flush with the deck and had steel lids bolted into position on rubber gaskets, being thus completely watertight under all conditions of weather. In passing, the cargo hatch covers in a tramp ship of the period consisted of a set of ill-matched wooden boards covered by a pair of patched tarpaulins wedged into the coamings; watertight steel hatch covers had another half century to wait before the idea took hold.

Quite a number of these whaleback steamers were built, some of them reaching 350 feet length by 42 feet beam, and one of the best known was

17 Whaleback *Sagamore*

the *Christopher Columbus*, a ferry boat based on Chicago which carried up to 5,000 passengers at a speed of 20 knots. This vessel, built in 1893, had seven turrets or casings on her whaleback deck, connected together by a hurricane deck.

Although the whaleback steamers were rarely seen outside their normal habitat at least one crossed the Atlantic and berthed at Liverpool. This was the *Charles W. Wetmore*, and she excited considerable attention and comment from the English sea-faring community, not only by reason of her submarine-like topsides but also because of her most unusual machinery, a compound steam engine with cranks at 180°.

The whaleback steamers were well in advance of the conventional cargo boats of the time, and it is surprising that their main features were not retained in subsequent Great Lakes vessels, if not in ocean-going ones. Their rounded decks and simplified shape made them good self-trimmers, their hatch closing appliances ensured reasonable immunity from heavy seas, and their slow, easy roll made them comfortable ships. They were, in fact, ideal from the ship operators' point of view, easy both to load and to unload either general or bulk cargo.

18 Whaleback *Sagamore* stern view

Quite possibly this view did occur to some shipowners, for in 1893 William Doxford & Sons Ltd., of Sunderland, built a Whaleback steamer on the McDougall design to the order of Wm. Johnston of Liverpool. This ship, the *Sagamore*, apparently had some difficulty in being accepted by the competent authorities (the penalty incurred for novelty in design) as she was registered in Belgium. She was 311 feet long b.p., with moulded breadth 38 feet 2 inches and moulded depth of 25 feet 3 inches, of 2,139 gross tons and, with machinery of 1,320 h.p., made 10 knots loaded. The *Sagamore* had four cargo turrets on her fore deck and one on her after deck, a bridge turret which also housed the donkey boiler and funnel, and an engine casing turret. She differed from the Great Lakes type in that her engines were housed amidships, and she had two holds forward of the machinery spaces, and one abaft. The accommodation was built over the two main casings and was of conventional type, being almost as wide as the ship's breadth.

The original idea of the cigar ship had been considerably watered down in the whaleback version, and the last link in the chain, before the cigar ship definitely settled for orthodox lines, was the turret ship—not to be confused with Ericsson's Monitor with its central turret.

The turret ships, many of which were built by William Doxford & Sons Ltd., could be considered as modified whalebacks, except that instead of having a number of individual turrets on the harbour deck they had a continuous turret of rectangular section from topgallant forecastle to poop, and the flat of this turret deck became the working deck and housed the hatches and casings. In this case, however, the stem and the stern were of conventional design.

In cross section the turret deck was barely half the beam, the turret side plating curving downwards from the deck and outwards to meet the shipside plating in a smooth elongated S bend, the fluting or harbour deck so formed extending for her full length and blending into the forecastle and poop structures. Like the whaleback, the turret steamer had no sheer.

Finally the wheel comes full circle and in the twentieth century, 1922 to be precise, we find a reversion to type in the motor vessel, *Adriana*. While this vessel is outside my terms of reference, her description follows so neatly upon the previous cigar ships that I cannot resist bringing her into the picture.

The *Adriana* was built by Cantiere Federale of Pietra Ligure, Italy, to the design brought out by Col. Vitulli Montaruli, the owners' managing director. The main characteristics were length b.p. 339·5 feet, beam

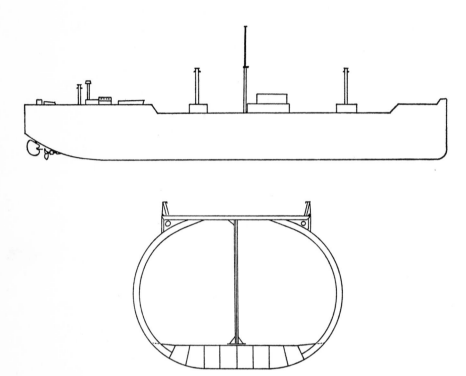

19 M/V *Adriana* profile and section

50·8 feet, depth 35·5 feet, deadweight 6,700 tons, speed 10·5 knots on twin screws at 2,000 b.h.p. She was therefore not just an experimental vessel but a full-scale cargo ship.

Her main characteristic was her oval midship section with a fairly narrow deck, slightly trunked, and the two shapes, top square section and lower oval cylinder, extended from forward to aft blending into each other at the extremities. The bow was of the standard cutwater type and the stern sloped up rather like a swim barge, with a balanced rudder but no deadwood. One would naturally question the directional stability of such a vessel, with circular cross section and no grip of the water, but apparently she was quite successful as a cargo ship.

With engines aft, she had four unencumbered holds in line, with an additional hold abaft the machinery spaces. She had Ansaldo type diesel engines and, after the fashion of the early motorships, she had no funnel, the exhaust from the motors being discharged through vertical pipes on the boat deck.

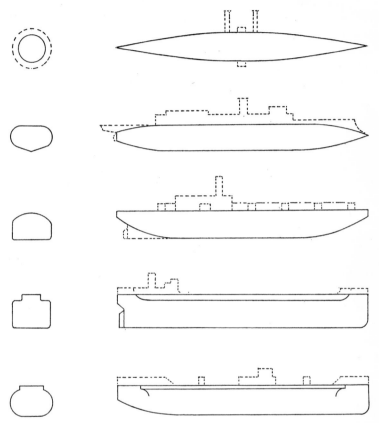

20 Development of the cigar ship, from top to bottom: cigar ship, *Polyphemus*, Whaleback, turret ship, *Adriana*

The advantages claimed for this novel (or was it old fashioned?) design of hull were a considerable reduction in the weight of steel used as compared with a square section steamer, provision for larger holds of the self-trimming type, and less wetted surface with consequent reduced fuel consumption. The promised reduction in weight, however, could not be fulfilled as the authorities quite rightly insisted on the normal scantlings being used for the ship until working experience suggested a re-appraisal of the design.

Summing up what we know about the cigar type ships, it would appear that in spite of their apparent strength, lightness and sea-kindliness, they never made any serious impact on history, and although the idea persisted for seventy years, they were not as successful as conventional ships.

However, here is a statement made by a naval captain who attended a trial run on the *Ross Winans*, and who, by virtue of his calling and from actual experience, can give us an objective appreciation of the cigar ship.

I have been asked to mention, which I am very happy to do, our experience with regard to the cigar ship. We went in her on a cruise. That vessel had very fine ends and a barrel-shaped frame. We were in a nasty sea, and although in a very small vessel, the pitching was almost nil. We could scarcely feel it, and there was certainly no uncomfortable motion. To my surprise, although the vessel was as round as a barrel in cross section, she did not roll when she was laid broadside to the sea, but remained perfectly upright in a sea in which most vessels would have rolled considerably. Steadiness was the remarkable feature of that ship.

In common with others I felt sorry when the prolongation of patent was refused to Mr. Winans, the talented inventor of that vessel, because I think he was carrying out experiments which would have been very valuable to our own country.

4 Circular ships

The two essentials in a sailing vessel or a steamer are that she must float in an upright position and that she shall sail in one direction only, this latter qualification being modified in certain cross-channel boats, ferries and canoes, etc., which can sail reasonably well in reverse. The implied requirement is, of course, that no vessel should sail sideways, although, as will be seen in a later chapter, the Portuguese Muleta does precisely that.

Primitive shipbuilders recognised these facts by trial and error and our conventional ships have consisted of an elongated structure ever since. Even builders of freak ships have kept to the basic principles of design in that a hull must be considerably longer than its width to have directional stability and to be of any use at all.

But in 1861 John Elder, the Glasgow shipbuilder, brought out a general design for a ship that would be completely circular in plan, and which, with its extraordinary beam and flat bottom, would have maximum stability, minimum draught and very little rolling in a seaway. A ship designed on such lines would make an admirable gun platform or an exceedingly comfortable yacht. As it happened his designs yielded both types.

The idea of a circular naval vessel appealed to Vice Admiral Popov of the Imperial Russian Navy, as part of his charge was the defence of the Black Sea coasts, a region of shallow waters with a limiting draught of thirteen feet. The conventional battleship of the day, the heavily armed and heavily armoured Monitor type, would require too much draught to be really effective here, and any orthodox war vessel capable of sailing in these shallow waters would be too small or too vulnerable to be of any use.

A circular vessel, however, with an immense displacement for very little draught, could be fitted with the heaviest armour available and equipped with the largest guns money could buy, and still float at less than the limiting draught.

Popov accordingly built two of these circular ironclads, which eventually became known as Popovkas (little Popovs) or occasionally as Cyclads, a mongrel mixture of the Greek *kuklos*, a circle, and ironclad. The first vessel, *Novgorod*, of 2,500 tons, was laid down at St. Petersburg in December 1871, and on completion the hull was dismantled and sent by rail to Nikolaiev on the Black Sea. The boilers, being too wide to go by train, were dispatched by sea on the steamer *Cesarewitch*. Re-building was commenced in March 1872 and the *Novgorod* was launched in the summer of 1873.

21 Circular Russian vessel *Novgorod*

The vessel, for all the world like a gigantic pocket-watch lying face upwards, was perfectly circular in plan, 101 feet in diameter with a maximum draught of 13 feet and a corresponding freeboard of 18 inches. The main deck had excessive round of beam of some 4 feet, which helped to discourage either sea water or enemy shot from lingering on board.

The deck armour was 2¾ inches thick, and the side armour, which extended to 6 feet below the deck level, consisted of two separate layers. The inner layer of 1½ inches thick iron plate corrugated 7 inches deep, was attached directly to the shipsides. The main or outer armour was in two tiers of plate, the upper one 9 inches thick, the lower one 7 inches thick, and these plates had heavy teak backing on to the corrugated inner plating. This side armour was covered by a layer of timber 2 feet thick, which was in turn sheathed in copper.

The bottom was quite flat and was equipped with twelve keels 8 inches deep, placed fore and aft, which served partly as docking keels and partly as fins to control her direction. The sides were vertical and there was a rounded bilge, and an overhang aft to protect the steering gear and, as far as possible, the propellers.

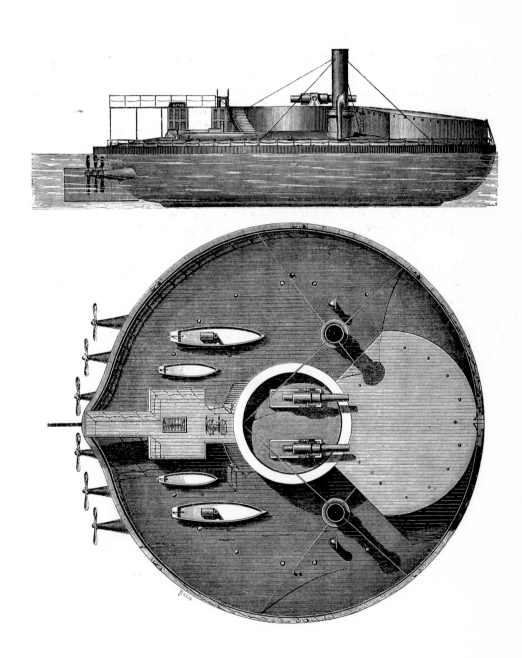

22 Profile and plan of Russian circular ships *Novgorod* and *Popov*

The pancake-like hull was divided horizontally by a tween deck and further sub-divided by a large number of water tanks placed around the shipsides, thus forming protection additional to the armour.

The business end of the *Novgorod* was the huge revolving turret at the centre, mounting two 8-inch-bore breech-loading guns, weighing some 11 tons each, on gun carriages. This turret was 29 feet 6 inches in diameter and 7 feet high, and was protected by 9 inches thick armour.

The turret rotated about a hollow pillar communicating with the magazine, the pillar serving as an ammunition hatch. The guns could therefore be traversed from forward to about 35° on each side, any further angle requiring rotation of the hull as well. Forward of the turret a light superstructure offered accommodation to the captain and officers, the crew being berthed below the main, armoured deck.

The *Novgorod* was propelled by six compound steam engines placed in a row athwartships, each driving its own screw, and taking steam at 60 lb. from eight boilers. The engines and boilers were divided into port and starboard engine rooms, the controls from each side being brought together to a master control station. By this means there were virtually two engines only, which could be operated by two engineers.

This engine handling was necessary because of the extreme difficulty of steering a circular ship by rudder alone. Without a keel to grip the water, and with a tremendous eddy of water round the stern of the circular hull, the rudder would have practically no effect, and it needed an external force, the jet stream from a set of propellers, to react against the hull and turn her into the required direction.

All six screws were 10 feet 6 inches in diameter, and their pitch varied from 10 feet on the two inboard ones to 12 feet on the outboard ones. The two inner screwshafts were somewhat lower than the others and their propeller discs protruded below the bottom of the hull. Thus, when the ship was drydocking, the propeller blade tips could foul the keel blocks or docking cradle and suffer serious damage, unless means were provided to tuck them neatly above the bottom. The central screws were accordingly made three bladed, and in the docking position they were placed with the upper blade vertical, ensuring that the other two would be well clear of any obstacle.

There are one or two points which might be mentioned here as having a special interest for vessels built in Russia. The Popovkas had a pair of steam ejectors to pump out the bilges, a form of bilge pumping which may have been known for many years but which only came into its own a few years ago. Also, as the technical press of 1875 commented, *Novgorod*'s engines and boilers were in poor condition after only two years of service.

On the other hand she was claimed to have been exceptionally steady in a seaway, although naturally prone to slamming damage because of her flat bottom.

Possibly because of the warming up of the cold war between Russia and Turkey, which resulted in a declaration of war in 1877, Admiral Popov built another circular ironclad, the *Vice Admiral Popov*, and launched her in 1875. This vessel was somewhat larger than her predecessor, being 120 feet in diameter with 18 inches side armour and slightly larger guns. She displaced some 3,500 tons but was generally similar to *Novgorod* in most other respects. The mere fact that a sister vessel was built at all suggests that the first vessel had fulfilled her purpose.

According to naval observers at the trials these vessels made six knots at full speed and they answered the helm very well indeed, turning on their centre the moment the three engines on one side were stopped or even slowed. With starboard engines ahead and port engines astern, the Popovka could pivot on her centre, or spin like a top. Answering the helm in a circular ship, however, need not necessarily result in a change in direction of sailing, and one is left with the impression that steering a Popovka was rather like steering a car on an icy road.

Livadia

The steam yacht *Livadia* was not a circular vessel but in most respects she belonged to that class of ships in that she was built by John Elder & Co. in 1880 to plans supplied by Admiral Popov along the lines previously tried out in the Popovkas, and aimed at maximum stability and comfort. She was, in fact, elliptical in plan, and her given name was that of the Imperial Palace at Yalta on the Black Sea coast.

She was ordered by Czar Alexander II, who was assassinated before the vessel was delivered in 1881. She was 235 feet long with a beam of 153 feet, displacing 3,900 tons on a draught of 6 feet 6 inches, quite a sizeable yacht, even for a Czar. But the Russian Imperial Family had always been lavish, even prodigal, in their yachts. In the space of fifteen years, there were, in quick succession, a number of large, luxurious official yachts: *Livadia, Polar Star, Derjava* and *Standart*, the latter being 425 feet long and requiring twenty-four Belleville boilers for her 15,000 horse power

E

23 Launching of the Russian imperial yacht *Livadia*

engines: a fitting pleasure boat indeed for the most powerful monarch in Europe.

The hull of the *Livadia* consisted of two parts, a lower 'turbot' shape which provided the buoyancy, upon which was superimposed a superstructure in the shape of an ordinary vessel. The 'turbot' base was considerably wider than the 'ship' portion and had sides sloping down to water level. The bottom was perfectly flat, but at the after end the stern frame skeg protruded well below the keel line to ensure sufficient immersion for the rudder. This necessitated trimming by the head to lift the stern clear when crossing a river bar.

The 'turbot' provided the working space for the ship and contained the engines and boilers, bunkers, stores, etc. It had a double bottom 3 feet 6 inches high and was subdivided into forty watertight compartments by means of two vertical bulkheads running right round the ship.

The 'ship' structure formed the hotel and navigating spaces, with the crew berthed on the lower deck, ratings forward, officers aft, and the Imperial suite occupying the whole of the upper and weather decks.

There were eight main boilers, all in line athwartships, providing steam

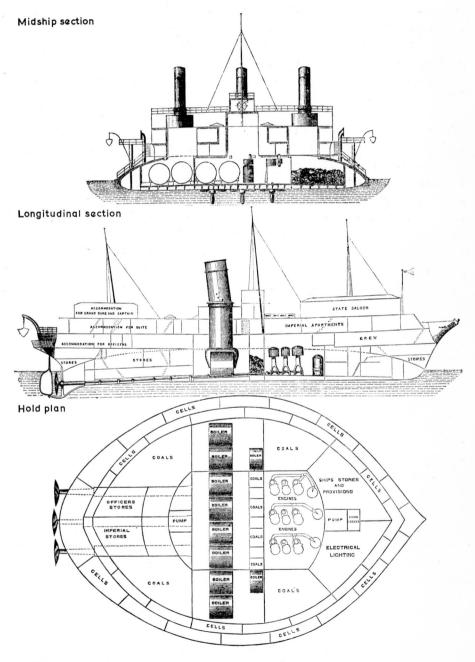

Midship section

Longitudinal section

ACCOMMODATION
FOR GRAND DUKE AND CAPTAIN

STATE SALOON

ACCOMMODATION FOR SUITE

IMPERIAL APARTMENTS

ACCOMMODATION FOR OFFICERS

CREW

STORES

STORES

STORES

Hold plan

CELLS

CELLS

CELLS

CELLS

CELLS

CELLS

COALS

BOILER

COALS

BOILER

BOILER

OFFICERS
STORES

BOILER

COALS

SHIPS STORES
AND
PROVISIONS

ENGINES

PUMP

BOILER

COALS

IMPERIAL
STORES

BOILER

COALS

ENGINES

PUMP

CHAIN
LOCKER

BOILER

COALS

ELECTRICAL
LIGHTING

CELLS

COALS

BOILER

BOILER

COALS

CELLS

CELLS

CELLS

24 The Russian imperial yacht *Livadia*, section, profile and plan

at 70 lb. to three propelling engines, also placed side by side, each driving its own screw; and to give point to her unusual breadth the three funnels were placed abreast. On trials on the Clyde she averaged 16 knots on 10,500 i.h.p.—this in spite of her bottom being foul after many months fitting out and with no chance of being dry docked for scraping and painting. (When a ship is completed she is invariably docked for cleaning before proceeding on trials—the loss of a quarter of a knot through dirty shell plating could result in a swingeing penalty against the builders.)

A close inspection of the *Livadia*'s plans shows that although designed as a yacht, the possibility of converting her into a super Popovka if necessary must have been implicit in the specification. This would account for the extraordinary degree of sub-division in the working spaces, with double lines of bulkheads enclosing a protective series of water tanks all round the shipsides, and the placing of the engines and boilers inside a citadel in the centre of the turbot. The removal of the Imperial apartments, the 'ship' portion, and the substitution of a suitable gun turret on the 'turbot' would have converted an innocent yacht into a truly formidable warship.

The *Livadia*'s debut was far from auspicious. Her boilers were among the first to be made from steel instead of the more usual wrought iron. The first boiler to be completed split under hydraulic test through all three shell plates, and was condemned out of hand. Three successive boilers showed similar cracks and were discarded pending a review of the design and the steel-making process.

Later, on passage to the Crimea, she sustained serious slamming damage during heavy weather in the Bay of Biscay and was forced to put into El Ferrol for shelter and repairs. Owing to her excessive breadth there was no dry dock which could accommodate her, and temporary repairs only could be carried out to the set up and leaky bottom plating. She was accordingly obliged to lay up in the Spanish port during the winter and continue her trip to the Black Sea in the following spring, floating on her tank top, i.e. relying on the water-tight double bottom to keep her afloat. Once arrived at her destination she was docked on the floating dock at Nikolaiev built for the Popovkas, repaired and placed in commission.

Although little is known of her subsequent career she outlived all her contemporaries and served for many years as a Russian naval depot ship. She was still in existence well into the 1920's.

The concept of round, flat vessels for war or peace might strike different people in different ways: as funny, impractical or eminently suitable for their purpose, as indeed the Popovkas appeared to be. They were a compromise between speed and sailing qualities on the one hand and a stable platform on the other, and they remind me, in nostalgic mood, of my childhood days in the sun-bleached Belgian Kempen, when a wooden clog, rigged with a jury mast and loaded with pebbles as cargo and with a tin soldier as skipper, served as a model yacht on the canal. The rounded shape and flat bottom were admirable for steady transport, but the rudder was useless and the clog inevitably fetched up on the far bank.

The circular design, in short, was merely the geometrical solution for maximum armour plus maximum armament at minimum draught.

The Mersey Docks and Harbour Board, however, had no such doubts about the practical aspect of a round vessel when Mr. G. F. Lyster, engineer to the Dock Estate, submitted plans for a ferry service between Princes Pier and the Woodside and Seacombe landing stages on the Cheshire side. The vessels would be circular in plan, carrying horses and carts in the centre under a glass roof extending for the full diameter, and passsengers in handsome, covered galleries arranged all round the deck. In order to give the greatest possible facilities of access to and from the vessels the landing stages would be constructed with semi-circular embayments into which the vessels would run, thus affording one-half of their entire circumference for embarking and discharging their passengers and traffic.

Instead of being propelled by paddles, as in the normal ferry boat, these vessels would use chains moored to each shore and stretching across the river bed, the chains passing over drums or gipsies, one on each side of the ship, and driven by powerful winches below deck. As a precaution against damage from other vessels' anchors, guard chains would be laid alongside the guide chains.

The main consideration for the proposed use of circular ferry boats was not that they could load and unload in a semi-circular dock: a conventional ship in a narrow-fitting U shaped dock would achieve the same effect. The circular form was thought to be one that would present less broadside and less resistance to the action of the tides than any other. This proposed ferry system was, however, never adopted.

Before leaving the subject of circular ships, let us examine one of the anomalies which their peculiar shape could produce in regard to registered tonnage. The Thames Yacht Tonnage rules of those days stated that:

$$\text{Tonnage} = \frac{(L-B)\ B^2}{188}$$

where L and B are length and breadth respectively. In the case of the Popovkas, where length and breadth are equal, i.e. where L=B, the tonnage becomes freakish indeed:

$$\text{Tonnage} = \frac{(B-B)\ B^2}{188} = 0$$

5 Twin hulled vessels

To most people the term 'catamaran' evokes nothing more than a mental picture of a new type of yacht placed in a special category by Yacht Club rules and sailed by shaggy young men smoking very large pipes. If pressed for details they would probably suggest that the word had been coined by yachtsmen to describe a type of boat evolved within the last twenty years.

The word 'catamaran', on the contrary, is Tamil and describes exactly the double canoe found in the Indian Ocean and, to a lesser extent, its cousin the outrigger canoe, both of which have been in constant use since history began.

Twin hulls, however, were not peculiar to the South Seas; they were fairly well known to the western world, and in particular to Britain, and were built by all sorts of people who had no interest whatever in Southern India. All they wanted was a steady floating platform, and their common sense told them that next to a raft a deck spanning two boats was the best solution.

This idea was used by Demetrios Poliorketes, one of the generals who succeeded Alexander the Great and who invaded Rhodes in 305 B.C. Unable to make any headway against the city walls he attacked from the sea, using pairs of galleys lashed together, upon which were built tall towers mounting catapults and archers.

Coming down the time scale to the seventeenth century we find considerable mention of Sir William Petty's *Experiment** by both those gabby but extremely shrewd columnists, Pepys and Evelyn. Thus John Evelyn in 1675:

Sir William amongst other inventions, author of the Double-bottom'd Ship, which though it perished and he censured for rashness, yet it was lost in the Bay of Biscay in a storme, when I think 15 more vessels miscarried; The vessel was flat-bottom'd, of exceeding use to put in Shallow Ports and ride over small depths of water: It consisted of two distinct keeles crampt together with huge timbers, etc: so as a violent streame ran betweene. It bare a monstrous broad saile; and he still persists it practicable and of exceeding use, and has often told me he would adventure himselfe in such another could he procure sailors, and his Majestie's Permission to make a second 'Experiment' which name the King gave it at the launching.

* Built in 1662, this was one of the earliest of western twin-hulled vessels which must not be confused with the Australian *Experiment* built in New South Wales in 1832. This latter vessel was an orthodox single hulled side wheeler, the paddle shaft being driven by a team of horses. I believe it was James Watt who coined the expression horse power, but I doubt if he intended it to be taken so literally.

Profile

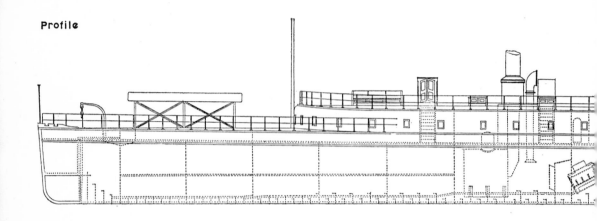

Main deck plan

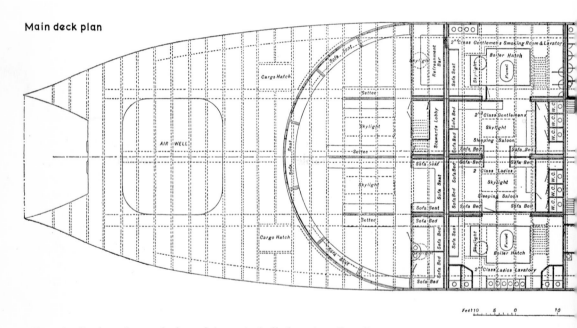

25 Longitudinal section and plan of the twin hulled packet *Castalia*

The *Experiment* was launched in December 1662, and a note in Evelyn's diary simply states: 'She was lost in a storm in 1665, Pepys was also at the launching.'

Samuel Pepys makes a number of references to this early catamaran, most of them very brief. Thus we meet with a casual remark such as: '... both Sir William (Batten) and I on board the *Experiment* to despatch

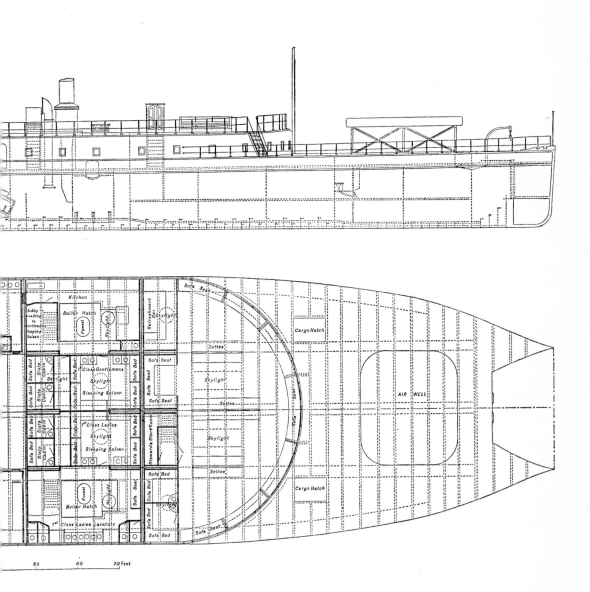

her away, she being to carry things to the Madeiras with the Indy fleet . . .'
Or again:

*. . . Mr. Grant showed me letters of Sir William Petty, wherein he says that his
vessel which he hath built upon two keeles, hath this month won a wager of £50 in
sailing between Dublin and Holyhead with the pacquett-boat, the best ship or vessel*

the King hath there; and he offers to lay with any vessel in the world. It is about thirty tons in burden and carries thirty men, with good Accommodation . . . in their coming back from Holyhead they started together, and this vessel came to Dublin by five at night and the pacquett-boat not before eight the next morning: and when they came they did believe that this vessel had been drowned or at least behind, not thinking she could have lived in that sea. Strange things are told of this vessel.

From these entries we learn that the *Experiment* was a fairly large vessel for her time, requiring a crew of thirty, that she was very fast and that she was considered eligible to make an ocean voyage to Madeira and back.

Another early vessel in this class was the *Edinburgh*, built at Leith in 1786 by Patrick Miller. This vessel was 73 feet long with a total breadth of 23 feet, and had three hulls held together by crossbeams, each hull having its own rudder, with the three tillers interconnected. Propulsion was by manually operated paddle wheels.

Robert Fulton's warship *Demologos* was built at New York in 1814. This vessel consisted of two wooden hulls with a steam-driven paddle wheel in between, there being no masts or rigging to be damaged by gunfire. The vulnerable paddle wheel was thus efficiently protected by the ship itself.

Several twin hull vessels were built in the early part of the nineteenth century, but left very little mark on history. *Prinzessin Charlotte* was built at Spandau in 1816. *Union* (1821) and *George Fourth* (1823) were twin hulled wooden ferry boats built by James Brown at Perth for service on the River Tay. All that is known about the latter is that she cost £4,330 14s. 10d.

Gemini, built specially to cater for Thames river traffic to and from the Great Exhibition in 1851, was a complete failure. On a trial run she got as far as Gravesend and there broke down, never to sail again.

Alliance was built in 1862 on the Clyde as a passenger ferry.

A later twin hulled vessel, the steam tug *Rosse*, invented by Captain J. Rosse and built in 1882 on the Hudson, was unusual in that propulsion was by means of a huge belt running fore and aft over two drums placed between the hulls and driven by a steam engine. Buckets or paddles were fitted to the outer surface of this belt, rather like the modern bucket dredger, and her inventor claimed that she could sail at full speed along a canal without undue wash upon the banks.

Castalia

The *Castalia*, the first large-scale sea-going twin hulled steamer, was inspired by Captain Dicey of the Indian Navy, no doubt from his experience of coastal craft in the Indian Ocean and the South Pacific. He conceived the idea of two vessels secured side by side, the one acting as counterpoise to the other, each in its turn preventing its fellow from rolling. From this arose the question of constructing either two separate ship-shaped hulls or two separate halves of one hull, and the latter arrangement was decided upon.

The *Castalia*, named after Lady Granville, was built by the Thames Ironworks and Shipbuilding Co., for the Channel Steamship Co. and was completed in 1875. She was 290 feet overall length, 17 feet beam for each hull with a space of 26 feet between hulls, giving her a total beam of 60 feet, equal to that of a crack North Atlantic passenger steamer. All this was on a draught of 6 feet 6 inches.

In cross section the ship appeared as a normal hull split down the middle, and the two halves separated to form the paddle-wheel race. These two half hulls were joined for most of their length by a lower and an upper deck, the connection being provided by carrying up the four engine and boiler room bulkheads in each body to form four main transverse webs spanning the race. Together with the upper and lower decks these webs formed immensely strong box girders and gave complete freedom from any working between the two hulls.

This ship was specially built for the middle passage and plied between Dover and Calais; as was the case with most cross channel packets in those days she was made double ended to avoid having to turn round in those extremely narrow harbours. Each hull, therefore, was equipped with a fore and aft rudder, and the rudders at each end of the ship were coupled together by an endless chain working on ths Rapson slide principle. Each half hull had its own pair of diagonal engines, the paddle wheels of both engines being placed inboard in the space between the hulls, and each wheel could be worked independently. A heavy iron girder ran midway between the two wheels and carried the bearings for the outer ends of the paddle shafts.

The promoters required a minimum speed of 14 knots to compete with existing packets and ordered engines of 1,250 i.h.p. driving paddle wheels 22 feet diameter with 20 fixed floats per wheel each 10 feet long by 2 feet 3 inches wide and with a dip of 3 feet 8 inches.

Midship Sections

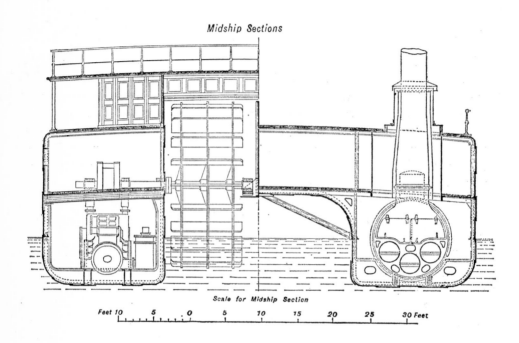

Scale for Midship Section

Feet 10   5   .0   5   10   15   20   25   30 Feet

Frame Sections

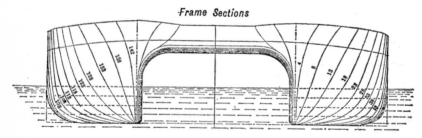

26 Transverse sections of the twin hulled packet *Castalia*

As originally proposed she was to have eight smallish boilers, but this design was altered to four bigger boilers, each 7 feet diameter and 6 feet long, of much larger grate area. With this new arrangement the speed was very disappointing, the vessel barely doing 9 knots at maximum permissible revolutions, as the boilers primed so badly that the engines could not be worked up to their full power. Several consultants, including the eminent engineer John Penn, took turns in redesigning the boilers to stop this carry-over of water into the engine cylinders, but to no avail. Eventually the Channel Steamship Co. contracted with Maudslay Son & Field for new, larger boilers 12 feet diameter and 10 feet 2 inches long and new paddle wheels 21 feet in diameter with shorter floats and greater dip.

This extra weight increased the draught to 7 feet, and the results of the measured mile trials gave 11 knots on 1,500 i.h.p., a very low coefficient of performance indeed. Most naval architects of the day had assumed that in the case of a twin hulled steamer with paddles placed between the hulls the water would be carried away by the wheels from the paddle race faster than it would flow in, and consequently that there would be a hollow formed just ahead of the wheels. It was quite a natural assumption in fact, but it was not borne out in practice.

To test this theory, and in an endeavour to find how the power was being dissipated, the builders carried out a daring experiment. They set the *Castalia*'s bows against the quay wall in Victoria Dock, started up the engines ahead and then got into a small boat between the hulls at the fore end, paying out the painter more and more and allowing the boat to drift into the tunnel under the deck until it almost reached the revolving paddle wheels, which in that confined space must have looked and sounded like a miniature Niagara Falls.

To their surprise and dismay, the builders noted that there was hardly any movement of the water immediately ahead of the wheels, and that ' . . . a piece of batten was floated up to within an inch of the floats and returned to us; was again thrust towards the wheel, was struck by the float and immediately disappeared.' With the water streaming out astern from the paddle race like a mill stream the designers could only conclude that the water fed into the paddles was drawn up from under the keels, and not from the bows. This was proved to be the case, for at sea the water tended to build up in the wheel race ahead of the paddles and choke them, a large proportion of the engine power being required to beat the water down before the wheels could get a purchase on it.

Paddle wheels can be as efficient as good propellers but their diameter and position on the ship are critical. The immersion of the floats, i.e. the dip, and hence the speed of the vessel, depends very much on the position of the bow wave crest, which should be just slightly ahead of the wheel. There is also a maximum ship speed for every size of wheel which is independent of revolutions or horsepower, as will be seen from the speed power curves of a conventional paddle steamer, where the floats have been widened to increase the overall diameter. Here it will be observed from the trend of the curves that no matter what additional power was given, the speed in knots would not be increased beyond a certain figure.

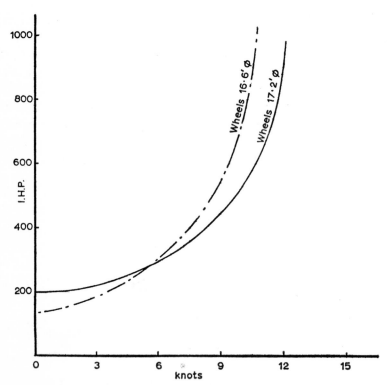

27 Speed/power curves for paddle engine

As far as sea-keeping qualities are concerned the *Castalia* seems to have fulfilled Captain Dicey's promise of a steady ship, for in an article on her in *The Times* for 1875 we read:

Leaving Dover we encountered a strong gale from the south-west, which being abeam tested her rolling qualities very fairly, if the term 'rolling' can be applied to her movements. For, strictly speaking, she does not roll, but as each wave passes, the windward hull lifts to it and falls again, the wave passing across the space between the hulls to lift in turn the leeward hull, but not to set up a roll, for if it were possible to stop the next wave from passing she would remain motionless, whereas in any single-hulled vessel the oscillation set up would continue for some length of time, and she would gradually come to a state of rest, and it is the above peculiarity that gives its chief value to this form of vessel. These movements of necessity cause an alteration in the horizontal deck platform, but not more than $3\frac{1}{2}°$ on the above occasion, and it was the opinion of her able commander, Captain

Pittock, that no weather she was likely to encounter on this station would give more than 5° of inclination, the present steamers rolling 14–15°.

With regard to pitching and scending, I may add that while at Calais on the above-mentioned day, the wind veered round to the north-west, and so on the return passage we had a strong sea ahead, into which the mail steamer was pitching, taking in the water through her hawser pipes and over her bows, sending it forth in white sheets over her waterways, while on the 'Castalia's' low deck forward might be seen at work an engineer, repairing a damaged float nearly the whole of her passage, her oscillation in a fore and aft line not exceeding 2½°.

In spite of this good write-up, however, she was not a success. Broken paddle floats had to be renewed or repaired every voyage and, while she appeared to be reasonably popular with the travelling public, she failed to make the economic grade and was withdrawn from active service in the winter of 1875.

She was eventually purchased by the Government, converted into a smallpox hospital and lay moored in the Thames for the next twenty years.

Calais Douvres

The *Castalia*'s owners decided to build a second twin hulled steamer and placed an order for a larger, faster ship with Andrew Leslie & Co. of Hebburn in 1876, the engines to be supplied by Black, Hawthorn & Co. Ltd., of Gateshead.

Before starting on the design the builders carried out one of those full scale experiments which excite such great interest in the public at large. They borrowed two Woolwich paddle ferries and tried them out at full power both singly and lashed together a convenient distance apart. From the figures obtained a suitable horse power was chosen for the contemplated mailboat.

This new vessel was named *Express*, but the owners experienced financial difficulties before she could be completed and eventually went into liquidation. With such a problem child on their hands the builders had no choice but to complete the construction, on the principle that a ready built vessel would be more likely to find a market than a half-finished one on the slipway. She was, in fact, sold to the London, Chatham and Dover Railway Co., renamed *Calais Douvres*, and placed on the middle passage to take the place of her predecessor.

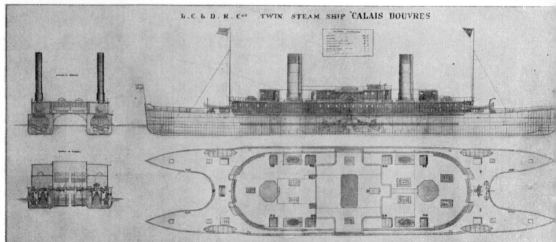

28 The twin hulled cross channel packet *Calais Douvres*

29 *Calais Douvres*—general arrangement

Unlike the *Castalia*, which was virtually one ship split into two and joined together again, the new ship consisted of two separate conventional hulls joined together precisely in the fashion of her prototype: by bringing the two forward and the two after engine room bulkheads in each hull right up to meet each other thus forming with the lower and the upper decks two enormous cross girders, all accommodation being placed in this tween deck space.

The *Calais Douvres* was slightly bigger than the *Castalia*, being 300 feet long overall, with a deck beam of 62 feet, on a draught of 6 feet 8 inches. As before each hull had its own system of boilers, engines and independent paddle wheel, the two wheels being placed alongside each other in the space between the hulls. A longitudinal wrought-iron girder divided this space and carried the outer bearings for the paddle shafts. The wheels were equipped with feathering floats, heavy iron plates hinged about the wheel rims, each fitted with a crank worked by a radial connecting rod revolving about a 'jenny nettle', a bearing 12 inches forward of the main shaft centre. This offset provided an inclination to the floats relative to their position on the wheel, so that they were almost vertical to the water when immersed and thus exerted maximum force. These two 'jenny nettles' were also fitted to the centre girder, and it might be appropriate here to point out that while this vessel, like her sister, was double ended and could sail 'ahead' in either direction, there was only one true ahead direction. The paddle floats fitted at this period were either slightly curved or of aerofoil section, and were consequently designed for one direction only at maximum efficiency. Again, for economy's sake, to use the steam expansively the designed valve settings could be efficient in one direction only. Hence, although as a ship she was truly double ended, her engines still had to conform to thermodynamic principles just like any lesser engines.

Mailboats normally have rather fine entrance and run curves, but not so the *Calais Douvres*. She had exceptionally powerful machinery and to provide additional displacement for this weight without increase in draught her builders gave her rather blunt lines fore and aft. Her four rudders, one at each end of her two hulls, were shaped into the contour of the plating, giving extra buoyancy, and as in the previous vessel the rudders at each end were locked together and worked as one.

The engines in each hull were twin cylinder diagonal, with cylinder bore 63 inches by 6 feet stroke and at full power gave the ship a speed of 14¾ knots at 4,300 i.h.p. a fantastic increase in power over the 1,250 i.h.p.

F

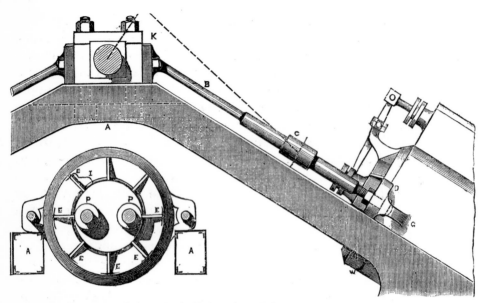

30 Shaft alignment of the twin hulled packet *Calais Douvres*

of the slightly smaller *Castalia*. She was, in fact, over-powered, although the original experiment with the two Woolwich ferries showed that a speed of 14 knots would require a minimum of 3,600 i.h.p. This power demanded a consumption over the twenty-four hours of something like 220 tons of coal, rather heavy for a cross channel steamer.

This enormous power was in some ways her undoing, which was also contributed to in part by an odd detail in design whereby the centre line of the cylinder did not coincide with the centre line of the crankshaft. This offset, called the désaxé system, was employed in the 1920's in one of the earlier marine diesel engines, in which the cylinder centre line was about 2½ inches ahead of the crankshaft centreline. The claims made for this system were that the length of the connecting rod was reduced in the ratio of 3·8 to 4 and therefore the total height of the engine was correspondingly reduced; secondly that the bearing pressures on the ahead and astern guides were equalised, giving a lower guide pressure with normal ahead running; thirdly, as the crank would be slightly over the centre with the piston at top centre, a better impulse could be obtained at the commencement of each firing stroke.

As a very junior member of a team who worked round the clock for three days in the 1920's to get one of these désaxé-type engines going,

I was not enthusiastic about the design, and when we finally got it to work the smoother running and more efficient combustion were not particularly noticeable in the clanking, hissing and general uproar of a large marine diesel engine running with blast injection. However, that was not the point. The important fact was that the extra stresses on the framework of an engine built on the offset principle had been allowed for in the design by heavier columns and bedplate. In the *Calais Douvres*'s engines, where the centre line offset appeared to be of the order of 12 inches, there must have been an enormous out of balance force on the guides. These guides were substantial round bars, one on each side of the cylinder, taking the side thrust from the connecting rod through the crosshead and guide eyes. In later-type engines, where guide shoes and guide plates were (and still are) used, any wear could readily be taken up by adjusting the shoe plates, but in the earlier type of diagonal paddle engines it was an expensive business to rebush the guide eyes when worn. Consequently, when the guide eye bushes wore oval, some of the side thrust inevitably was taken up by the piston rod and, through it, the piston rod stuffing boxes on the cylinder top.

In these engines the cylinder top was cast integral with the cylinder, the piston being removed through the bottom of the cylinder, and any serious defect to the top involved the renewal of the complete cylinder.

In the *Calais Douvres*, cracks appeared in the webs supporting the stuffing boxes in three of the four cylinders, some of these cracks being serious.

On two cross channel passages she sailed with one cylinder badly cracked and out of commission, another cylinder cracked but still usable, and a third believed to be cracked.

It is difficult at this distance in time to find out what her true value was as a cross channel steamer, but here is the view of a seasoned sailor as he awaited her arrival at Dover:

I was on the Admiralty Pier on one occasion when there was a good deal of cross sea, the wind was about W.S.W. and the tide was ebbing, which many gentlemen here know would produce very rough water indeed in the neighbourhood of Dover. After waiting some time the Ostend boat arrived, one hour and forty minutes before the 'Calais Douvres' made her appearance, and the trains were kept waiting one hour and forty minutes for the arrival of the 'Calais Douvres'. She came through the mist which enveloped her and showed herself, and I watched her with the keenest interest. She rolled, or she moved; not an honest roll, but I may call it a wobble, which if not the ordinary roll of a Channel steamer, was quite as objectionable to her passengers.

She approached nearer and nearer, and with the aid of a powerful glass, I watched her keenly, and as she was coming straight end on to where I was standing on the Admiralty Pier, and that part between the two hulls seemed to me to be completely choked with water, which sufficiently accounted to my mind for the very slow progress she was making in comparatively smooth water for so large a ship, she being 300 feet long. You would not have expected so much motion in an ordinary Channel sea with a ship of that length, but she seemed to me to be completely choked between the two hulls, and that was enough to prevent her making rapid progress. She took green seas all over that lower deck. In fact, I very much doubt if it would have been safe to have stood on that day on that lower deck. Not having been on board, I am only speaking of what appeared to me to be the case from the Pier.

She came in, and I must say she steered very well indeed. I was told that there were 460 passengers on board, and I should think from the observation which I had the means of making that that was about the number, but I do not hesitate most solemnly to declare that at least 400 of those were sea-sick, for I do not think in my 40 years' experience in the English Channel, or in my 40 years' experience of crossing the Atlantic, I ever saw so many people sea-sick in one day as there were there.

My son was with me, and we both counted the people as well as we could, and we afterwards noticed that a man and a boy were employed on the deck of that ship for half an hour and upwards in washing up the basins which had been used. That is very clear proof that those travellers that day had not derived any benefit from a slow, large ship.

There was not a particle of her deck that was not wet with the spray blowing over, and she is not protected as a comfortable vessel ought to be from the wind or the spray, because there is nothing but wirework all round, just to prevent you tumbling overboard; there is no protection for ladies, whose dresses are apt to be blown up on the deck of a ship if they are not screened by high bulwarks. The ordinary Channel steamers have very high bulwarks, and they are a great protection against the weather, and they put up weather cloths fore and aft which keep off the wind and the spray, but there was nothing of the kind in the 'Calais Douvres'.

I went below to examine every part, to see her under circumstances of a roughish passage, although I had seen her before. The cabin windows had all been closed and the heat and offensive smell in this part of the vessel made it utterly impracticable for anyone to remain there. It was impossible from the heat of the boilers that anybody could have remained for a quarter of an hour in those cabins without being almost parboiled. I assure you that I do not exaggerate in any word that I use, the heat was most excessive, and at this moment, if you go on board the 'Calais Douvres' you will find that the partitions and the bulkheads, or many of them, are cracked, and all of them are blistered from the excessive heat from the boilers. They are close to the boilers in the lower part of the vessel. That is an objection on rainy days, when there is no suitable place to go below and lie down.

Rather a jaundiced view of the vessel and apparently not that of the travelling public, if we can believe the London, Chatham and Dover Railway Co., who claimed that in one season, making a round voyage each day, she carried 50,000 people and netted £22,000 or 15% of capital cost. The *Calais Douvres* was fairly popular with passengers during her brief career, but she required careful nursing in wintry weather, and the maintenance of her massive engines and paddles plus the cost of keeping her in commission proved too much for the owners and she was withdrawn from active service in 1887, to be used as a hospital ship in Dover Harbour.

Captain Dicey, designer of the *Castalia*, struck the final blow. He held that Messrs. Leslie had infringed his patent and brought a lawsuit against the builders, which was subsequently settled out of court. It is difficult to imagine the basis of the litigation, as he could hardly claim exclusive rights for a type of vessel that had been in use for thousands of years. But his claim must have been valid enough for it to have been settled by the builders.

The *Castalia* and the *Calais Douvres* were popular with their passengers, but they were not technically successful. Both vessels were tricky to handle in anything but moderate weather, and prone to paddle damage. They were also uneconomic, for the following reason—almost the whole of the power required by a steamer to attain her speed is absorbed either in wave making or in skin friction, and it is the latter which accounts for the greater loss. In a carefully designed hull some of the power used at the bow to push the water aside and under the forefoot is returned by this same water in closing in at the stern. With skin friction, however, there is no such bonus. Skin friction is another form of ordinary friction, and while it can be reduced slightly by special butts on the riveted plates, it just cannot be eliminated. In a cross channel steamer the drag will affect the water up to three feet from the ship's plating, the layers of water next to the skin of the ship travelling with it at the same speed, the layers further out travelling at a reduced speed but still in the same direction, and so on until the motion dies out several feet from the ship. In a twin hulled ship, there is much more wave making and skin friction than in a single hulled vessel of the same carrying capacity in passengers and cargo.

To sum up, in *Castalia*, with engines based on the power requirements for an equivalent ship with a single hull, the speed was too slow and she could not compete with conventional packets. In the other case, *Calais Douvres*, the power was calculated for a twin hulled vessel, resulting in an enormous increase in horsepower as compared with the orthodox steamers, and a heavy increase in running costs.

Twin hulled steamers were not confined to Europe or America. They were fairly well represented in Australia, especially in the Darling-Murray-Murrumbidgee River complex.

A twin hulled steamer, the *Kangaroo*, was in use as a traffic ferry in Hobart, Tasmania. This vessel was double ended in the usual ferry style, and was built of the local wood in 1855, her particulars being 110 feet long, by 11 feet 6 inches beam and over 7 feet depth for each hull. The paddle wheel, worked by a two cylinder 30 h.p. engine, was placed between the two hulls. After a series of changes of ownership she was withdrawn in 1926 and her engine removed.

Another catamaran-type ship, the *Bunyip*, plied on the Murray and Murrumbidgee Rivers in New South Wales. This vessel, also of wood, was built in Adelaide in 1858 for Captain Randell and partner, and consisted of a pair of twin hulls connected by cross girders, with a paddle wheel in the space between the hulls, each hull measuring 100 feet long, 12 feet beam and 5 foot 8 inches deep. In 1862 she was rebuilt by closing the two hulls together, removing the central paddle wheel and replacing it in the stern, forming a sternwheeler. The sternwheel was driven by a pair of high pressure oscillating steam engines, one cylinder in each hull. The vessel had two decks, the lower for cargo in bales, the upper for passengers, and in this respect would bear a superficial resemblance to the American Western River steamers.

The *Bunyip* was destroyed by fire (the usual fate of these Australian river boats) in 1863 when sailing on the Murray River with twenty people on board. Several of them were lost, together with the cargo of wool.

A most unusual feature about this twin hull, and one which strikes an ultra-modern note, was the small bow thruster, a transverse paddle wheel driven by an oscillating steam auxiliary engine fitted at the forward end between the two hulls. This wheel served to push the bows round some of the narrower bends in the river and so assist the steering, although report has it that the steering was not the *Bunyip*'s strong point. No men-

31 Twin hulled steamer *Gemini* at Mannum Wharf, S. Australia

tion is made of the form of steering but we need not necessarily assume that she was fitted with twin rudders coupled together. For all we know the vessel may have been equipped with a rudder on one hull only, which would have made it very difficult to steer her round a narrow bend in the river.

The *Gemini* must surely be one of the oddest of ships even against a background of bizarre ships, a genuine freak and a veritable phoenix in the shipping world. It started life on the Murray River and must not be confused with the *Gemini* built in London for the 1851 Great Exhibition and described earlier in the chapter.

Now by definition a twin hulled ship is assumed to be built of two identical hulls, or, alternatively, of two mirror-image hulls; one left- and one right-handed. Common sense tells also us that these two hulls should be built simultaneously, but with the *Gemini* this was not so, and her name is not strictly descriptive.

Captain Randell, previously mentioned as being in charge of the *Bunyip*, had had a small wooden paddle steamer built near Adelaide in 1853 by labour totally unskilled in the art of boatbuilding. This ship was named the *Mary Ann* and was the first steamer to navigate the Murray River, being 55 feet long by 9 feet beam. The engine was made at Adelaide and the boiler, which was rectangular, had to be bound by chains for safety as it behaved like a concertina when steam was raised. The *Mary Ann* was not very successful, so the owner had the hull rebuilt and lengthened by about 20 feet. Even the larger hull was not a success, so Randell ordered another hull to be built, with the same length and depth as the original, but considerably more beam. He clamped the two hulls together to form a 'twin' hulled vessel and named her *Gemini*. The registered particulars have an odd ring about them: 'First hull 75 feet length×9 feet 6 inches beam×6 feet 4 inches depth, second hull 75 feet length×11 feet 6 inches beam×6 feet 4 inches depth. Overall width 23 feet 9 inches.' The paddle wheel, 14 feet in diameter, was placed between the two hulls and worked by a bigger engine sited in the new hull, while the boiler was fitted in the old *Mary Ann* hull to maintain the balance.

This vessel's register closed in 1875 after a fairly successful career, and when she was broken up part of the hull structure was utilised in the dumb barge *Nil Desperandum*, later fitted with an engine, still under the same owners. The vessel eventually became known as the *Black Swan*, and her register closed in 1904. Part of her hull was used to build the Murray River paddler *Alpha*, owned at Adelaide, and this vessel carried on well into the middle of the present century, being last reported in 1963 as 'lying wrecked at Mildura'. She certainly seems to have completed her century.

6 Jointed ships

Jointed ships were to the nineteenth century what Flying Saucers are to the twentieth. Ever since the end of the Second World War, U.F.O.s have been in the news from time to time, and many of us have met people who swear they have seen them late at night on a lonely moor, with glowing side lights, roaring exhausts, and little green men with pointed ears. It is only when pressed for details that these people admit that they didn't actually *see* the Saucers; it was the chap next door who heard about them down at the pub. In describing the jointed ships, I am leaving the safe world of hard, proven fact for the treacherous realm of circumstantial evidence: the massive iron bulk of a Monitor to the elusive wraith of a Flying Dutchman.

Of all the vessels described in this book the jointed ships are the least authenticated. While all the other steamers were described in the technical and lay-Press and were registered with their competent authorities as commercial ships, it has been impossible to obtain a detailed account of a jointed ship, or particulars of any registration of such a vessel.

We have, therefore, to fall back upon descriptions of these vessels given by laymen who, however observant they may be and however accurate their notes, are still not able to convey precise technical details such as the hinged joints connecting the several sections of the ship.

Now it is impossible to draw a line between the jointed ship and the barge train, and it can be demonstrated that the former is merely an extension of the latter. Barge trains were common on the Mississippi from the earliest days of the steamboat, the method in general use being to group a number of barges together and couple them to a steam towboat at their stern (in this context the towboat *pushes*, the tug-boat *pulls*).

This arrangement was carried a stage further in 1863 when a special barge train was built for the River Indus. This consisted of a paddle steamer towing up to five barges, the bow and stern of each barge being semi-circular, each barge locking its bow into its neighbour's stern. The towing paddle steamer was of conventional shape with a semi-circular stern, and the first barge had a semi-circular concave bow and stern. Each following barge had a convex bow and hollow stern, the whole system being locked together with triangular drawbars working on ball and socket joints in such a way that, while the barge assembly formed one unit, a certain amount of sideways movement was allowed for between barges, and any one could be disconnected at will.

Particulars of the train were as follows:

Item	Length	Breadth	Draught	Tons
Steamer	200'	20'	2'2"	185
1st barge	40'	18'	10"	18
2nd, 3rd and 4th barges	100'	18'	10"	39
End barge	100'	18'	1'4"	63

The last barge was fitted out with passenger accommodation, and it will be noted that the whole train drew very little water.

A peculiar feature of the steamer was its vaguely amphibian ability to creep over sandbanks. The paddle wheels projected 6 inches below the level of the keel, and were made exceptionally robust. In the event of stranding the paddles were disconnected from the main engine, connected to a heavy duty turning gear, and used as crawlers to ride over the sand bank, the barges in tow floating easily in her wake.

This system was not successful, as in descending the Indus the barge train jack-knifed in the strong current and the end barges over ran and sank the steamer.

A similar arrangement was to be found on the Rhône in those days. Navigation on this river had previously been carried out with self-propelled lighters 18 feet broad, 9 feet deep and upwards of 500 feet long, an immense length to depth ratio, which made them very weak indeed. Inevitably some of these lighters broke in two, and it was proposed to form a craft composed of a number of sections, each of which would constitute a barge in itself, the whole being tied together to allow a certain degree of freedom between units. The vessel would then be able to 'walk' upon an uneven surface, fully loaded, without fear of major casualty.

The tug for this barge train was of fantastic design, and for ingenuity and one-up-manship put our Indus crawler very much in the shade. Here is a contemporary engineer's description of it:

Upon the Rhône a paddle tug is in some cases employed which is propelled by a large heavy wheel 20 feet diameter, which is mounted at the end of a wooden frame like the bucket ladder of a dredging machine. The frame is susceptible of motion up or down through a trunk or aperture in the bottom of the boat, and at the end of the frame the wheel is mounted. It is turned round on its axis by means of a chain passing over a pulley on the paddle shaft, and also passing over segments bolted on the side of the wheel. The wheel is thus turned upon its axis, and as it runs along the bottom of the river, with great spikes projecting from its edge for engaging the ground, the vessel is propelled forward in the same way that a locomotive is propelled forward upon a railway, and the slip incident to the ordinary means of propulsion is thus prevented. The hinged frame enables the wheel to rise and fall with the inequalities of the river bottom without the propelling efficacy of the chain being impaired. The boat uses this instrument of propulsion only in ascending the river, which is very rapid, and when the great wheel is in action the paddles are disconnected from the engine and revolve freely with the stream. In descending the river the central wheel is hauled up by means of suitable gear, worked by two small engines and the pulley on the engine shaft from which the chain derives its motion is thrown out of gear, while the paddles are thrown into gear, and the vessel is then propelled by her paddles like a common steamer.

A more complicated barge train was developed by J. Bourne, exclusively for long, winding, shallow rivers in the East, and was built and tried out on the Clyde before being despatched abroad. The train consisted of a steamer and five barges, articulated to one another by hinged joints, so that the whole train presented only a single bow to the water and therefore suffered less resistance in ascending a river than if each barge were being towed one behind the other in the usual manner. The steamer for the train was 230 feet long, quite a sizeable vessel to start with, and it drew four barges each 130 feet long with an end barge of 160 feet. The overall length of the train was thus over 900 feet and it carried 3,000 tons on a maximum draught of 3 feet.

Propulsion was by means of paddles driven by compound engines developing 1,000 i.h.p., the steam being at 100 lb. per inch, superheated at the boilers and reheated between the h.p. and the l.p. cylinders. And all this in the 1860's!

In this particular steamer the paddles had feathering floats, far too vulnerable to be allowed to walk the ship over a sand bar. In the event of stranding the engineer, instead of sweating it out down below hammering rusty bolts out of a rusty coupling to engage the turning gear, could nip up on deck for a breather and, lazily leaning over the rail and spitting meditatively into the water meanwhile, could watch the frantic captain getting his ship afloat in the good old-fashioned way.

Because of the length a certain amount of lateral flexure was allowed in the joints between the units to enable the train to round a bend in the river, and longitudinal bending was also necessary to allow the separate portions to adjust themselves on the mud when aground.

It had been found that a train of common barges towed apart by ropes turned in the wrong direction; M is a bevelled pinion on the same axis; N is a bevelled pinion, which works at one end of the horizontal axis O with pinion M; P is another bevelled pinion at the other end of the axis O; Q is a pinion working with the pinion P; S is a | indicating when a sufficient quantity has been wound on to the bobbins; also, the manner of giving the necessary tension to the yarns, by causing them to pass round the rollers J or o.

MACSWENEY'S PATENT JOINTED SHIP.

THE present system of steam transport by water labours under some disadvantages, from each vessel being a rigid structure, and not admitting of the means of saving a portion of the hull, in case of accident. It is proposed to remedy this defect, by having the | is believed by the patentee, will enable it to attain a degree of speed far beyond any hitherto achieved. The joints of all the sections are constructed to one gauge to admit of the section specially appropriated to the engine and crew being transferred from one set of sections to another. By this means it is proposed that one engine

32 MacSweney's patent jointed ship

presented a number of hazards in a swift current, for if the towing steamer or front barges grounded, all the others ran into her and caused serious damage to each other by collision. By using the articulated system this type of injury could not occur for, while the joint between the units allowed freedom of movement in the alignment of the barges, they were held together to form one complete assembly.

In spite of the care taken in the design of these hinges, however, accidents could and did happen, as we have noted above.

Now all the above systems of linked vessels, although presenting interesting features to a seaman, would not qualify for a place in a nautical freakshow, and they are mentioned here merely as an introduction to the real jointed ship. The barge train was a number of true vessels locked together to form a large craft, while the jointed ship was a true vessel that could be broken down into several rudimentary ships capable, if necessary, of navigating on their own.

The pioneer of the articulated ship was MacSweney, who in 1856 brought out his MacSweney's Patent Jointed Ship, which was built by

Pierce and Co., for the London coal trade. This ship was made up of three sections, each section complete in itself and capable of being connected to or disconnected from the parent ship at will. The action of the hinged joint was in the vertical plane only, and the joints were standardised so that any section could be accommodated in any part of the train.

The forward section was the towing member, a paddle-driven steamer which also housed the crew, and the two following members were the cargo carriers, each section being fitted with masts and sails.

The idea of the jointed ship was to allow any of the sections to be uncoupled for loading or discharging while the rest of the ship carried on in service, in much the same fashion as a shunting locomotive in a marshalling yard. In theory each unit could be sailed by means of her own fore and aft rig. But actually one supposes that she would have to be towed alongside by the fore part before being unshackled. With the sections hinged to each other to allow of vertical movement only these barge-like structures would need to have swim ends, and a swimbarge needs a budget plate or deadwood, and a rudder on the end of that, before it can sail on its own and steer; the masts, therefore, could have been left out of the design altogether without affecting the usefulness of the ship.

Connector

Another jointed vessel, and probably the better known to cognoscenti of freak ships, was the *Connector*. This vessel belonged to the Jointed Ship Company with registered offices in Rood Lane, London, and served as a collier between the capital and the North of England. She was built at the Joyce shipyard in Greenwich in 1858 and made her maiden voyage to Hartlepool where a number of manœuvring tests were carried out on the hinged sections.

This vessel was built in three or four sections—the accounts differ— the forward section housing the crew and the after section the officers and machinery, and she must have been one of the first screw-driven steamers on this trade.

Here are some accounts of her, taken from the Press and covering a period between 1858 and 1863:

The vessel's projectors, a few days since, invited a party of scientific gentlemen to an experimental trial trip in the Thames. The vessel left Blackwall and proceeded down the river to Erith Reach where, having dropped anchor, in a few seconds, with

33 Jointed ship *Connector*

one circuit of a lever on deck, the fore section (all the sections are perfect ships) was completely disconnected and the other parts propelled across the river whence the centre portion on which the visitors were assembled, was as rapidly left free. While the party took lunch, the steam or stern section returned for the part left moored on the opposite shore and, having brought it over, in the space of five minutes, the two separate parts were united. Though the water was much disturbed by passing vessels, the trip was very interesting and gave general satisfaction

The 'Connector' has been subjected to the most severe tests in the heaviest weather and proved herself thoroughly seaworthy.

A jointed steamship, the same, we believe, formerly employed for a short time in the Newcastle and London coal trade, was tried on the Thames on Wednesday.

One of these curious jointed iron steam vessels, which are asserted to possess great advantages for coasting and inland traffic purposes over the ordinary screw steamers, is now lying off the pier at Hungerford Bridge. Except for her great length and narrowness, there is nothing very peculiar in her outward aspect, but the singular extremes of these dimensions, in a vessel of such light draught, at once attracts attention. Still more curious, however, is her appearance when the swell of a river steamer reaches her, when the joints come into action and the whole of the long hull undulates in a snaky sort of fashion, so unlike the steady rise and fall of common ships that, at first glance, the 'Connector', as the ship is called, seems coming to pieces. She seems in truth as if her back was broken in many places, which is actually the fact, though, in the case of this small steamer, the divisions in her length are the new principles of construction, the advantages of which she is built to illustrate and, as her builders hope, to develop.

Every section has rough bow and stern of its own, so as to enable it when detached, to be moved by sails in the water, all except the last section or joint, which, as containing the motive power, is of course properly shaped as regards the stern, although the bows are the same as the other sections. The joints themselves by which the different parts are bolted together are very powerful and move easily, allowing the different sections to rise and fall with the slightest motion of the water. Each section is a perfect wrought iron portion of the hull, capable of being disconnected from the rest of the ship with perfect ease, almost in a few seconds.

In all these articles, written at different times by various observers, we get the very strong impression that there were, or had been, other jointed steamers built along the same lines, and that possibly a steamer built like a carpenter's folding rule was not such an odd sight in the 1860's as it would be today.

It is unfortunate that none of the observers gives much information on the type of coupling used to connect the separate sections, as it must have been extremely simple if a joint could be 'disconnected from the rest of the ship with perfect ease, almost in a few seconds'.

This might appear a simple matter to anyone thinking in terms of railway coach couplings, where both wagons are perfectly still and level, but the operation might present some difficulty at night time, with the ship lying in a tideway and a cold wind blowing across the river. Each section could weigh a hundred tons or more, and, with a tendency to surge and heave against its neighbour and react on its hinges, it might not be such an easy matter to disconnect the hinges, and certainly not a safe manœuvre.

Before passing judgment on the mechanics of the jointed ship it would be necessary to hear the crew's remarks after unshackling a section on a wet wintry night!

The sectional ships, however, must not be identified only with the nineteenth century. The notion has been continued well into the twentieth century. At the present moment a barge train is operating on the Seine composed of a pusher tug and two cargo barges, the complete arrangement being clamped into one unit by means of two steel cables extending between the forward barge and the after tug, the intermediate barge being sandwiched between the two, the cables being extended by means of hydraulic machinery. To avoid metallic contact between barge and barge, a rubber cushioning strip is fitted at the bow and the stern of these barges.

The jointed ship was also reintroduced in the early twentieth century, although for totally different reasons. The old-time passenger vessel, with its several tiers of light-scantling promenade and boat decks, had its strength mainly in the hull girder from the weather deck downwards. This meant that, with the neutral axis of the ship girder below water level, any bending of the ship in a seaway (and all ships bend in a seaway) imposed an enormous tension or compression on the light uppermost deck, which was not made to withstand those stresses. The top deck was accordingly discontinued at about a quarter its length from each end of the vessel, and this discontinuity was covered by a brass toeplate extending across the deck. A measure of the ship's bending in heavy weather could thus be observed by the movement of the deck beneath the toeplate.

Up to now I have dealt with ships built up of separate sections, each a true ship in its own right, and coupled together to form a jointed ship, the joint in this context indicating merely a connection between any two sections of the unit which could be made or broken at will to allow any part to be added or removed. The fact that this connection allowed relative movement in adjoining sections was generally incidental, a horizontal hinge arrangement being the easiest to manipulate. There never was any intention of building a vessel to undulate over the waves, as vessels built in the sixties of last century were fairly small, heavily built and presented no strength problems to their designers. Thus the word *jointed* has so far been used, implying a connection between static vessels, as opposed to *articulated*, conveying the idea of relative movement.

The concept of a purely articulated ship has recently been put forward by the Japanese, surely the most sophisticated shipbuilders of our time, and, although it occurs outside our terms of reference, the idea is so ingenious that it merits inclusion in this review.

The purpose of the design was essentially to reduce the longitudinal

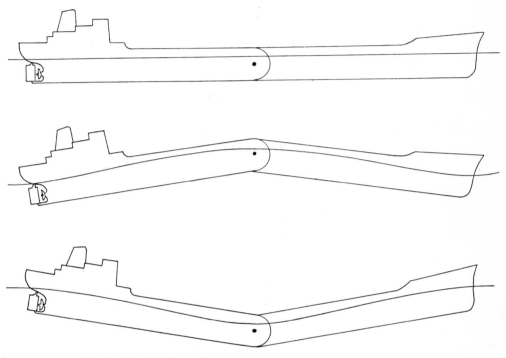

34 Proposed articulated bulk carrier

bending stresses in, say, a bulk carrier or tanker, in contrast to the *Connector* where fuller utilisation of the various parts of the vessel was the guiding principle.

The specification calls for a ship's hull comprising a fore section and an after section hingedly connected together about an axis transverse to the hull to allow free hogging and sagging, the axis being built at or near the mid-depth of the hull, and the confronting ends of the two sections having semi-cylindrical projections and recesses, these being co-axial with the axis.

The diameters of the semi-cylindrical projections and recesses are substantially equal to the depth of the hull in way of the axis, and the arrangement resembles an ordinary door hinge.

A tube is fitted at the centre of each projection, flanged to the sides, so that when the two sections of ship are in line the centre lines of all these tubes will coincide. A very heavy hinge shaft is then threaded through each set of tubes on port and starboard side and locked into place.

G

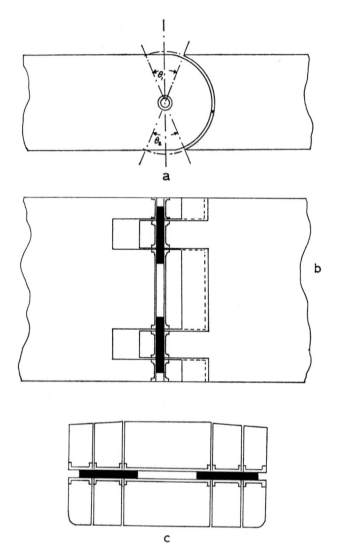

35 Hinging arrangements for articulated vessel, (a) profile, (b) horizontal
section, (c) transverse section

Referring to the side elevation the angle θ_1, subtended from the shaft
centre, indicates the maximum relative rotating angle between the fore
and after sections of the hull in the sagging condition, and the angle
θ_2 that of the two sections in the hogging condition.

These two angles depend upon the radius of the semi-cylindrical projections and upon the radial gap distance between the opposed ends of the sections. These angles can be set as desired to suit the type of waters in which the vessel is designed to work, and an ocean-going vessel would have larger maximum angles than a coastal vessel.

To finish on a lighter note, an unusual and ingenious type of articulated canal lighter was built by Charles Wye Williams, the founder of the City of Dublin Steam Packet Company. In an endeavour to promote cheaper travel in Ireland he designed a boat for passengers on the Limerick-Lough Dearg canal of a speed which should equal that of a trotting horse. This required a fairly long vessel, but the locks on this canal were too short for a craft of any length. Williams solved the problem in a delightfully Irish fashion: to a square-ended middle body he attached a fine lined bow and stern, hinged at deck level, so that they could be wound up vertically by a winch when passing through the locks.

7 Early submarines

If asked his opinion on the origin of the submarine, the man-in-the-street would probably suggest that it was specially invented by the German Navy just before the 1914–18 War. His argument would be based on the submarine's dependence for its action on the internal combustion engine and on electrical propulsion, both of them essentially products of the twentieth century. The submarine, as far as he is concerned, is as much a feature of our century as, say, the motorship or the aeroplane.

As an underwater fighting ship the submarine does, in fact, belong to the twentieth century, but as a freak vessel it goes back many centuries. Its development runs parallel with that of conventional fighting ships, though only appearing now and again to break the surface of history as a good submarine should.

There is no doubt that earlier references to this type of craft refer to diving bells or a loose form of air chamber fitted over a man's head and shoulders, and it is difficult from this distance in time to sort out practical experiment from armchair philosophy. There are very few authenticated instances of submersible vessels before the beginning of the nineteenth century, as most enthusiasts for underwater navigation became victims of their invention before they had time to write their memoirs.

Roger Bacon declared that the Greeks under Alexander the Great built vessels that could navigate beneath the surface of the sea, but one of the earliest attempts at a submarine appears to be that of Cornelius van Drebbel, who is alleged to have built one manned by twelve rowers which, during the reign of James I, travelled some distance under water in the Thames. Contemporary sources state that the submersible was made of two identical rowing boats fitted together along their gunwales like the two halves of a walnut, with the oars protruding from the shell through leather seals. It is said that the boat navigated for several hours at a depth of fifteen feet, that the vitiated air inside the hull was refreshed by means of a 'chymical liquor' invented by the builder's son-in-law, Pierre van Drebbel.

No mention is made in this account of how the vessel was submerged and brought back to the surface, or how the coxswain found his way about under water; but apart from that the story falls to pieces by the fact that it is impossible to row under water, just as it is impossible for a man to walk about in water up to his chin. Rowing depends on the oars working in two media, the power stroke in water and the return stroke in air. If both power and return strokes took place under water the vessel would simply rock back and forth.

A number of notables toyed with the idea of a submersible boat: Bishop Wilkins in 1680 put forward a good theoretical case, and others were Papin, Taisnier, Stapleton and John Williams, but most of these were mainly concerned with some form of diving bell in which men could go down to the sea bed for discovery, pearl fishing or dock repairs.

In 1772 Dionis of Bordeaux is stated to have carried ten passengers five leagues below the surface of the Bay of Biscay without the necessity for renewing the air, and one is left wondering at the identity of these ten passengers: were they convicts impressed into this service as guinea-pigs, with the promise of a free pardon upon their safe return, or were they simply day trippers getting the eighteenth-century equivalent of a trip round the lighthouse?

The earliest recorded submarine boat was that built by Captain David Bushnell, of Connecticut, in 1775–6, and variously called the *Turtle*, the *Tortoise* or the *Coconut*. This vessel was constructed of oak in the shape of a pear and floated with its base uppermost. It was made roughly in two halves with a horizontal flanged joint, and the upper half was fitted with a brass conning tower equipped with glass bull's-eyes.

This vessel had two ventilating tubes with non-return valves at their outer ends to close when submerged, and a water inlet valve on the bottom. Thus the submarine could be submerged or surfaced simply by partially flooding with the foot operated valve or by discharging the water by means of a force pump.

Propulsion was by screw propellers, there being a hand-operated propeller in the upper lid of the vessel for diving and another in the horizontal plane for travelling under water, and it is interesting to note that the description of these screws antedates Ericsson's official invention of the screw by several decades.

The reason for this quaint submersible vessel lay in its equipment designed to blow up an enemy ship. This consisted of a tube let into the shell of the *Turtle*, through which a special screw auger could be projected and screwed into the keel or planking of the enemy vessel, and left in. This auger contained an automatic explosive charge fitted with a time fuse, and the whole arrangement was rather like a rudimentary limpet mine. Unfortunately for Captain Bushnell the screw auger was useless against copper sheathing, and his invention never made the headlines.

There was one feature about this submarine boat, however, which showed the captain to be a more practical inventor than most of his kind. A load of loose ballast was attached to the bottom of the boat which, in an emergency, could be released from inside by the one-man crew. This ballast was attached to the vessel by a 50-foot cord, and could be retrieved when required.

We hear no more about submarines until the turn of the century, when Robert Fulton demonstrated his *Nautilus* to the French authorities at Brest in 1801. There is surprisingly little information available about this vessel, but one gathers that on trial it remained at 25 feet below the surface for one hour, and that on another occasion, possibly due to some defect, it remained under water for 4½ hours, air for the crew being supplied from an iron globe containing one cubic foot of compressed air.

The *Nautilus* made no impact on history and we have to wait for another half century before our next submarine appears on the scene. This was the *Marine Cigar*, built in 1851 on Lake Michigan by Lodner Phillipps and patented in 1852. The claims made by the inventor are not exactly modest, as will be gathered from the following write-up in one of the contemporary magazines:

It has two double hatches, one on the top, and one at the bottom, and may have side hatches if required. The upper hatch is sealed down when the vessel is submerged; when the upper hatch is open the bottom one is shut, and vice-versa. It has two sight domes, which are used when the vessel is on the surface and it has four interrupted keels to prevent it turning over when submerged. When in deep water, lights with reflectors are placed opposite some of the bull's-eyes seen on the sides, and owing to the shape of the vessel, the bull's-eyes nearest the fore part enable those within to see their way in the water.

Should the vessel run into anything, it can be extricated without injury, having on its point or bow a thimble or outer case which is so constructed that by reversing the screw, the boat would be backed, leaving the thimble. Having a glass tube properly marked, the exact depth of water from the surface is always shown. Fresh air is supplied as necessary from tanks containing many atmospheres compressed. The boat is sunk by admitting water into tanks through pipes and is raised by expelling the same. It can be kept stationary or at any required depth of water from 1 inch to 200 feet, and in this lies the secret which makes the boat effective. It has, likewise, a secret mode of loading guns under water, but no doubt its greatest use will be in the many ways it can be employed in examining ships' bottoms, repairing and building docks, wharves etc., having patent tools for working through its sides, likewise for pearl fishing. Being able to go to sea in any weather, there will be no difficulty in commencing diving operations immediately one is built.

It may be propelled by hand-power or by electro-magnetism with a screw of Mr.

Phillipps' invention, fitted to a shaft on a universal joint by which the rudder is dispensed with. It is to carry 20 to 30 men, and is 60 feet long by 7 foot 6 inches diameter. The first boat built on this principle at Michigan City was tried out with complete success.

The inventor goes on to claim that his boat weighed only eight tons, that on trial in Lake Michigan it remained under water for four hours with no air hose or outside air supply, and that the boat was propelled near the lake bottom at about three miles per hour. During this dive some baulks of timber 14 inches square were sawn through in the sea by the crew acting from inside the vessel, to demonstrate the possibility of using tools below water from a submarine. The inventor concludes by mentioning several ways of attacking and sinking enemy ships by mines and torpedoes, or by attaching clockwork bombs to their keels.

Lodner Phillipps was not merely content to navigate below the surface of the sea; he very properly fitted a depth gauge in the form of a graduated tube to show him the depth of water. But his statement that the vessel could remain stationary up to 200 feet below the surface was surely exaggerated. At that depth the water pressure on the hull is nearing 100 pounds to the square inch, or $6\frac{1}{2}$ tons to the square foot, and it is very doubtful if a crudely built iron tank of that diameter, could withstand such a pressure. Even if it did it would still be necessary to pump the ballast from the tanks by handpump against 100-pound discharge pressure before the submarine could be surfaced.

But it is possible that the inventor did try to reach 200 feet depth in his ship on the last, fatal dive in Lake Michigan.

In 1853 we find brief mention of W. Bauer of Munich, who invented a submarine to be driven by a gas engine supplied with air drawn through pipes extending above the surface of the water, and he thus antedated the German submarine schnorkel tube by nearly a century.

The notion of a submarine as an effective weapon of war really came to the fore at the beginning of the American Civil War. As described in a previous chapter, the Southern States, having built their floating battery *Merrimac*, were playing havoc with the government vessels in Chesapeake Bay. The Federal Government accordingly invited a Frenchman to build them a submarine to blow up or sink the *Merrimac* and paid him a fee of $10,000 for his services. The resulting vessel was cigar shaped (the classical shape for a submarine, apparently), was propelled by sixteen oars with collapsible blades, and used lime to purify the air. When it was complete and ready for diving trials, with the water looking cold, black and very, very deep, the Frenchman could not be found, and as nobody else understood how to work the submarine the trials were abandoned and the experiment written off.

Later on, however, as the Civil War progressed, the Southern States developed their own midget 'submarines' and nicknamed them Davids, either from the Biblical character matched against the Philistine giant or possibly from Captain David Bushnell of the previous century. These diminutive vessels varied in size among themselves, probably due to scarcity of materials, but they averaged 30 feet in length and carried a crew of five: four ratings to man the hand-operated propeller cranks with an officer in charge as navigator. They were made of iron and had the now normal cigar shape with either conical or wedge ends. Their weapon was the spar torpedo, an explosive charge attached to the end of a long pole which extended well beyond the vessel's bow.

One of these 'submarines', the *H.L.Hunley*, built in Charleston and named after her designer, was simply an old boiler some 26 feet long and 4 feet in diameter with the ends knocked out and replaced by bow and stern sections. The three-bladed right handed propeller was about 24 inches in diameter placed inside a shroud ring, on the after end of which was hung the rudder. Inside this 4 foot cylinder with its centreline propeller shaft, four resolute men would be crouched to work the cranks as best they could in such an awkward position, with their leader in control at the open access hatch. The smallest wave would lap over the hatch coaming and make things uncomfortable for the crew down below, a larger wave would simply swamp the vessel and drown the crew: with one man jammed in the access hatch there would not be the slightest hope of escape for the crewmen.

These 'submarines' were stated to be submersible, and able to attack underwater, and that they could travel at 4 knots on the surface, but these claims require careful examination. Any vessel ever built is submersible in that it can be filled with water and sunk, but up till then no vessel had proved conclusively that it could be navigated below the surface, attack the enemy and return safely to base. Also, four men sweating on the handles working a rudimentary propeller would hardly move a vessel 30 feet long, and certainly not propel it at 4 knots. And yet . . . it is easy to dogmatise: the fact is that many of the 'submarines' were built, and at the retaking of Charleston alone, nine of these Davids were captured.

From contemporary descriptions, one gathers that these small vessels were not submarines in the normal, accepted sense. When attacking, they filled their ballast tanks until the hull was almost submerged, and only the entrance hatch showed above water. They thus presented a minimum target to the enemy, and as they attacked by night, the small area of the vessel showing on the surface of the water would hardly warrant a second glance from the lookout man on the enemy ship.

Floating level with the surface, and with an open hatch as conning tower, made these Davids extremely vulnerable in attack, as the wave resulting from the spar torpedo explosion tended to flood or capsize them, and this in fact happened to many of them. There is only one recorded instance of a Government ship being destroyed by a David: the *Housatonic*, a Federal sloop, sunk off Charleston by the *Hunley* with a spar torpedo. This *Hunley* had made several torpedo attacks on other ships, and on three previous occasions had been swamped and sunk, drowning most of her crew in each case. The present attack, although sinking the enemy, proved fatal to the *Hunley* which was herself destroyed. But what superb courage these Confederates showed, to volunteer as crews for these midget 'submarines' with the knowledge that in the event of an attack, whether the enemy lived or died, they themselves would most certainly perish. This was not the thoughtless courage of a spontaneous heroic act on the field of battle, to the accompaniment of bugle calls and flying flags, with a background of cheering from the gallery. This was something entirely different: these 'submarine' crews knew their ship for what it was: an iron coffin. There was nothing impulsive in their courage, this was the real thing.

While the Davids were not very effective as fighting ships they served as a good deterrent to the Federal ships in much the same way as declaring a certain area to be mined is nearly as good as actually sowing mines in it, and very much cheaper. The Federal Government accordingly decided to fight like with like, and gave orders for the construction of a torpedo. This word, the scientific name for the electric ray, originally meant an underwater explosive charge with a time fuse; by extension it came to denote the vessel conveying the charge to the target, finally assuming the modern meaning of an underwater explosive missile. The Davids were considered as torpedoes in that they laid their explosive charges under or against the enemy ships by means of their spar, and the vessel ordered by the U.S. Government would simply be a mechanically propelled super David.

She was constructed at Fairhaven, Connecticut, in 1865 in the record time of three months, to the designs of a local naval constructor. She was

84 feet overall, with a moulded beam of 19 feet and 10 feet depth of hold. Built entirely of timber, her launching draught was only 4 feet, which was increased to 7 feet 6 inches when her machinery, armour, stores, bunkers and equipment were on board. Being a flush-decked vessel she had the barest minimum of superstructures and appendages: two funnels, two watertight entrance hatches and a low conning tower, standing about 3 feet high, with a sloping coaming. The deck itself was considerably arched both transversely and fore and aft, rather like a whaleback, but with a hard deck angle to the shipsides. This deck was armoured with 1 inch thick iron plating, extending down the sides to below water level.

The conning tower, which offered the most direct target to an enemy shell, was protected by 12 inches of armour composed of several layers of 1 inch thick plating. This turret alone weighed 11 tons.

The vessel's hold housed huge ballast tanks which, when filled, increased the draught to gunwale level, leaving only the deck exposed, and the method of attack was similar to that of the Southern States' Davids. For this purpose she had very large steam-driven centrifugal pumps in her engine room, which could flood or pump out the ballast tanks in a matter of minutes.

Spuyten Duyvil

She was named *Spuyten Duyvil*, archaic Dutch for 'Devil with a Syringe', a very appropriate name when one comes to examine the torpedo-laying machinery, for torpedoes still had to be placed, they were not yet self-propelled. This machinery was designed by Captain Wood, Chief Engineer of the U.S. Navy, also in the space of three months, and proves that in those days the position of a Head of Department in the Navy was not necessarily a sinecure.

The lower part of the bow of the vessel, instead of being made solid as usual, was composed of two hinged iron flaps which, when closed, corresponded to the general shape of the bow. They were kept in place by chains when the vessel was under steam. Within the space enclosed by these two flaps a sluice valve led into the torpedo-loading chamber, at the top of which was a water-tight manhole giving access from inside the vessel. This loading chamber was, in fact, a water lock which could be pumped out by one of the main ballast pumps.

The after end of the water lock contained an 18 inch gun-metal ball-and-socket joint complete with gland which carried the tubular iron spar

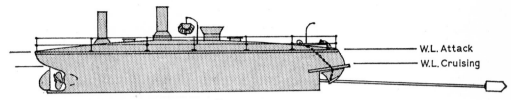

36 Spar torpedo boat *Spuyten Duyvil*

for the torpedo. The end of this tube, 5 inches diameter and with a bore of 3 inches, which projected into the loading chamber, was furnished with a bell-mouth casting of gun-metal with a light sheet metal casing to support the torpedo. The torpedo had a knob at the rear which engaged in a clip at the end of the tube. Inside the tubular spar a long iron rod, operated from inside the ship, could push the knob clear of the clip and so release the torpedo from the spar.

Abaft the ball-and-socket joint the spar was led through a swivel tube working in vertical guides, and this swivel could be raised or lowered by a steam control cylinder and thus alter the elevation of the spar, and hence the torpedo, acting on the ball-and-socket joint as a fulcrum. The spar could be withdrawn into the ship until the tube bell mouth was inside the waterlock for loading the torpedo, and then pushed out to its full extent, some twenty feet, for attack. This operation was carried out by a steam winch driving an endless chain, and the motion was reversed merely by reversing the direction of rotation.

The torpedoes themselves were to be operated on the principle of the modern hand grenade, where the firing mechanism is held in the safe position by a pin, which when withdrawn allows the fuse to touch off

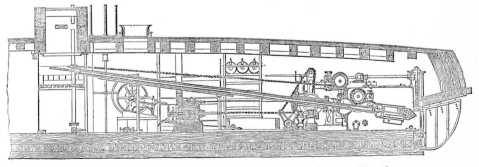

37 Arrangement of spar withdrawal gear in torpedo boat *Spuyten Duyvil*

the explosive. In the case of the torpedoes the method of firing was to be as follows: the bow flaps were opened out full, and, with the sluice valve shut, the waterlock was pumped out, the access hatch opened and a torpedo fitted to the end of the tubular spar. A length of cord was then tied to the torpedo firing pin and the other end made fast to the end of the tube. With the access hatch closed and the sluice valve opened, the spar was then run out to its full extent and the angle of elevation adjusted by the swivel tube, to place the torpedo below the enemy ship's bottom. By operating the internal rod the torpedo was released and by backing ship smartly, and at the same time drawing in the tube with cord attached, the firing pin was pulled out and the torpedo exploded.

It will be appreciated that to approach an enemy to within twenty feet and carry out this rather tricky operation in the face of heavy fire would have required courage of a very high order. In the event, the Civil War was over before *Spuyten Duyvil* was completed, and the vessel was never taken into action.

But even if it had been finished neither it nor the smaller Davids were, in fact, submarines inasmuch as they remained buoyant with their navigators conning from the surface, and in the case of steam-driven craft, with their boilers still working.

Several more or less successful experiments were made with true submarines. Charles Brun designed one for the French Navy in 1863, propelled by an 80 h.p. compressed-air engine. The American engineer Merrian tried out a small egg-shaped craft propelled by hand, the only significant feature of which was that the propeller was fitted on a swivel and was driven through a universal coupling; it could therefore also act as a rudder.

The first true submarine, that is a vessel that could navigate below the surface under its own power and emerge when required, was designed by George William Garrett round about 1879. He first built a small experimental vessel, powered by hand, in which he carried out diving trials in Liverpool Docks. Satisfied with the results, he had a full-scale vessel built in Birkenhead by Cochran & Co., and such was his confidence in her that she was named *Resurgam* (I shall rise again) at the launch.

Built of iron in the now familiar cigar shape, she was 45 feet overall length and 7 feet in diameter, conical at each end with a cylindrical middle-body sheathed in wood and faired to the cones. A short conning tower protruded from the top of the shell, with a watertight hatch as a lid and bull's-eyes all round; this tower contained the steering and control gears.

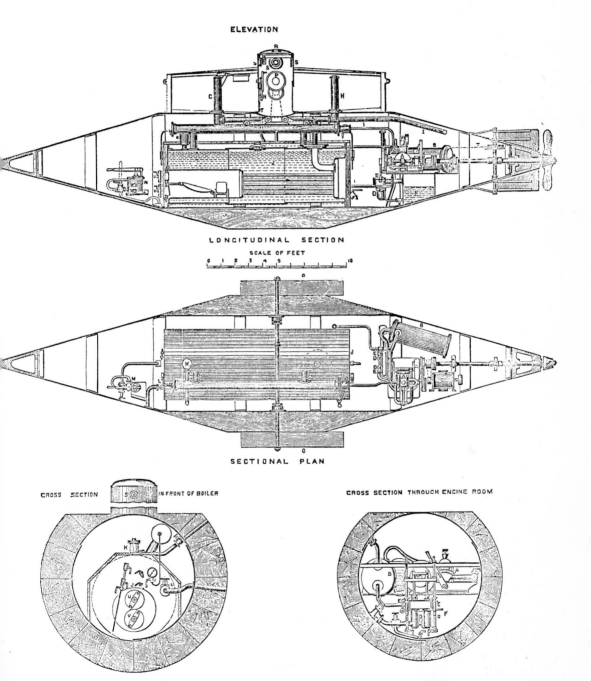

ELEVATION

LONGITUDINAL SECTION

SCALE OF FEET

SECTIONAL PLAN

CROSS SECTION IN FRONT OF BOILER

CROSS SECTION THROUGH ENGINE ROOM

Garrett's submarine

The secret of Garrett's success with his submarine lay in its inherent safety: it did not require to be flooded to submerge, and consequently if anything untoward happened in manœuvring it bobbed to the surface when all machinery was stopped, a sort of fail-safe arrangement. In previous submarine-type vessels the only way to get them below the surface was to let them partially fill with water until they sank of their own accord. It was then up to the crew, working in the dark, in a confined space and breathing foul air, to pump for dear life and get the water out again before they became overcome. It is small wonder if they had no time or energy to man the propeller cranks, with the thought of pumping an unspecified amount of water out of their craft before they breathed pure air again. The *Resurgam* had no ballast tanks whatever, and her only pump, other than those required for working the engines, was a hand-operated bilge pump. She was built to float fairly low in the water, and had port and starboard diving fins fitted amidships, controlled from the conning tower. Diving was therefore dependent on propeller speed and the angle given to the hydroplanes, much as in the case of a modern submarine.

Most of the interior of the vessel was taken up by the boiler, in the middle-body, and by the propelling engine, condenser and pumps at the after end. An unusual feature of the machinery was a rotary vane blower driven from the main engine and used to provide forced draught to the boiler, by means of which up to 150 lb. steam head was obtained before diving. Both the air suction pipe and the short boiler flue pipe, which projected above the deck, were fitted with automatic non-return valves, and the furnace and ashpit doors were closed on airtight joints when diving.

Garrett claimed that with a good head of steam the *Resurgam* could sail twelve miles under water, and that the air contained in the submarine before diving was sufficient for the three-man crew during that time without needing renewal.

This vessel was lost off the Welsh coast, but the nature of the accident was never known.

Thorsten Nordenfelt, a Swede, took the idea of Garrett's submarine a stage further in the vessels he designed for Turkey in 1885. These vessels carried out exhaustive trials in the Sea of Marmora without apparently impressing the Turks to any noticeable extent. By all accounts they were excellent sea boats when sailing on the surface and, having no buoyancy at their ends (i.e. no lift to the seas), they did not pitch but simply rose bodily over the waves.

They were built, as usual, as an elongated cylinder tapering to a point at both ends, and were 100 feet long overall, with a maximum diameter of 12 feet, and displaced 160 tons. They were, in fact, quite sizeable vessels, and Nordenfelt claimed the following merits for them:

1 As the hull always maintained a reserve buoyancy it would float to the surface as soon as the screws were stopped (a claim originally made by Garrett for his *Resurgam*).
2 Vertical movement in the water could be effected by the main propeller with hydroplanes, or separately by using small independent diving propellers.
3 Vessel could steam underwater for 30 to 40 miles on the steam stored in the boiler and in the steam accumulator.
4 No reserve air need be carried, as experience had shown that, provided the boiler was efficiently blanked off when diving, the air contained in the hull was sufficient for several hours without becoming foul.

The Nordenfelt submarine, named after the designer, had three ballast tanks, one of 15 tons at each end, and a smaller one of 7 tons amidships. The whole of the interior was taken up by the propelling machinery, there being a large marine boiler, a steam accumulator and a compound main engine driving the screw through an inclined shaft with universal couplings.

The accumulator contained a heat exchanger at its base, live steam from the boiler being conveyed through the coils of the heater, giving up its latent heat to the water in the accumulator and being returned to the boiler via the feed pump. By this means a large store of superheated water was stored in this pear-shaped tank which when released into the main boiler at a lower pressure flashed into steam.

The diving propellers, both forward and aft, were each worked by an independent three-cylinder steam engine, the cylinders being placed in 'star' formation round the crank. This type of steam engine will start immediately from any position, and it was essential to have the diving propellers under fine control. When the submarine was under way the hydroplanes at the bow maintained longitudinal stability. These fins were normally under the control of the captain, but had an emergency safety device whereby, upon release of the controls, they returned to their normal fore and aft centralised position.

In order to utilise the steam pressure as much as possible the main engine was built with large-bore cylinders, which could accommodate low pressure steam. All pumps and ancillary gear in the engine worked on a

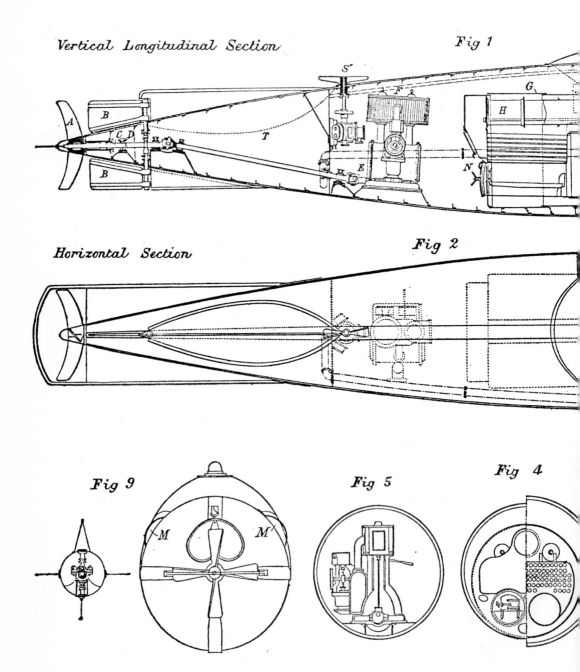

Vertical Longitudinal Section   *Fig 1*

Horizontal Section   *Fig 2*

Fig 9   *Fig 5*   *Fig 4*

39 Nordenfelt's first submarine

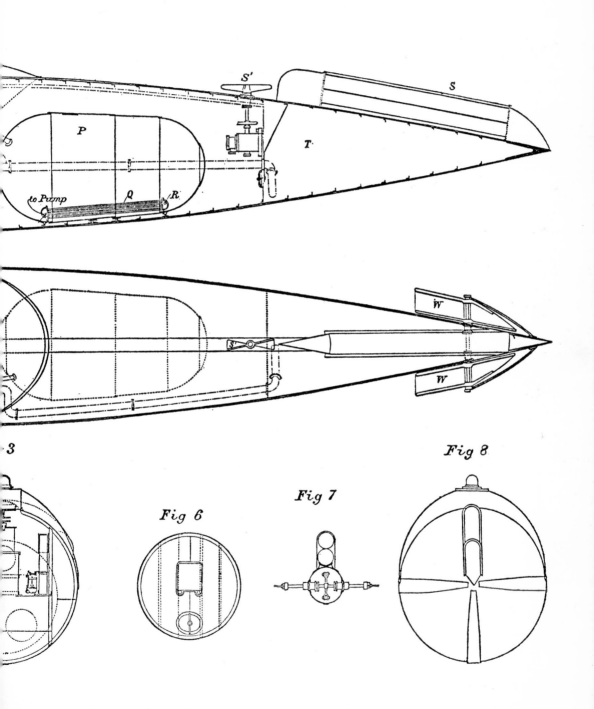

Fig 6

Fig 7

Fig 8

vacuum produced by a large air pump. In fact the power produced by the machinery in this vessel was developed as much below as above the atmospheric line on the indicator card.

The air supply for the crew and boiler was drawn in through the open conning tower by a centrifugal fan and delivered via the engine room to the boiler front. After passing through the furnace, combustion chamber and return tubes, the flue gases were led through a large tube in the top of the boiler and out through the hull of the ship immediately abaft the conning tower, into a stumpy funnel. In diving trim this funnel was unshipped and passed down into the stokehold, and the deck opening was secured; the flue pipe at the top of the boiler was sealed off by a smoke-tight lid, and the firing door and ashpit were also sealed, as in the *Resurgam*. When submerging the *Nordenfelt*'s ballast tanks were filled until the deck was awash, but reserve buoyancy was always retained, and actual diving was commenced by the vertical diving screws, the diving level being maintained by the combined action of the main propeller and the bow vanes.

Nordenfelt's submarine No. 4, still with the same name, was much more sophisticated than the prototype and basically was not very far removed from the modern submarine. This new vessel, built in 1888, was a departure from the conventional cigar shape, being cylindrical with wedge ends, and had a number of ballast tanks at both ends and amidships. She was 125 feet long, 12 feet in diameter and displaced 160 tons on the surface, or 245 tons submerged. She had two 10 feet diameter boilers, one 11 feet long, the other, a boiler-cum-accumulator, being 20 feet long, which gave her an underwater cruising radius of 50 to 60 miles.

Her main engine was a 4-crank double compound unit, still a favourite in modern steamers, developing 1,200 h.p. at 15 knots, and here again vacuum was used to a large extent to work the auxiliary machinery, there being two sinking engines (for driving the diving propellers), two fan engines and two sets of steering gear, apart from the numerous pumps attendant on the main engine, ship's service, torpedo compressors, etc.

The interior of the ship was divided into five sections. They were, starting from forward: torpedo chamber, officers' quarters, boiler room, engine room and crew's quarters. Access between forward and aft was by creeping over the boiler tops, an unpleasant manœuvre in a coal-burning ship.

There were two conning towers, each with a glass cupola on top just large enough for the occupant's head, the captain's tower being at the fore end, the engineer's at the after end.

Each boiler had its own short smoke stack, and these were removed in diving and blanked off as previously described.

While the various *Nordenfelt* ships may not have made much difference to their respective navies as submarines, they excited favourable comment as torpedo boats of the David and *Spuyten Duyvil* types, i.e. in an attack *à fleur de l'eau*. With their ballast tanks flooded until only the conning towers were visible they could steam at about six knots and discharge their torpedoes at will without presenting a worthwhile target to the enemy.

It is interesting to note that on the trials of *Nordenfelt-4* on Southampton Water Mr. Garrett acted as captain.

The conventional submarine of the twentieth century takes over from the *Nordenfelt*, but before leaving this subject I must mention another quaint submarine vessel of a different type, strangely reminiscent of an earlier age. This was the *Argonaut*, and her successor *Argonaut II*.

The *Argonaut* was built in 1897 by Simon Lake and carried out cruising and diving trials at Baltimore and in the Chesapeake Bay. She was then taken round to show her paces in New York and made no fewer than a hundred dives and covered a distance of over a thousand miles with a crew of five.

The principal claims made by her inventor were:

1 She could be perfectly controlled while submerged and could be maintained immovable at any depth.
2 She could travel on any type of bottom.
3 Greater speed could be obtained when submerged than when running on the surface.
4 No greater perceptible power was required to run the vessel submerged up a steep hill than on a level bottom, due to her buoyancy.
5 The crew were as comfortable when submerged as when on the surface. The *Argonaut* remained below at one time for ten hours and fifteen minutes. During this time the bottom door was opened, clams and oysters were picked from the bottom and the cook prepared a hot meal of clam fritters, coffee, baked beans, etc.
6 Communication could be maintained with the outside world while the boat was submerged.
7 The *Argonaut* was useful for repairing submarine cable, and its divers could readily pass into and out of the vessel.
8 Although storms raged on the surface the vessel, when submerged, would not be affected.

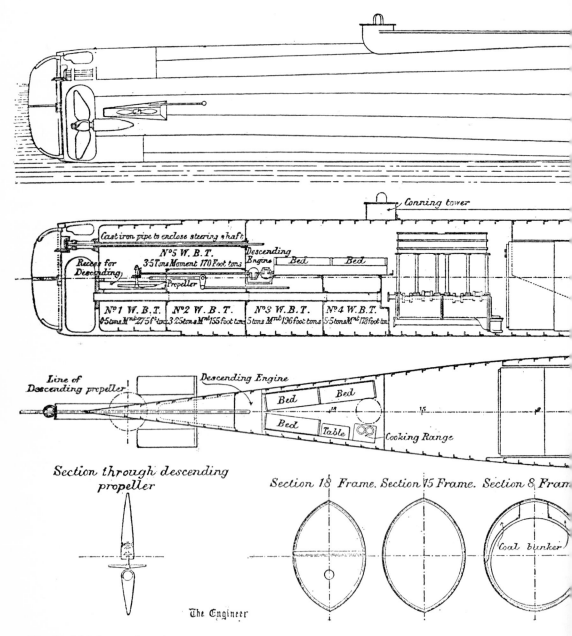

Cast iron pipe to enclose steering shaft.

Nº5 W.B.T.
3·5 Tons Moment 170 Foot tons

Recess for
Descending

Descending
Engine

Bed

Bed

Propeller

Conning tower

Nº1 W.B.T.	Nº2 W.B.T.	Nº3 W.B.T.	Nº4 W.B.T.
0·5 tons M^{nt} 27·5 f^t tons	3·25 tons M^{nt} 155 foot tons	5 tons M^{nt} 196 foot tons	5·5 tons M^{nt} 178 foot tons

Line of
Descending propeller

Descending Engine

Bed

Bed

Bed

Table

Cooking Range

Section through descending
propeller

Section 18 Frame. Section 15 Frame. Section 8 Frame

Coal bunker

The Engineer

40 Nordenfelt's later submarine

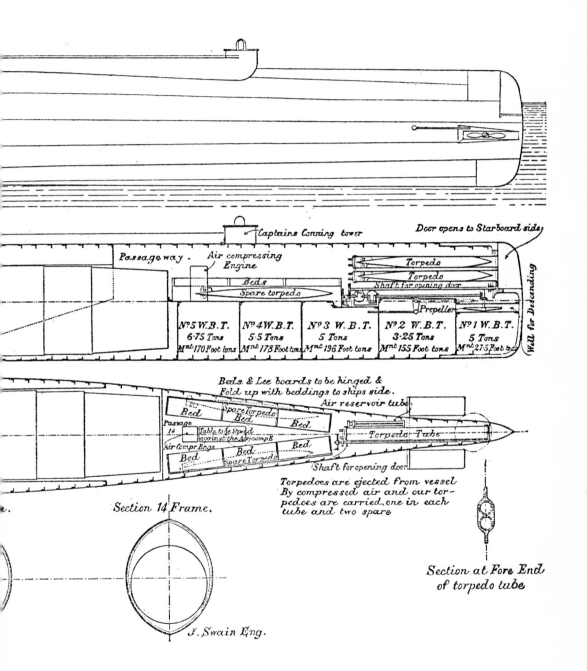

Captains Conning tower

Door opens to Starboard side

Passage way.

Air compressing Engine

Beds

Spare torpedo

Torpedo

Torpedo

Shaft for opening door

Propeller

Well for Descending

No 5 W.B.T.	No 4 W.B.T.	No 3 W.B.T.	No 2 W.B.T.	No 1 W.B.T.
6.75 Tons	5.5 Tons	5 Tons	3.25 Tons	5 Tons
Mnt 170 Foot tons	Mnt 178 Foot tons	Mnt 196 Foot tons	Mnt 155 Foot tons	Mnt 27.5 Foot tons

Beds & Lee boards to be hinged &
Fold up with beddings to ships side.

Air reservoir tube

Bed

Spare Torpedo

Bed

Bed

Passage 14

Table to be stowed against the Air compr E

Torpedo Tube

Air Compr Engs

Bed

Bed

Bed

Spare Torpedo

Shaft for opening door

Torpedoes are ejected from vessel
By compressed air and our torpedoes are carried, one in each
tube and two spare

Section 14 Frame.

Section at Fore End
of torpedo tube

J. Swain Eng.

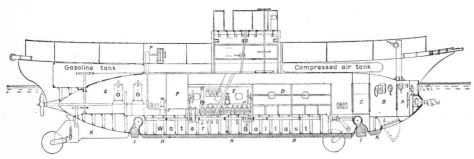

41 Submarine *Argonaut II*

This vessel was not so much a submarine as an ambulating diving bell, retaining contact with the surface. She had a tubby little hull 36 feet long and a diameter of 12 feet and displaced 57 tons when submerged. She was powered by a 30 h.p. petrol engine, both for surface and underwater cruising, and this engine also supplied power for electric light, pumping tanks and compressing air, the compressed air being stored in heavy steel cylinders.

There was the usual conning-access tower, and the vessel could be navigated from the fore end, where a glass port and shielded searchlight were fitted.

Fresh air was drawn into the ship and the engine exhaust gases were expelled through two 40 foot long pipes extending well above the surface of the water; her effective diving range was thus limited to about 40 feet depth. The two unusual features about this submarine were a pair of wheels to ride along the bottom, powered by the propeller, and the canny method of diving to any specified depth. In diving trim and with all hatches secured a heavy, solid weight on a cable was dropped to the sea bed from a recess in the vessel's bottom, and the ballast tanks were partially flooded to reduce buoyancy to a minimum. Then the cable was wound in on a winch operated from inside the hull, and the vessel was gradually pulled down to whatever depth was required, remaining in that position until the cable was released, when she would drift up to the surface again.

Argonaut II, a logical successor to the previous boat, was built at the end of 1899 and so just qualifies for inclusion in this review of odd ships. Like the *Polyphemus* and the *Livadia* she had a basic hull forming the business end of the vessel, with a ship-shaped structure surmounting it containing the equipment and non-perishable stores.

The pressure hull was 66 feet long with a diameter of 10 feet, and weighed 100 tons, and the very large conning or control tower, still part of the pressure hull, extended through the superstructure into the ship-shape bridge. This 'ship' structure housed the large containers holding a forty-eight-hour supply of air at 4,000 lb. p.s.i. and the gasoline tanks for the two 60 h.p. engines, which not only turned the propeller but also powered the two forward wheels.

The ship structure had a fiddle bow and a bowsprit, the latter being a hydraulic buffer to protect the vessel against collision.

The pressure hull had a pair of driving wheels at the fore end on spring shock absorbers, and a trailing wheel which also acted as a rudder. Navigation could be from the conning tower when sailing on the surface, or from a control station in the nose of the vessel where sight ports and a searchlight were fitted as in the previous vessel. There was also a bottom hatch through an airlock for access to the interior by divers.

The method of diving was similar to the first *Argonaut*, but in the second vessel there were two heavy weights which were first lowered to the sea bed and down which the submarine climbed, rather like the native pearl diver pulling himself down to the bottom of the sea. An added refinement lay in the detachable keel, a weight of three tons, which could be released in an emergency and allow the buoyancy of the hull to overcome the pull of the two working anchors.

In *Argonaut II* the air and exhaust schnorkel pipes, instead of being rigid, were flexible hoses anchored to a small raft floating on the surface. They had non-return valves at their open ends to prevent the ingress of water.

These then were the submarines of the nineteenth century: they had moved out of the experimental stage but still had a long way to go (seventeen years in fact) before they could mount a 12-inch gun, and a lot further still before they could be considered as safe as surface vessels.

The dangers that engendered a distrust of submarines are not hard to find. What seems comparatively simple to operate on the surface becomes exceedingly complicated when carried out in the dark in a confined space, with the air becoming slowly more and more foul, and panic just round the corner. In these circumstances the reasoning part of the brain ceases to function, and it is only by constant practice that orders can be carried out in an unthinking fashion.

And, apart from the merely mechanical side, there is that dangerous situation which every submarine must face every time she dives: a period of negative stability when the ballast tanks are being flooded, with consequent free surface. This effect of free surface will be appreciated by every father who has had to empty the baby's bath down the sink: however carefully he carries the bath, he is bound to stagger with the slopping of water from side to side.

In addition to loss of transverse stability there is the very acute danger of change of trim. As soon as the submarine is below the surface the longitudinal centre of buoyancy moves along to coincide with the geometrical centre of the pressure hull, but as the centre of gravity remains fixed there may, probably will, be a sudden change of trim, requiring careful and constant alteration to suit diving depth. It is very doubtful if these altering conditions of trim were appreciated by the early submariners, and ignorance of the laws governing floating bodies was probably the cause of most submarine fatalities.

8 Portuguese inshore craft

There is as much difference between the ships described in preceding chapters and Portuguese local craft as there is between a dwarf and a pygmy. While both may measure the same height the one is a victim of glandular maladjustment and is therefore abnormal, a true freak; while the other is a perfectly normal member of a race of small people. The vessels described below are not freaks in the usual sense but they are definitely odd in shape and in the purpose for which they are used.

Portuguese literature is singularly free from mention of these boats and it is impossible to state categorically that any particular vessel is derived from any definite source. It is, however, well known that Portugal at one time or another was visited or colonised by Cretans, Phoenicians, Carthaginians, Greeks, Romans, Norsemen and Moors, with, possibly, an emphasis on the Near Eastern peoples. Just as the anthropologist will discern traces of Semitic influence in the features of the humble folk in the fishing settlements of Povoa de Varzim, Costa Nova, Peniche, Cascais, etc., so will the archaeologist find remnants of an Eastern culture in their usual clay ornaments, decorations and household utensils. Little models of the Cretan bull are still on sale in the market places up country, and figurines of Ashtaroth, the Phoenician goddess of fertility, are yet to be found not very far from Lisbon. The Moors occupied the South of Portugal for many centuries and naturally they left their mark in the swarthy skins of the peasants.

The Phoenicians were the earliest navigators and builders of deep sea vessels. They influenced Cretan, Greek and later Roman shipbuilding, although they kept the secrets of ocean navigation to themselves. It was they who finally broke through the Straits of Gibraltar to explore and settle in the Atlantic countries. The Portuguese fisherfolk on the West Coast claim descent from those early Phoenician colonists, and point to their main fishing town, Peniche, as being the Latinised version of Phoinike, the Greek for Phoenicia. This is plain rubbish, of course (the Phoenicians spoke Aramaic, a Semitic tongue, and would presumably identify themselves in their own language). But there can be no doubt that the mantle of deep sea navigation did fall upon Portuguese shoulders as they it was who opened up the commercial world in the fourteenth, fifteenth and sixteenth centuries. In those days all great discoveries were made by either Portuguese captains or Portuguese pilots, and names such as Corte-Real (Newfoundland), Dias (Cape of Good Hope), Tristão da Cunha (the island of), Fernandes (Labrador), Cabral (Brazil), Peixote (Japan), are household

I

words. The most famous, perhaps, was the man who discovered the Straits of Magellan on the first circumnavigation of the world, and whose name appears on the maps in an Anglo-Spanish form, simply because few people outside his own country could pronounce it. (The real spelling was *Magalhães*, and should be pronounced as *Ma-ga-lyah-insh*.)

The Portuguese also inherited these old Mediterranean sailors' skills in boat building, together with their ancient designs and, as often as not, the skill to use their ancient tools. In fishing villages throughout the country the timber is sliced up into curved planks by means of the pit saw, and artisans still use the bow drill as a matter of course.

Most of the vessels described in this chapter are still in use although the internal combustion engine is fast making them obsolete. Among them the *Muleta* is a true nineteenth-century product, but before discussing this freak we will consider some of her forerunners.

The Saveiro

Portugal is fortunate in her many wide, sandy beaches extending for mile upon mile, clear of rocks and reefs, and backing on to open sand dunes and clear country beyond. This open coast line, however, presents few harbours and offers little shelter to coastal vessels—any fishing must be from craft which can be drawn up on to the beach, and it is not everyone who would care to launch a small boat from those beaches into the huge Atlantic breakers for a living. Portuguese fishermen, born sailors every one, solved this problem very neatly many, many, years ago, and in doing so must have used an instinct for ship design inherited from some of their Mediterranean forebears.

A form of beach trawling, using a special trawlnet, the *arte de xavega*, has been developed on the sandy shores. It consists of rowing a boat out to sea with the net on board, one warp of which is anchored on the beach, shooting the net at the proper moment and place, and returning to the beach with the other warp. After beaching the boat, the net is hauled ashore and emptied. Quite a simple operation in essence, but a major feat of organisation when one comes to consider the size of the boat, the weight of the net and the number of the crew. A rudderless rowing boat over 50 feet long, displacing 15 tons, carrying up to 44 rowers with only four oars among them is an unusual sight at any time, and this boat is more unusual still in that her overall length is roughly double that of her bottom. This is the Saveiro type, the heaviest boat engaged in the *xavega* (pro-

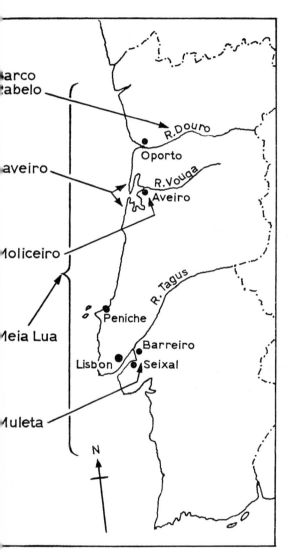

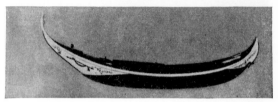

Above : Portuguese coastline showing regions where indigenous craft are to be found

bt, from top to bottom : Barco Rabelo, Saveiro, iceiro, Meia Lua, Muleta

nounced *shavga*) type of trawling, and it is to be found only on the beaches in the immediate vicinity of Aveiro, in the province of Beira.

The wooden hull is crescent shaped, with a high curved prow and stern to offer less surface to the breakers, and with a flat bottom suitable for drawing up on to the beach. The shape can be said to conform fairly well to the curve of the sea between the rows of heavy waves, and average dimensions are 55 feet overall length, 14 feet beam at the gunwales, 12 feet across the bottom, 4 feet 6 inches depth amidships, and with a loaded displacement of 15 tons at 3 feet draught, the freeboard being a scant 18 inches for open Atlantic sailing. The height of the stem from the keel line is about 17 feet, that of the stern about 12 feet.

The bottom is almost flat for about half length, rising in a smooth curve to meet the stem and stern beaks. These extremities have a greatly exaggerated sheer line and the general impression is that of a slice of water melon. The hull proportions are truly fantastic, especially when the boats are seen drawn up on the beach: an overall length to bottom length ratio of 2 to 1, and a 4 to 1 ratio in the depth at end and at amidships.

The ships are invariably gaily decorated with intricate designs and with religious motifs on bow panels. They are constructed of local pine, and being flat bottomed have neither keel nor keelson, the longitudinal strength being provided by the side planking $1\frac{1}{8}$ inches thick, reinforced by a 6×2 inch shelf running inside the gunwale for full length. There are some twenty-seven frames made in two halves scarphed into each other, those at the extremities being made into solid floors.

The planking is carvel type and the flat bottom is reinforced by wrought-iron rubbing strips for beaching. At the fore end a small locker is contrived to keep the few items of equipment: a bailer, an anchor, odd rope, etc. For general equipment the vessel is parish rigged.

In view of the Saveiro's great length, a considerable part of which is unsupported, the entire structure appears to be weak, and indeed when the vessel is being drawn down the sand for launching the bottom may be seen to flex and the side seams to open. A slight amount of leakage, however, does not materially affect the seaworthiness of this type of boat as the actual time afloat may be a few hours a day only, and its life span is estimated at from eight to ten years. There is no rudder, nor could there be on such a curved stem, but neither is there a steering sweep, as one would expect. The ship is steered entirely by means of the oars.

Each boat has two sets of nets, one in use, the other being overhauled, dried and recoiled ready for use. These trawlnets differ considerably from those used by North Sea trawlermen. The upper and lower sides are similar, but no otter boards are employed to keep the mouth open, the hauling speed not being sufficient for them. The net is laid as the vessel makes a wide sweep round the fishing grounds and the wings are gradually drawn together as the warps are slowly hauled in from the beach.

Compared with the British net the *xavega arte* is enormous, the belly measuring some 120 feet long by 25 feet wide at the cod end, of a mesh varying from ·3 inch to 2·5 inches, and the wings are about 700 feet long. As would be expected each warp is about 4 miles long, i.e. they must extend from the fishing ground to the beach, for the Saveiro is not a trawler, it only transports the net to the site, the actual trawling being done from the shore.

The net, and its warps, may weigh up to 7 tons, and has cork floats and clay weights to spread it, while small barrel floats are fitted at the tips of the wings where normally the otter boards would be placed.

To appreciate the scale of the gear, the North Sea trawlnet has lower wings about 70 feet long while the cod end is only 15 feet wide, with other dimensions in proportion.

The launching of the Saveiro is a thrilling sight, much more so than a bullfight. Not only is it a highly organised battle against the elements but it is also an exceedingly dangerous one, where many fishermen are in mortal peril even before they set foot in their boat.

Planks are laid along the beach in two rows to form a firm surface to support the rollers as the ship is manhandled down to the water's edge, as, of course, there are no power-driven winches to help. When in the water, but before being actually waterborne, the net is carried down in a long procession from the drying frames in the sand dunes.

Once the net is correctly stowed on board, and seven tons of net and warps take some stowing in a rowing boat, the actual launching takes place. As already pointed out these long, straight, sandy beaches are extremely vulnerable to the prevailing northerly winds and there is a very strong current in addition to the monster Atlantic breakers; there is precious little in the fisherman's favour.

The vessel still not quite waterborne, two check ropes are attached to ring bolts at the stern and brought back on to the beach, one on either side; each is in charge of a man who controls it by means of a half hitch round a post driven into the sand. A third rope, similarly attached to the bows, is taken well up the beach to windward and checked on a pole, this rope serving to keep the vessel's head to the sea. The vessel is now manhandled until it just starts to move with the waves, when the crew jump aboard and get the oars out, while the shore gang, numbering some thirty men, proceed to push the vessel out through the breakers by means of a long forked pole attached to a crutch in the stern. This pole, about thirty feet long, has the butt trailing along the sand and acts as a brake by digging in as the waves tend to force the Saveiro back on to the beach.

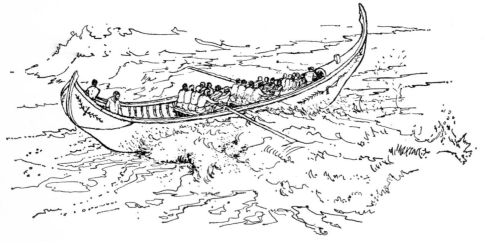

43　Launching the Saveiro

During the forward movement the men stationed at the check ropes pay out as required or check when ordered to, and the whole of the operation is under control of the skipper in the stern.

Notwithstanding the precautions taken during launching, however, it has been known for check ropes to part and the forked pole to break, or for an oar to be caught off balance by a wave, in which case the heavy vessel simply empties its crew into the water and rolls over on top of them.

The method of fishing is fairly straightforward. One warp is made fast to a post up on the beach and the Saveiro, complete with full crew and nets, is rowed out to the chosen fishing ground which may be anything up to four miles out, according to the season, the wind or current or simply to the skipper's hunch, paying out the fixed warp as she goes. The net is then shot, the vessel meanwhile drifting to leeward, and after making a wide curve to open out the wings, the second warp is brought back to the beach alongside the first. The vessel is then beached, and the second warp, with a turn round one of the bitts, acts as a handy brake on the return passage through the breakers.

With the vessel beached she is turned round on rollers and prepared for the next run.

In the meantime two teams of oxen, consisting of several pairs yoked together, take charge of the two warps and gradually draw the net on to the beach. Each warp is provided with different knots at intervals in its length to enable the shore gang to gauge the distance of the net from the shore and to ensure both wings being drawn up together. As the cod end appears rollers are placed below it to aid its progress and the end is opened well beyond reach of the waves.

It will be seen that fishing from these beaches is a communal affair, not a private enterprise, and a lot of the sheer muscle power is supplied by youngsters—with the usual small boys' genius for being trampled underfoot!

The Saveiros south of the town of Aveiro usually mount four oars, and those to the north two, the oars being the size and weight of telephone poles. They need to be worked in a very special manner as most of the available room in the waist of the boat is taken up by the net and several miles of warps.

In the 4-oared Saveiro the crew consists of 46 men, 44 oarsmen, the skipper, and the mate, the latter being the fishing master. In the 2-oared boats there are 32 oarsmen, a skipper and mate. In the first case there are therefore 11 men to an oar, and in the second case 16.

The oars themselves, made of chestnut or eucalyptus, are about 33 feet long with a 6 foot long by 7 inch wide blade. They are heavily reinforced and fitted with a wooden pad engaging with a $1\frac{1}{4}$ inch iron tholepin on the gunwale, the latter being strengthened in way by means of metal brackets. Owing to the dimensions of these oars the loom is too thick to be handled, and a light spar is attached parallel to and a few inches clear of it, to which the rowers apply themselves. Two iron rings shackled to the loom are equipped with several lengths of rope, on which additional crew members can haul.

The method of rowing may even be relevant to one of the greatest unsolved mysteries of ancient naval architecture: how were the rowers disposed in the biremes, triremes, quadriremes, quinqueremes, etc? Did these terms imply two, three, four or five men to an oar or, as some would have it, that the rowers were placed on five different decks. Or something of each? Thucydides, a most reliable observer and factual historian, tells

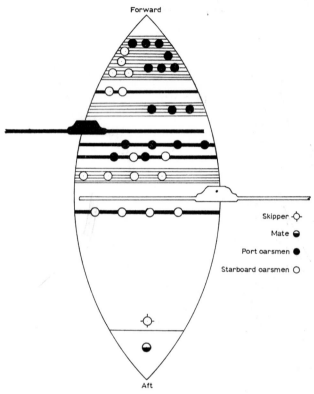

44　Two-oared Saveiro showing position of each oarsman

us that in Homeric days the ships carried up to a hundred men, every one of whom rowed, except the chief who steered. Now, allowing for the usual half crew rowing, the other half having a lay off, we still have fifty rowers. Did this mean fifty oars? In the huge Attic tesseraconteres, with the oars grouped in fours (banks or men), Thucydides states that the oars were fifty-three feet long. No man on earth, however Homeric in stature, could handle an oar that long and we therefore come back to the number of men manning each oar. This, however, raises another problem, as a large crew to each oar means a lot of men attached to a relatively short loom. The Byzantines solved this by fitting an apostis or out-rigger to their galleys, allowing more swing to the oar and giving a far better purchase. But the ancient tesseraconteres and penteconteres did not mount an apostis, and there must therefore have been some sort of compromise between the number of men to an oar and their position at varying deck levels. This is borne out by the names of the different types: the thranite on the weather deck, the zygite below him and the thalamite well below the other two, in some sort of tween deck.

In the crew of our Saveiro, there are 16 men to each oar in the two-oared vessel, and 11 men to each of the four oars in the other type. Would Thucydides call them hekkaidekaconteres and hendekaconteres respectively? The actual disposition of the 16-oar crew is as follows: three men sitting on a thwart, facing aft; six men standing, facing forward; and seven men in the bows pulling on the oar ropes. Like the Greek oarsmen each single man on each oar has his appropriate title, which places him in his correct position on board and defines his duties. The Portuguese language is very rich when it comes down to detail.

One point to note is the safety measure implicit in the check rope attached to the innermost end of the oar's loom, ostensibly to prevent the oar being lost overboard. At sea this rope is secured to a thwart or spar at such a length that it serves to prevent a wave thrusting the oar against the rowers and causing possible injury.

As in Homeric days, the skipper sits in the stern and directs the rowing, while the mate sits abaft him and pays out the warp.

Can it be that these humble fishermen have inherited from their remote ancestors not only the art of building multi-oared ships, but have retained the clue as to their use?

The Meia Lua

The Meia Lua (half moon) is also employed in beach trawling and is basically similar to the Saveiro. As both types have existed over the centuries it is now impossible to tell which was the prototype of the other. The Meia Lua is to be found here and there throughout the entire length of the Portuguese Atlantic seaboard, wherever the beaches are suitable for trawling and where the coastline offers some protection from the breakers.

Their construction is similar to that of the Saveiro, flat bottom for half the length, without keel, with carvel sides and exaggerated bow and stern curves, and built throughout of the local pine. Although they differ in size according to locality a typical vessel will be 27 feet long, 7 feet broad and 3 feet deep, with beaks 10 feet and 8 feet above the base line for stem and stern respectively. The framing consists of single timbers 14 inches apart and scarphed into each other exactly like the larger Saveiro.

K

The planking is 1 inch thick and is pegged to the frames with wooden dowels.

Instead of an inside shelf this vessel has a heavy rubbing strip fitted outside the gunwale as a slight concession to longitudinal strength.

Seven thwarts are fitted, and there are usually five oars a side, each oar being manipulated by one man only. In this type of ship the steering is done by a long sweep over the stern bearing against a wooden post.

As the Meia Lua is so much lighter than the Saveiro and fishes on grounds considerably closer to the shore launching is that much more simple. The vessel is pushed down to the water's edge on two long poles laid as rails, the net and warps are laid aboard and she is pushed out by her own crew. The nets are similar to those already described for the Saveiro, but much smaller and the warps are relatively short and easily stowed.

Generally speaking, the only features of the Meia Lua that differ from the Saveiro are the peculiar, graceful curves of the beaks and the eyes painted on the bows. No proper explanation has yet been given for the reason for these eyes—some fishermen state they serve to guide the vessel through the water towards the shoals of fish, while others aver that they keep away the Evil Eye. This latter explanation should not be lightly discarded; anyone who has lived for a time among Portuguese, Spanish or indeed any Mediterranean peasant people, will agree that witchcraft still flourishes, and that the Evil Eye is very much to be avoided. In Portugal a ram's horn is hung from the axletree of every country cart and inside the forecastle of every ship, from trawler to liner, precisely as a protection against this evil influence.

In both the Meia Lua and the Saveiro the lower part of the hull is painted black or dark blue, with red designs and religious symbols on a white background round the beaks.

Did not Homer describe his heroes' ships as 'sharp, dark prowed, vermilion cheeked, hollow-curved, stem and stern high and up-raised as the horns of an ox'? Surely a perfect description of our Portuguese *xavega* trawlers.

The Moliceiro

The River Vouga, a small unimportant stream in Beira province meandering westwards towards the dune country and the Atlantic seaboard, floods a hundred or so square miles of countryside with slightly brackish water.

This marshland embraces a number of small fishing communities all within hailing distance of the market town of Aveiro, the fishing being both lacunar and deep sea. The marshland consists of an extensive system of lagoons linked together by navigable canals, very similar to the Norfolk Broads, and it has developed a culture separate from the adjacent country-side. One aspect of this is the Saveiro for deep sea fishing. Another is the Moliceiro for lagoon dredging. This is the life of the *Ria*, a word which means 'wide, shallow lagoon with a river running through it'.

This *Ria*, stretching for miles parallel with the sea but separated from it by the dunes, is never more than six feet deep, and canals connect it with the neighbouring fishing villages of Costa Nova, São Jacinto, Murtosa and, of course, Ilhavo, a village scarcely bigger than a football field, which supplies half the Portuguese deep-sea fishing fleet with its crews.

The surrounding countryside is sandy, especially in the coastal sectors, but for many centuries it has been gradually nursed into good arable land by means of the waterweeds culled from the lagoon. These waterweeds, of various kinds, have the generic term of *moliço* and give their name to the vessels employed in their gathering and transport, and, by extension, to the general transport of goods and ferrying of passengers between villages; the industry supports a considerable percentage of the labour in the Aveiro district.

The Moliceiro is a long, flat bottomed vessel of shallow draught and very low freeboard, so low, in fact, that it is measured in quarters of an inch, and it is used exclusively in the lagoon and adjoining waterways. It is not a sea boat and would, indeed, have a very short life in a seaway owing to its design and construction.

When seen drawn up on the beach it has the appearance of a water-line model, even to the rudder, and this must be borne in mind when studying the sketches. A typical boat will have the following dimensions: length 50 feet, breadth 8 feet at the gunwales and a depth of about 2 feet, and, as there are no regulating authorities in the district, the freeboard is a gamble with Davy Jones.

The bottom is quite flat for about three-quarters of the length, with the bows curving upwards and backwards, reminiscent of the North American birchbark canoe, and, as is the case with most indigenous craft, gaily painted and decorated at the ends on a uniform ochre background of hull. The upper portion of the stem, about 12 inches of it, is hinged to allow it to drop when sailing below the canal bridges.

The cross-section is trapezoidal, being narrower at the bottom, and the gunwale has an inner shelf and an outer rubbing strip. As in the Saveiro and the Meia Lua there is no keel or keelson, and the frames, about two feet apart, are fitted in a similar manner to those vessels. A small decked-in forecastle is provided, serving as a food and equipment store and at times as sleeping quarters for the crew of two. Propulsion is by sail, poling or towing according to circumstances.

When sailing, the mast, which is about 25 feet high and stepped slightly forward of amidships, is fitted with a 12 feet yard and lugsail. Very little rigging is employed, but sometimes a back stay is fitted and usually the halliards are secured to windward and serve as shrouds. The forebrace is secured to the forward leech rope by means of several small lines set at intervals in the upper half of the sail and the sheet is occasionally run on a wooden sheet horse. Tacking is seldom resorted to—the lagoon is so shallow that poling would be quicker; but owing to the absence of keel a lee board is employed, looped to the mast.

To enable the vessel to be controlled by either member of the crew the rudder tiller is fitted athwartships, and a rope attached to one end of the tiller is carried forward, rove through a block on the stem head and brought back to be lashed to the other end of the tiller. With this arrangement the vessel can be steered from any position on board.

An interesting point to note with regard to the rudder is that, due to the sharp curvature of the stern, the top and bottom pintles are not in line with each other, which would appear to lead to excessive wear in the gudgeons.

On the starboard side, at the forward end, a small chain and staple are fitted, forming a loop. When mooring the Moliceiro a pole is thrust through this loop and driven into the sand. At other times, when for some reason or other this form of mooring is not desirable, a small anchor is employed. This anchor is about the most primitive type since anchors were invented, and consists of two sticks lashed together at their upper ends and secured to the extremities of a crescent-shaped piece of hardwood with pointed ends, the ensemble forming a sector and the whole being weighted with a large stone wedged into the frame. The holding power of this anchor is debatable; the stone by itself would do just as well.

The gathering of the waterweeds from the bed of the lagoon ('the harvest'), to which the Moliceiro is mainly devoted, is carried out by means of long wooden rakes. The weed is stacked in the bottom of the boat and as the cargo, and consequently the draught, increases, portable bulwark boards are fitted to the gunwales. They serve a triple purpose: they keep the seaweed in position, act as splashboards in view of the extremely small freeboard, and when the vessel is light, they are laid flat across the thwarts and serve as gangways for the crew when poling or working ship. To this end the inner surfaces are coated with pitch and sawdust to ensure a good footing.

The Moliceiro is built throughout of the local white pine and is usually constructed in one of the villages well away from the water's edge. The builders, having inherited their skill from generations of craftsmen, use no drawings whatever, and most of them cannot read or write.

All measurements are incorporated in one yard-stick: a squared pole some five feet long upon which are notched all the basic dimensions. This pole does duty for drawing office and mould loft; and, though hardly the last word in naval architecture, the resulting vessel, when seen afloat, will hold her own anywhere in this world for grace and line.

Upon completion the Moliceiro is loaded on a long trailer drawn by teams of bullocks and conducted to the lagoon; there the trailer is driven into the water until the vessel floats free.

The launch, incidentally, always takes place on a Saturday, irrespective of the date of completion, and is both a religious and a social ceremony.

Life on board the vessel is pretty arduous as in summer the crew may spend two or three nights on board, anchored in the lee of a sand dune. Cooking is done on a charcoal brazier placed on a stone hearth in the stern, and at night the men have to sleep on the soft side of a plank underneath the sail, which is draped over a pole as shelter.

The Barco Rabelo

Although port is an essentially Portuguese wine, grown, made and matured in the country, it always has been virtually a foreign wine in the sense that it is produced for export to England and Scandinavia. Most of the wine growers are British and live in Oporto, and very little port is consumed in the country—the average Portuguese palate is attuned to a drier, harsher wine with less alcoholic content.

The story of port is very simple. The grapes are grown in an area on the upper reaches of the River Douro (pronounced *Doh-roo*) and the raw wine is sent down in large barrels or pipes of between 113 to 115 gallons each to Vila Nova de Gaia, across the river from Oporto, where it is matured and carefully blended in the warehouses. Upon completion of its life cycle it is shipped either at Gaia or at Leixões, the sea port for Oporto. The part that interests us in the cycle is the means of transport between the vineyards in the province of Tras-os-Montes and Gaia.

Owing to the mountainous nature of the country, roads are few and far between, and, while there is a railway serving the various townships along the river, the only feasible method of transport for bulk commodities, and the only possible one for a temperamental cargo such as wine, is by water. The river flows along a deep, narrow valley from east to west, and in the neighbourhood of the wine-growing country, where the vines grow on terraces scooped into the precipitous hills, this valley becomes a gorge and the Douro a swiftly flowing stream with many rapids.

A sailing boat of large capacity has been evolved to navigate this river. It has a shallow draught for the upper reaches, and is capable of negotiating the rapids by virtue of its extraordinary manœuvrability, taking its cargo of wine downstream to the estuary by means of the current and the wind when favourable, and returning up-river empty by means of sailing or towing.

This class of vessel, the Barco Rabelo (literally: boat-with-a-tail), is peculiar to the River Douro, and has been employed in transport for many centuries. Strabo is alleged to have referred to them, and they figure in the 'Black Book' of Coimbra cathedral, the local equivalent of our Doomsday Book, as early as the ninth century. They are constructed throughout of the local pine but, contrary to the almost universal practice in Portugal, the planking is clinker laid, a fact which points to a Scandinavian origin.

The size varies to a very great extent, the largest vessels now seen measuring 60 feet long, 12 feet wide and 4 feet deep amidships. They can carry from 45 to 50 pipes of wine, or up to 25 tons of cargo. It is on record, however, that in bygone days vessels of this type were built to carry up to 100 pipes. When loaded the Barco Rabelo sits very deeply in the water with a freeboard of only a few inches and, as in the case of the Moliceiro, splashboards can be fitted along the gunwales. In passing it might be pointed out that a low freeboard seems to be the common denominator in all these indigenous craft.

The framing is similar to that fitted in other vessels already described, and there is neither keel nor keelson. Instead of the wall sides and the dead-flat bottom of the fishing boats, with their hard chine, the bilges of this river boat are generously rounded. The bows are low and spoonshaped, as in the Norwegian pram, while the stern is much higher with the sternpost ending in a broad, flat shoe provided with a steel thole pin (or rudder pintle) for the steering oar. The stern is decked in to form a store locker, while a low platform is incorporated in the bows to contain the ropes and gear necessary for working the ship.

The bridge is situated about two-thirds of the vessel's length from forward and consists of a tall wooden structure built up from the gunwales on strong stanchions, one at each corner, with crosspieces to form

45 Barco Rabelo under sail

a ladder on each side. The deck of the bridge, which extends the width of the hull, is about 3 feet wide and slopes slightly towards the stern. It is a good 12 to 14 feet above the bottom of the boat and even when the cargo is piled high above the gunwales the skipper still has an unrestricted view. The width of the bridge deck is laid with short fore and aft strips to afford a foothold when the skipper 'walks' the steering oar hard over.

This steering oar is the outstanding feature of the Barco Rabelo and gives it its name. It is an enormous sweep in the shape of an elongated letter S, and fits over the thole pin mounted into the shoe on top of the sternpost.

It is about 35 feet long and some 6 inches square in section, and is usually made in two pieces. A butt strap over the scarph projects to port and contains the gudgeon engaging on the thole pin. The loom has a counterweight at its inner end and this is so adjusted that the oar blade will float in the water at about the same draught as the vessel, certainly not more. There are a number of wooden pegs driven into the top of the loom to accommodate a check rope for taking a bend in the river, or for turning in a small circle. Owing to the tremendous leverage, and to the amount of swing which can be given to the loom, this steering oar is said to be able to spin the Barco Rabelo on the proverbial sixpence, and this, of course, is of primary importance when navigating the gorges or shooting the rapids.

The skipper usually steers with his back against the steering sweep, in much the same fashion as his colleagues throughout the world steer their boats, except that in the present case we are dealing with a 'tiller' up to 15 feet from the stern head. Should the blade of the steering oar catch the bottom or a nearby rock the reaction at the inner end would be sufficient to jerk the steersman off the bridge; hence the necessity for particular care in adjusting the blade immersion after every loading.

The mast is stepped slightly forward of amidships and carries a yard, often made in two pieces, at its extreme top. The square sail is bent to this yard and the braces and sheets are brought aft on to the bridge. The yard topping lift is usually made fast aft to serve as a backstay. A rope is attached to the top of the mast and passes aft of and below the sail, upwards and forwards of it, through a block on the mast head, thus entirely encircling the sail. The fall is secured to a cleat on the bridge. When the boat is under way the rope is hauled taut and the sail is bunched up at its lower end, allowing the helmsman on his lofty perch to see below the canvas. This manœuvre gives the sail its typical hemispherical shape when sailing before the wind. In this connection it may be pointed out that, as the only wind available in this deep valley of the Douro is along its course, there is no question of the Barco Rabelo tacking, a form of progress impossible in such a narrow waterway and for which, moreover, the rig is not designed.

Navigation of the Douro is possible only by day, as no lights or buoys are provided, and the wine boat is tied up to the bank at night, when a tarpaulin is draped over the steering oar and bridge erection to form a tent for the crew. Should the wind prove unfavourable on the upstream voyage the vessel is either towed up by its crew or, when the nature of the banks do not allow of this being done, anchored in midstream until the wind changes. Time is not important to either master or crew: these happy, carefree creatures are not slaves to the machine and they do not fight the elements, they co-operate with them.

When rapids are encountered the Barco Rabelo is hauled up by means of oxen hired for the purpose or, if freights are scarce and money is tight, by the crew themselves. In the latter case the ship's portable gear is sometimes carried on the men's backs to reduce the draught to a minimum.

When drifting down river, should there be no wind and once clear of the rapids in the upper reaches, the mast is unstepped and with its yard is floated alongside.

The Barco Rabão

The Barco Rabão (literally: little-ship-with-a-tail) of the lower reaches of the Douro and its estuary down to the bar, is similar to the Barco Rabelo but on a smaller scale, being in fact, derived from it. It rarely exceeds 25 feet long and has the disproportionately long steering sweep but no bridge, the helmsman standing on a high thwart placed in the same relative position as the bridge on its prototype.

This vessel is propelled by oars or by sail and has a variety of rigs: square sail as on the large vessels, lug sail, sprit sail, etc. A peculiar rig sometimes met with gives the craft the appearance of a butterfly. It consists of twin sprit sails set athwartships, one on each side of the mast, each sail being supported by a diagonal boom let into a noose at the mast step, the booms with the mast forming a broad, inverted arrowhead.

The Barcos Rabão do not engage in the transport of wine except as ordinary merchandise; they are the general purpose boats of the lower Douro and are used for cargo and passenger ferry service.

The Muleta

The Muleta (Portuguese=crutch) is the only Portuguese freak vessel which can be truly contained within our terms of reference of bizarre ships of the nineteenth century. All the other vessels described in this chapter existed since official records were kept and they are still in existence, though fast dying out. The Muleta, on the other hand, is not mentioned before the beginning of the nineteenth century and the last one was dismantled on or about 1900, although the hulk was in use well after that time as a general purpose boat. The genus thus fits very neatly into our list of freaks.

The Muleta was peculiar to Seixal and Barreiro, small towns on the south bank of the Tagus and quite near to Lisbon, and was at one time a very common sight in the estuary. Unfortunately its freakish method of progress in a fairly crowded sea lane, coupled with the advent of the steam trawler, caused it to fall into desuetude and it gradually disappeared towards the turn of the century. The Muleta was unusual not only in regard to its shape and its rig but also to its method of fishing.

Average dimensions were about 50 feet long by 12 feet beam and 7 feet depth of hold. The hull planking was carvel laid and the framing followed the modern plan: keel and keelson, double frame timbers, deckbeam shelves and knees, etc. While not a sea-going vessel she was built like one, and a partial deck was provided, extending from forward for about 30 feet and from aft for about 10 feet. The waist, i.e. the space between the two portions of deck, was left open and served for access to the underdeck spaces, this cockpit being provided with ladders forward and aft, while a gangway was thrown across it for access from one end of the vessel to the other.

The stem was semi-circular in profile and was protected by an iron cut-water fitted with ornamental spikes set radially for its full length from deck to keel. Above the rounded stem a sharp beak jutted forward and upwards at an angle of about 20 degrees to the vertical and served as an abutment to the fishing mast. This beak was from 4 to 5 feet long, and, together with the whole of the fore end of the hull, was gaily painted.

The stern was rounded and, as in the case of the Moliceiro, the rudder forepiece followed the curve of the stern and had the pintles out of alignment. And here again the rudder tiller was placed athwartships and was controlled by a tackle at each end, the fall of each being made fast to its own cleat and not, as one would have expected, being connected to each other as with the orthodox relieving tackle fitted to larger rudders. Under these conditions steering would need to be carried out by two men, one man hauling in on one tackle while the other paid out on his.

Two iron rubbing strips encircled the hull, one just below the deck level, the other at about water level, and both were fitted with large wrought-iron ornamental knobs spaced about 3 feet apart. This vessel also had removable bulwarks and leeboards like the Moliceiro.

It will thus be seen that the Muleta represented a curious blend of the archaic and the modern; with a design and details from an earlier civilisation, upon which have been superimposed the paraphernalia of a more modern age. The curved stem and the forward jutting beak of the Muleta bear a striking resemblance to those of the Maltese Speronara: a direct descendant of the Phoenician vessels, ram and all. Also the highly ornamental and knobbly rubbing strips round the hull below deck, quite useless from a practical point of view, could quite reasonably be compared with the hypozomata or girding cables in Greek vessels—cables rove through the hawseholes, brought round the hull under the wales and tightened up at the stern by means of poles, to hold the ram ship together.

In spite of the apparent confusion of masts and spars there was only one true mast, rather stumpy, stepped about amidships and inclined forward at an angle of about 15 degrees to the perpendicular. This carried the 50 foot yard with its main lateen or latin sail, by means of which the vessel proceeded to and from the fishing grounds in the normal manner.

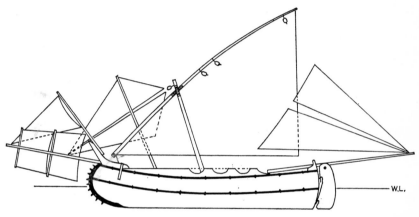

46 Sail plan of Muleta

When fishing a light pole mast was fitted into a socket at the foot of the beak and long booms were thrust out both forward and aft, to which were bent a number of sails of various shapes and sizes. The forward or jib-boom carried two square sails on short yards, and the light pole on the beak carried a flying jib, the tack of which was attached to the end of the jib-boom. A peculiar type of sprit sail, in halves permanently fastened to each other, was supported on a boom resting on the deck about midway between the main mast and the beak. The tacks of both halves of this sail were made fast to the inner end of the jib-boom.

The after boom carried two try-sails controlled through blocks on the main yard.

The fishing grounds of the Muleta were the river and the estuary of the Tagus, from the bar up to the home ports of Seixal and Barreiro. The vessel sailed down river with the tide and, upon reaching the mouth at low water, would shoot the trawl and drift upstream with the wind and the incoming tide. Both booms were run out and the warps of the net were made fast to their ends. The square sails, flying jib, sprit and trysails were then set and the vessel proceeded upstream in sideways fashion, like a crab. The auxiliary sails were adjusted to suit the wind and current and served mainly to steer the ship, as the rudder under these conditions would be ineffective. It will now be understood why Muletas were never very popular with the Lisbon pilots and seafarers generally.

9   The *Great Eastern*

No review of bizarre ships would be complete without some description of the *Great Eastern*, for, although this vessel was in most respects a conventional passenger-cum-cargo carrier with orthodox hull, machinery, rigging and equipment, she was as much a freak as the odd looking vessels described in previous chapters; after all, a giant is a freak just as a two-headed calf is a freak. The *Great Eastern* had nothing that other vessels didn't have, she simply had a lot more of it. She held the record of being the largest ship for half a century, being exceeded in length only by the *Oceanic,* built 1899, and in sheer size by the *Lusitania,* built 1906.

The mere fact of her being bigger than other ships would not make the *Great Eastern* outstanding, until we compare her with the largest ships existing at the time, and do a little mental arithmetic. Her standard length was 680 feet between perpendiculars and when she was laid down in 1854 the largest vessels at that time were *H.M.S. Warrior* (380 feet long) and the P. & O. passenger vessel *Himalaya* (340 feet long). In other words the *Great Eastern,* being twice as long as her biggest rival, was roughly eight times as large.

With such an enormous increase in size everything had to be scaled up to suit: machinery, masts, rigging and equipment, launching arrangements, all had to be designed from data derived from smaller vessels but which had not hitherto been proved for the sizes now contemplated. In short, all design data had to be extrapolated from existing engineering tables.

Apart from her record for size the *Great Eastern* held a number of other records, some of which have never been broken. She was the 'mostest' vessel ever built, and was:

1 The only merchant vessel ever to have five funnels, although the Russians had a five-funnel cruiser shortly after the turn of this century, the *Askold,* euphemistically known as the 'Packet of Woodbines'.

2 The only vessel ever to have simultaneous screw, paddle and sail propulsion.

It is true that a small vessel, *H.M.S. Bee,* built in 1842 had both paddles and screw, and was used as an engineering training ship at the Royal Naval College, Portsmouth. This vessel, however, had a single side lever engine which could be coupled at will to either a paddle shaft or a screw shaft. The *Great Eastern* had an entirely independent set of engines, housed in a separate engine room, each with its own set of boilers and controlled by its own squad of engineers, firemen and trimmers, for both screw and paddles.

3 The first merchant vessel to have her master knighted.

4 The safest vessel on the Western Ocean service, as she never lost a passenger. This in itself is a remarkable record for that criminally reckless age when the government had no control over a vessel's seaworthiness, crew, cargo, life-saving appliances or fire-fighting equipment, and when the master's authority was absolute. In the early days of steam, ships were driven for all they were worth and very few lived to be broken up—speed was far more important to owners than comfort or even safety. A ship in those days died fighting, usually taking most of her crew and passengers with her, and the record of sailing casualties on the Atlantic passage in the 1860's was appalling.

Some critics might point out that the *Great Eastern* never carried many passengers anyway, but that is not quite the point: she was an essentially safe ship

5 She was the ugliest vessel of her time. The steamer of the mid-nineteenth century still retained the graceful outlines of the sailing ship, with her clipper bows, raking masts, tapering yards and a beautiful sweep in the sheer line; even her paddle boxes blended sweetly with the hull contour. The *Great Eastern*, however, with her straight stem and stumpy counter, slab sides and total absence of sheer, and with a series of perpendicular masts and funnels set out like fence poles, was about as dainty and glamorous as a coal barge.

Hence, although we must salute her designer's courage and enterprise in building such an immense vessel, we reserve our opinion on his aesthetic achievement.

Now the *Great Eastern*, her social history and her impact on the latter half of the nineteenth century have been very well described by many competent writers, and anyone interested in the history of this giant ship will have already read one or more of their books. I therefore propose to confine my comments to the more technical aspects of the vessel's design, construction and service, and the following brief historical notes are merely included to complete the picture.

The *Great Eastern* was conceived by that engineering genius of the nineteenth century, Isambard Kingdom Brunel, in 1851 and was the logical successor to his two other vessels, both of them famous after their own fashion. His earliest, the *Great Western*, a wooden paddle steamer of some 2,300 tons displacement built in 1838, just missed by a few hours being the first steamer to cross the Atlantic, being beaten in this by the *Sirius*.

His next venture was the *Great Britain*, completed in 1845 and the largest ship in the world at that time. She was also the first screw steamer to cross the Atlantic. Although no freak she was unusual in some of her character-istics and unique for her day in that she survived stranding in Dundrum Bay, N. Ireland, for eleven months without breaking up. She had six masts, five of them stepped on deck in tulips like tall candlesticks, and a 6-bladed wrought iron propeller driven by chain and sprocket wheels, through a hollow intermediate shaft. Probably the most peculiar features about this ship were the arrangements made for her launching. She was built in a section of the Cumberland Basin in Bristol, the narrow entrance of which was blanked off to allow the dock to be drained. Now it had been under-stood by the owners that the dock entrances to this basin complex were to be considerably widened before the hull reached completion, and con-struction was accordingly commenced. Unfortunately, the harbour works were not put in hand as agreed and when the launching date arrived the owners were left with a remarkably big ship imprisoned in a very small land-locked basin. Eventually they obtained permission from the authori-ties to widen the locks, allow the *Great Britain* to pass through, and restore the entrances to their original condition, this Cesarean operation being performed at their own risk and cost.

Brunel seems to have had little luck in the launching of his big ships, but we must give him credit for building them to last. During a series of changes in her social status, the *Great Britain* had her masts cut down, her engines and propeller renewed, then removed entirely to become a full-rigged ship on the bulk cargo trade. Finally, in 1886 she limped into Port Stanley in the Falkland Islands and remained there as a coal hulk until 1936 when, at long last, she was beached at Sparrow Cove where she lies to this day.

His third and final vessel, the *Great Eastern*, started building in 1854, was ready for launching in November 1857, but due to bad luck and bad management was not afloat until the end of January 1858. Her acceptance trials in September 1859 were marred by tragedy when an economiser over one of the boilers blew out, killing five men and injuring many more.

On her maiden voyage to North America she ran out her screw shaft bearing and the ship had to be nursed all the way home, where a new screwshaft was fitted. On the third voyage, during a gale in the North

Atlantic, she lost both paddle wheels and snapped her rudder head just above the steady bearing, and had to struggle back home with screw engines alone and a temporary rudder repair.

In August 1862 she struck the Great Eastern Rock, a pinnacle of rock at the entrance to Long Island Sound, and ripped a hole in her starboard bilge some eighty-three feet long. Other ships drawing less water had been blithely sailing over this pinnacle for years, and it took a vessel with a draught of thirty feet to discover the rock; her owners, faced with a bill for many thousands of dollars and months of demurrage, must have considered this a high price to pay for the honour.

This series of major damages, involving expensive repairs, and made more costly still by there being no dry dock anywhere in the world suitable for a ship of this size, ruined her owners and she was laid up in 1864 through sheer lack of funds to run her.

Between 1865 and 1874 she was chartered for odd voyages, mainly for laying cables, and one might say that she spent more time cable-laying than carrying passengers. In 1875 she was laid up at Milford Haven where she remained for eleven years until she was purchased by a large department store in Liverpool and was anchored in the Mersey as a show-boat-cum-bilboard. After a brief visit to Dublin and Greenock as a show-boat, where she must have appeared as some proud, savage queen decked out as a clown for the amusement of her captors, she was broken up at Birkenhead in 1889.

During her lifetime this vessel ran through fortune after fortune and destroyed her designers, builders and all her successive owners with grim impartiality, yet she spent most of her life at anchor.

Her principal characteristics were:

Length B.P.	680 feet
Breadth over sponsons	120 feet
Moulded breadth	82 feet
Depth	58 feet
Draught	30 feet
Gross tonnage	18,914 tons
Displacement	27,384 tons
Speed	14½ knots

The *Great Eastern* is always referred to as Brunel's great ship and it might be pertinent to enquire exactly what part he played in her construction. As the owners' technical adviser he was, of course, responsible for approving the design and checking the quality of workmanship, but as these functions are undertaken every day by owners' superintendents the world over who certainly lay no claim to building their respective ships, Brunel must have had considerably more voice in the creation of the ship than would appear at a casual reading of her history.

When we say we built our own house we usually mean we engaged a builder to construct it to our own design or specification. When we talk about designing our own house we simply mean that we produced a draft arrangement of the living rooms, leaving the professional architect to deal with such things as foundations, strength calculations, drains, water and electricity lay-out, approval of plans, etc., about which the amateur designer knows nothing at all. Building a ship entails all the above problems plus many thousands more, and both the design and the execution of the work are rightly the job of the shipyard, the more so when we are dealing, as in this case, with the biggest ship in the world. Even in the 1850's, when shipbuilding was still an art rather than a science, a structure of this size had to be worked out in detail on paper before even a single plate could be ordered, and this required many hundreds of plans. (Nowadays a similar sized vessel would need thousands of plans.)

Even a genius like Brunel could hardly have had the specialised knowledge required to deal with such items as the power and design of the main propelling machinery, the boiler capacity, the pumping arrangements, rigging and sail plan, passenger accommodation, catering requirements, etc., which only a large yard with a competent design staff can supply.

The *Great Eastern* was, in fact, evolved by the Millwall yard of J. Scott Russell, erstwhile professor of natural philosophy at St. Andrew's University and professional shipbuilder, and it is he who claims the honour of having designed the hull on his wave-line theory. On the other hand we can be certain that some of the ship's novel features were suggested by Brunel, such as the longitudinal framing with transverse web frames, double bottom extending up the sides to form a double skin below water level, double main deck, and bunker space for some 12,000 tons of coal.

He also, in the face of the many set-backs incurred in the launching and fitting out, when the management were fighting a losing battle with bad luck and when morale was generally low, provided that nervous energy to see the construction to a satisfactory conclusion, even though the effort cost him his life.

L

The idea of longitudinal framing seems to have been derived from his experience in designing bridges, and he thought of a ship simply as a gigantic box girder.

The double bottom was new in that age, but had been tried out in the *Great Eastern*'s predecessor. The *Great Britain* had a form of double bottom construction, but in that case the tank top was for strength purposes, not watertightness. In the case of our great ship, however, the double bottom extended up the shipsides to slightly above water level, and the tank top thus formed an inner, watertight skin for the major part of the ship's length. The two skins of plating, $\frac{3}{4}$ inches thick and almost 3 feet apart, contained the heavy longitudinal structure and formed with the transverse frames an exceedingly strong cellular framework or honeycomb. The space between these two skins was used as a huge ballast or fresh-water tank, conveniently sub-divided into sections which could be flooded or pumped out at will.

It was this double skin that saved the *Great Eastern* when she struck the rock entering New York Harbour. As the inner shell remained intact she could have sailed home quite safely floating on her inner bottom.

Although a double bottom is retained in modern ships the inner skin extending up to water level has been discarded as being too expensive and unnecessary. We can also be sure that had this pinnacle of rock in New York Harbour struck a few inches deeper into the *Great Eastern*'s bilge and pierced the inner shell she would have sunk like a stone. Although she had a dozen transverse bulkheads, sub-dividing her length into a number of compartments, few of these bulkheads were water-tight. Nearly all were pierced by a non-watertight access doorway, and any one space flooded would result in general flooding throughout the ship.

In the old-fashioned sailing ship, where the hull consisted of one huge hold space, any minor leakage through the seams which could not be controlled by the hand pumps spelt disaster. As these old wooden ships' planking was usually strained and their caulking loose, and as, moreover, their hand pumps were not always as efficient as they might be, sailing ships were indeed a poor insurance risk.

The modern ship depends for her safety on a certain degree of sub-division, depending on her trade, and this is effected by fitting a series of transverse watertight bulkheads throughout the length, spaced apart a distance, so that with one compartment flooded the buoyancy of the intact compartments will be sufficient to keep the ship afloat. In larger ships, built to a two compartment standard, two adjacent compartments could be flooded without the vessel sinking.

Of course the bulkheads will be watertight, and any openings in them will be fitted with watertight doors. Furthermore, unless designed for a specific trade, the compartments should not be divided by a longitudinal bulkhead but should extend from port to starboard; otherwise damage to, say, the port side would flood the port compartment leaving only the starboard side intact and buoyant. While the loss of buoyancy of this port section would not of itself be sufficient to sink the vessel it would seriously affect the transverse stability, and, by heeling the vessel over, might place some of the deck or superstructure openings below water and thus flood neighbouring compartments.

All the above is of great importance to a ship in the event of a collision at sea, but would be of little help in an accident involving a tear along a ship's side, as was the case in both the *Great Eastern* and the *Titanic*. The only fact we can go on is the ratio $\dfrac{B}{B-D}$ where D is the length of the tear and B is the spacing between bulkheads. The emphasis is still on watertight bulkheads.

Another of Brunel's ideas was that of building a ship that would sail to Australia and back without bunkering. This was no gimmick, as in the 50's and 60's of the last century there were no bunkering stations on the Cape route. Coal had to be shipped out to various ports of call on the way to Australia and the vessel to do this job was the sailing ship. The steamer was still dependent on sail for her very existence, and, in passing, it may be noted that it was on the Australian run that sailing ships could still be economically employed until the turn of the century.

It cost money to charter a sailing ship to place caches of coal along the route via the Cape, hence the exorbitant cost of steamer passages to the East. On the other hand every ton of coal carried on a ship means a ton less of cargo, and as the *Great Eastern* was designed to load 12,000 tons of coal in her bunkers this meant 12,000 tons less cargo in her holds. It was not so much a shipowner's dilemma as a nightmare.

Twelve thousand tons of coal is a fantastic amount of fuel, but the ship's daily consumption at full speed was 384 tons, or 290 tons at cruising speed, giving a coal consumption of 1 ton per mile. With 12,000 tons on board she would just about make the Australian coast before her fuel ran out.

Building the ship presented no insoluble problems in naval construction, but her fitting out was considerably helped by the newly launched floating derrick owned by the Patent Derrick Co., and this was especially useful in handling such heavy lifts as the engine bedplates, cylinder castings and shafts, which had to be lifted over the weather deck and lowered down into the hold. Some of these single lifts weighed 40 tons, no mean feat when one considers the span of the lift from the floating platform to the centre line of a very beamy ship.

Apart from the fore and after peak the *Great Eastern* had no large tanks, but a great number of smaller tanks formed by the double bottom, double skin and double main deck; and this is as good a place as anywhere to dispose of the persistent legend of the riveter being boxed up in one of the tanks and his skeleton being discovered by the ship's breakers thirty years later. A ship's tank is like a room in a house, it just cannot be built without some means of access into and out of it. In a riveted ship (welded ships came in very much later) there is no room to hammer a rivet inside the tank, the head-room being barely 3 feet. Hence the rivet is inserted from *inside* the tank and pointed from *outside*. To do this the red-hot rivets have to be passed into the tank through a manhole, there being no other way to get them there, and both the rivet boy, who receives the rivet from the heater and gives it to the holder-on, who inserts the rivet and holds a spring hammer against the head, must have free access with the outside of the tank to be able to do their job at all. In short, it is just as impossible for a riveter to box himself up inside a tank as it is for a glass-blower to bottle himself into one of his own hand-blown bottles.

However, the access openings in these tanks are secured by watertight covers or lids and it is always possible, in spite of the many precautions taken, for the tank lid to be fitted in place with someone inside the tank. This would be extremely bad luck for the workman concerned, but he would hardly have to wait to get out until the ship was broken up. The structure inside the tanks has to be periodically examined for corrosion or thinning of the plates and bars, for loose rivets and wastage generally. The water tanks have to be periodically scaled and cement washed against corrosion and the dry tanks and void spaces painted. It is hard to believe that during the whole of this monster ship's lifetime no one ever ventured into her tanks to check up on her general well-being.

Launching a ship, as all naval architects will agree, is the most worrying part of the whole construction, and at any launching ceremony, amid the laughter and jollification, the most serious man is the shipyard designer, whose job depends on several thousand tons of steelwork sliding down the ways at the drop of a trigger. It is bad enough when the ship in question is similar to a previous order, where the calculations can be checked against factual results. It is worse when the ship is of novel construction or larger than the usual run. It is a nightmare when one is launching a ship twice as long or eight times as large as any ever built, and where the curves for launching calculations extend outside the graph of practical experience.

Due to her enormous length the *Great Eastern* could not be launched stern first into the Thames, and she was accordingly built broadside to the river on a specially strengthened way. After the hull structure was completed up to the weather deck, and her paddle wheel frames had been shipped, two launching ways were constructed at right-angles to the ship's keel, about 80 feet wide and about 140 feet apart, leading down into the water at an inclination of 1 in 12. These ways were fitted with a series of railway lines running down them, 8 inches apart, and with their surfaces coated with black lead. Two wooden cradles were then built upon the launching ways to support the weight of the hull when the shores had been knocked out and the keel blocks removed. The undersides of these cradles were shod with iron plates 7 inches wide and 1 inch thick, fixed at right-angles to the railway lines on the launching ways, and resting upon them.

At the top of each launching way there was a gigantic winch, with its cable leading round a block on the end of the cradle then back to a secure anchorage up in the yard. The purpose of these two winches was to check and control the speed of the cradles as they slid down the ways, by means of their hand brakes.

Unfortunately the use of two iron surfaces in contact with each other, and the consequent friction between them due to the immense weight of the vessel, do not appear to have been taken into account by the designer; nor did he appear to have foreseen the probability of one cradle sliding down the ways faster than the other.

At the first attempt to launch the *Leviathan* (her original name) on 3rd November 1857 several things happened almost simultaneously. The forward cradle started to slide down the ways and its winch started to pay out the check cable. Several spectators standing on the winch, presumably unaware of its function in the launching operations, were tossed into the air and seriously injured, and in the ensuing panic someone applied the brake and brought the cradle to a sudden halt. Meanwhile the after cradle hadn't moved an inch. A second attempt to launch her resulted in the after cradle sliding for some fifteen feet until the heat generated by the sliding friction of iron upon iron welded the two together and stopped everything.

It took another three months to get the ship afloat, jacking her down the ways an inch at a time.

Side launching is not so unusual in this country, but it is confined to small ships and certain narrow waters where stern launching would be impossible. In North American shipyards, however, especially those on the Great Lakes, many ships are launched sideways, ships almost as long as our *Great Eastern*, and as far as one can ascertain there have been no hitches at the launching ceremony. As a matter of interest, having described an unsuccessful side launch, it is only fair to explain how the Great Lakes yards launch their very long steamers.

Ships intended to be launched sideways are constructed close to, and parallel with, the water's edge and can be built upon an even keel instead of on an inclined plane (which, incidentally, helps the shipwrights in erecting the bulkheads and framework). Some 50 to 60 ground ways are constructed between the keel blocks and at right-angles to the keel. These are about 24 inches wide and some 10 feet apart, with a declivity of between $1\frac{1}{2}$ to 2 inches per foot. (Note that the declivity of the *Great Eastern*'s ways was only 1 inch per foot.) They extend from the ship's inner bilge into the water as far as possible. The sliding ways are usually built parallel with the keel, in short lengths straddling 3 to 4 ground ways. These sliding ways are built up by means of wooden blocks and crib work to support the ship's bottom, and the series of short cradles are tied together to form an integral structure. The half-dozen ground ways at each end of the ship are the trigger ways to hold the vessel solid until the launching. They contain the dogshores or hydraulic triggers and rams, to release the ship. The next half-dozen ground ways from each end form the guide ways and are equipped with heavy ribands or guides on their sides to prevent any fore and aft movement during the actual launching.

When the hull is completed the keel blocks and shores are removed and the vessel will lie upon the cradles for almost her full length. The whole of the ship's weight on the inclined plane of the sliding ways will now rest on the triggers at both ends, and the vessel should start sliding as soon as the triggers fall. To be certain of success, however, some strain is generally taken on the hydraulic jacks forward and aft of the triggers while these are still in position, to give just that little impetus to the ship when the triggers are released.

One of the principal factors in a successful launch is good lubrication between the sliding and ground ways. These are made of timber, of sufficient surface to allow a maximum of 3 tons per square foot on the grease, and the grease itself is not just any oily slush scooped out of an engine sump. It consists of two layers of hard tallow on each way, applied hot and ironed smooth as glass with flat bars, and with a sandwich coating of soft soap between. The soap, having very little resistance, enables the sliding ways to start moving with very little pressure from the jacks; once moving, the heat generated by the friction softens the opposing layers of tallow, allowing them to take up the lubrication.

Like everything else about her the *Great Eastern*'s propelling machinery was of monstrous size. It is only in recent years that diesel engineers have attained that elusive figure of 2,000 h.p. per cylinder, at one time considered to be the ultimate in design of reciprocating machinery. Yet a hundred years ago this power was achieved in the paddle steamer *Scotia*, which developed 4,600 h.p. in two cylinders with only 25 lb. boiler pressure. When required to produce a more powerful engine than any previously built our ancestors had no choice but to tackle the problem in the only way known to them: to scale up the machinery to a gigantic size. They had no way of 'changing gear' as it were, of fitting an alternative type of prime mover or even of raising the boiler pressure. In the 1850's marine boilers using salt feed could not steam over 25–30 lb. without foaming and priming, that is, carrying water over into the engine with a possibility of cracking the cylinder. Compound, triple and quadruple expansion engines were still a long way ahead in time, while oil fuel burning, the steam turbine and the diesel engine belong to the twentieth century. The only solution was to build a bigger engine.

This trend could be observed in the passenger ships just before the advent of the steam turbine, the classical case being that of the wing engines of the triple-screw steamers, *Olympic, Titanic* and *Britannic*, probably the most powerful marine steam reciprocating engines ever built. These four-cylinder giants had a stroke of 6 feet 3 inches. The imagination boggles at a four-cylinder engine with a stroke of 14 feet, yet that is precisely what Scott Russell fitted to the paddle shaft of the *Great Eastern*.

A detailed and more technical description of this paddle engine is given in a separate chapter devoted to marine engines and here I shall confine myself to a general description of the propelling machinery.

This law of engine size increasing in direct proportion to its output with static steam conditions had the expected corollary: as ships grew bigger their engine room capacity had to increase accordingly at the expense of the payload or cargo deadweight. Also, with such gigantic engines, it was impossible to build a twin-screw installation, the compromise being one screw engine and one paddle engine.

The *Great Eastern*, therefore, was a composite ship inasmuch as the machinery was concerned, there being a huge paddle engine amidships developing 3,410 i.h.p. at 10·7 r.p.m. and driving paddle wheels 56 feet in diameter and weighing 836 tons, and a four-cylinder horizontal *vis-à-vis* engine driving the screw. This latter engine had cylinders 84 inches in diameter, with a stroke of 48 inches, and it developed slightly under 5,000 i.h.p. at 38 r.p.m. The screw engine drove a cast-iron built-up four-

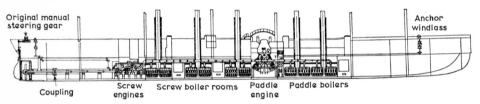

47 *Great Eastern*, longitudinal section

bladed propeller 24 feet in diameter and weighing 36 tons (the *Queen Mary*'s propellers weighed only 35 tons each).

These massive engines had ten boilers between them, four for the paddle engines and six for the screw engines, although as the main steam pipe connected up with all the boilers each engine could draw from a common supply.

The machinery spaces extended from the mainmast to slightly forward of the aftermost mast, that is, more than half her length, and together with the coal bunkers extended for the full breadth of the hull up to the tweendeck level.

The disposition of the machinery was in the modern fashion, there being a crossbunker at the fore end followed by two boiler rooms, an auxiliary machinery room, main-paddle engine room, then three boiler rooms separated by two crossbunkers, ending up with the screw engine room and the shaft tunnel. The coal bunkers were placed at the ship's sides, and extended the length of the machinery spaces, being cross connected by the crossbunkers which extended the full width of the ship.

There were certain novel features in this machinery installation, some of which were incorporated in later steamers, others which could have

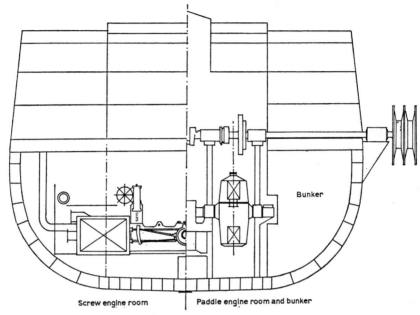

Bunker

Screw engine room   Paddle engine room and bunker

48 *Great Eastern,* transverse section

been but were not. One of these was the provision of a crew's working alleyway extending from forward to aft of the machinery spaces, nowadays an accepted part of a modern passenger liner and colloquially referred to as the Burma Road. Another was the possibility of entering the stern tube, after pumping out, with the vessel afloat, in order to inspect the screwshaft and check the weardown. A third innovation was to make the bunkers self trimming right down to the boiler firing doors, and so reduce the number of coal trimmers per watch. In the bad old days of coal-burning passenger ships, where many thousands of tons of coal were carried in a maze of inter-communicating bunkers, the work of the trimmer was similar to that of the coal miner in many respects (except that of pay) in that he had to sweat it out eight hours a day stripped to the waist shovelling coal at one end of the heap and wheeling it against the roll of the ship to tip it down a small coal hatch to the lower bunker and thence to the stokehold. Sometimes both wheelbarrow and trimmer followed the coal down the hatch to appear in the boiler room in a cloud of dust rather like Mephistopheles in amateur pantomime.

The two engine rooms were very small in relation to the size of their respective engines; as both engines drove their air and circulating pumps from the main shafts, each engine room contained one big engine and nothing else. The engine room could almost be said to fit the engine like a glove, as the fore and aft bulkheads forming the side bunkers were recessed in way of the oscillating cylinder gudgeons to allow of the bearing keeps being lifted.

To a modern marine engineer, accustomed to having the main propelling engine surrounded by a host of pumps, dynamos, heaters, distillers, switchboards, compressors, and all the paraphernalia for the hotel requirements of a modern luxury liner, the *Great Eastern*'s engine rooms would appear very naked indeed. Where in the modern turbine engine room there is a veritable maze of steam pipes above the platform and fuel and water pipes below it, there was very little of that in our monster ship, which was probably just as well when we consider that the main steam pipeline amidships was 3 feet 9 inches in the bore. In the case of the *Canberra*, the largest ship built since the war, and developing 90,000 h.p., the main steam pipeline is barely 10 inches bore.

Immediately forward of the paddle engine room was the auxiliary engine room, containing several independent pumps for ship's use and an acetylene gas generating plant. It is not known if this plant was used to any extent—it must have constituted a perpetual hazard to the ship, with the possibility of a gas main developing a leak through flexure of the hull. Another auxiliary engine room abaft the screw engine contained a donkey engine which could drive the windlass and mooring winches.

Apart from fresh and sea water being supplied for passenger use there is no record of any refinements such as we are accustomed to in modern steamers. The hardy passenger of the 1860's did not expect electric light, steam heating, air conditioning or a private bathroom, and if he did he did not get them. All he was entitled to in return for his fare was something to eat and a place to sleep in. The *Great Eastern*, in keeping with the standards of the period, no doubt kept a good table, at least as regards quantity, and the first class cabin was probably as good as those obtaining in contemporary vessels, i.e., a small stuffy box with no artificial light and precious little ventilation. The illumination supplied to passenger cabins in those days consisted of an oil lamp standing in a glass box let into the alleyway bulkhead in way of the partition between two cabins. One lamp, consequently, sufficed to light up the alleyway and two adjacent cabins. As these lamps were kept on a low wick in the interests of safety and economy it was almost necessary in some cases to hold a lighted match very close to a lamp to see if it was still lit!

However, it took more than that to discourage passengers in the days when bathrooms were unknown and perfume was a necessity. Before the 1850's people slept in their underwear, but judging from contemporary photographs travellers at sea didn't even bother to undress to that extent when turning in; they simply kicked off their boots.

The *Great Eastern* was built with hand steering gear, and here again she holds the record for being the biggest ship ever designed to be steered by hand. The gear was the simple type normally found in the sailing ships of the day; we must not lose sight of the plain fact that she was built and rigged as a sailing ship.

The rudder head projected through a gland in the main deck and was fitted with a steering quadrant low down near the deck. The quarter-masters stood on a platform above this quadrant, where there were four large steering wheels fixed on a barrel shaft. A chain from one corner of the quadrant made several turns round the barrel and was attached to the other corner, the steering being of the so-called indirect type. Normal watches were eight men at the wheels at any given time, but this number was considerably reinforced in heavy weather, as the kick from the helm in rough seas would have been brutal.

With the steering position immediately above the rudder, and the navigating bridge spanning the paddle boxes several hundred feet away, it was impossible to navigate the ship at first hand, as it were. There being no engine room telegraph (this only came into being in the '70's) callboys were placed at strategic positions along the deck and in the engine room to relay directions for manœuvring the engines; the time element was not that important as it took several minutes to stop the engines and start up again in reverse. But steering was a different matter, and in the North Atlantic there was very little margin for misunderstandings. Steering had to be immediate and positive, and the only way to ensure it was to have visual signals. This was accomplished by fitting a vertical compass card in a binnacle on the bridge, covered by a moveable brass plate with an aperture sufficient only to show one point of the compass at a time. By means of a light inside the binnacle the required steering order could be read and understood by the quartermasters and immediately carried out. By daylight this position would be indicated by a projection on the brass plate.

In 1867 the *Great Eastern* was fitted with a steam steering gear designed by McFarlane Gray, then principal at the Board of Trade. This system had an engine driving the steering wheel barrel shaft through gearing the cable from each corner of the quadrant being retained, and a purist could consider the final effort as a steam-assisted hand gear. Apart from the steam engine taking over the sheer muscle power required for steering McFarlane Gray's steering system enabled the master wheel to be fitted on the bridge, directly under the eye of the officer on watch. This wheel, by means of rods and bevel gears extending between bridge and poop, a distance of about 400 feet, transmitted any movement direct to the engine control valve and thus eliminated the exchange of light or hand signals between bridge and steering gear.

The beauty of this system, which has been retained in all subsequent steering gears, was the hunting mechanism, whereby the action of the rudder opposed and cancelled the movement of the steering wheel: the rudder position always coincided with the amount and direction of helm shown on the steering wheel control column.

In spite of the size of the *Great Eastern* and the luxury of her public rooms the navigating bridge and the steering platform were still those of the sailing ship. Captain, officers and crew were expected to carry out their duties exposed to the elements in all their nastiness—there was no steam-heated wheel house or chartroom to retire to in really bad weather, and any cups of cocoa brought round to the helmsmen on duty would certainly have a salty flavour not wholly accounted for by being made of brackish drinking water.

Earlier on it was stated that the mooring winch or capstan immediately forward of the steering wheels was driven through a system of shafts by a donkey engine installed in a small auxiliary engine room situated at the mouth of the screwshaft tunnel, and it might reasonably be asked why the steering gear could not have been driven from the same shaft. There are several answers to this, the principal one being that nobody had ever thought of a steam steering gear before, the shipping mentality still being geared to human muscle power. Secondly the donkey engine was non-reversing, and a steam steering engine must be able to run efficiently in both directions. Thirdly, being a heavy engine difficult to start (and in those days no engine was easy to start; muscle power came into this as in everything else on board) and situated in a part of the ship completely cut off from all communication with the bridge, steering by this engine would have been impossible.

Now this ship had been designed as a sailing ship as well as a steamer and she was complete in this respect, having six masts, named for the days of the week, five of them fabricated of iron plates and one, the mizzen, just forward of the bridge, of timber in order not to interfere with the compass. Her sail plan was difficult to categorise, as she was square rigged on the main and mizzen masts and rigged fore and aft on the foremast and the three jiggers. With two independent engine systems it is doubtful if she used the sails much, although possibly a steady sail would have come in handy on the Western Ocean. In the early years of her life she is usually shown with the sails, but these tended to disappear in later illustrations.

The main yards, supplied by Ferguson of Millwall, were the largest of their kind, being 124 feet long and 33 inches diameter at the bunt, and each yard weighed from 15 to 17 tons. It might also be noted that there were no steam auxiliaries on board to handle the yards or sails, just plenty of human muscle power.

We must not lose sight of the purpose in creating such a large ship as the *Great Eastern*: she was built for the Australian trade via the Cape of Good Hope and her designers presumably intended her to use her sails as much as possible on the leg from the Cape to Australia to eke out her coal supply. This passage, the notorious Roaring Forties, is one of the loneliest in the world, the density in shipping working out at about one ship to every hundred thousand square miles of ocean. This is the empty sea, where a ship can roll steadily 30° from port to starboard and back again all the way across, and where the waves are so immense that they obscure everything. This is also the sea, stretching right round the bottom of the world, where the 'wall of water' can be met with: a freak breaker that by some interplay of wind and opposing waves has formed itself into an almost perpendicular cliff of solid water advancing with the wind; to meet it beam on would be fatal to any ship. These are the seas which the Psalmist may have had in mind when he sang about 'They that go down to the sea in Ships: and occupy their business in great waters; These men see the works of the Lord: and His wonders in the deep'.

The *Great Eastern* was built for this sort of weather and there is no doubt that she would have made a gallant attempt at running her Easting down on sail alone, but what crew could expect to control yards weighing 17 tons by hand, or set sail on them with a total wind pressure of several tons? Add to this the uncertainties of hand steering, and we see that, although built as a sailer, this ship was in practice essentially a steamer.

Between 1865 and 1874 she spent several periods laying a network of submarine cables throughout the world: Britain to U.S.A., France to U.S.A., India to Suez, etc. In this work she was most suitable, having staying capacity as regards stores and fuel, manœuvrability with her screw and paddle engines, and the space to carry the necessary cable.

For cable laying, the middle funnel and a pair of boilers were temporarily removed and three large cable tanks fitted in their place. In those pioneer days of submarine cable laying the work was not at all straightforward, as the crews were dealing with something entirely new, and all credit must be given them in making a success of it. The old type cable twisted under tension and formed loops and kinks on the sea bed when the tension was released. Or the tensioning brake might be too tight when paying out from the drum, resulting in a taut cable over the sea bed; then, when the cable was raised to repair a fault the tension on the Lucas grapnel, due to the catenary effect over some distance, would snap the cable.

(Incidentally the modern method of ensuring correct slack is by means of a drum of piano wire mounted at the stern sheave, the end of the wire being attached to the submarine cable. This drum of wire is free to revolve but is controlled by a brake, which keeps the wire taut, while the cable runs out with a certain degree of slack. The length of wire run out gives the distance covered by the ship, and should be slightly less than the amount of cable paid out).

In Mediterranean countries where people still quote proverbs at each other there is a saying that whatever is born crooked will never grow straight, a saying which describes our *Great Eastern* perfectly. The vessel must have been designed under an unlucky star, as very little went right with her throughout her entire career. She probably originated the saying that any vessel that sticks on the launching ways will be a Jonah ship all her life.

Some of the troubles were obviously due to sheer bad luck: the Great Eastern Rock, for instance. Some were due to her immense size and the tremendous strains involved: running out her screwshaft bearing during the first voyage, and smashing both paddle wheels and snapping the rudder head on the third voyage. Others again were due to plain bad management, one of these being the fiasco of her launching, when the whole operation came to a sudden and expensive stop by panic braking of one cradle.

Another incident, a fatal explosion, took place during acceptance trials in the Channel. The two pairs of forward boilers were each fitted with an economiser or feed water heater built around the base of each funnel, thus ensuring that any residual heat from the furnace gases would be extracted. The method of 'feeding' was to pump sea water through this

economiser by a small banjo pump, and thence into the boiler, there being
an overflow pipe leading half-way up the funnel to act as a relief. Unfortunately, during construction someone had fitted a cock to this relief
pipe, and someone else had shut it. On trials an engineer had difficulty
in pumping his boilers through this economiser, and accordingly by-passed
it, thus making it, in effect, a pressure vessel with no inlet or outlet, and,
moreover, with no relief pipe. As the economiser was full of hot water,
absorbing additional heat all the time, the water eventually changed into
high pressure steam and burst, killing five men and injuring many more,
blowing the forward funnel out and causing heavy consequential damage
in the saloons.

Many of the troubles which plagued the *Great Eastern* are still encountered in modern new construction, but somehow they do not have such
sinister overtones. Stupid spectators still attempt to get too close to the
launching ways at the ceremony (I have even seen a young man taking
a film at a launching while standing between the wooden ways, with the
ship bearing down on him like an express train). And even in present-day
computerised shipyards stopcocks or blank flanges fitted to tanks and
pipes for testing purposes are apt to be left on. But they always seem to be
discovered before anyone gets hurt.

The *Great Eastern*'s failure as a passenger vessel was primarily due to the
inability of her successive owners to recognise her worth in the trade for
which she was designed, and this fact is bitterly summed up by her builder
John Scott Russell:

*The fuel shown in this plan (i.e. a section through the bunkers) amounts to 12,000
tons. Working the engines at high pressure, with great expansion, that quantity
of fuel would carry the ship once round the world; but as yet the engines have not
worked in the manner intended, it being unsafe to trust the owners with a mode of
working requiring so much skill.*

*Hitherto, therefore, the engines have been worked without their proper degree of
expansion, and without the economical development of their fuel and power. When
the ship shall fall into the hands of skilful owners and managers, there will be no
difficulty, with a much less expenditure of fuel, in maintaining the 14 knots an hour
for which the ship was designed and which, with a much larger expenditure of fuel,
she has already performed; but it would be unsafe to trust such skilful working to
any but owners and managers who have shown by a long term of capacity and ability
their trustworthiness for such work.*

All improvements in machinery, and especially in steam navigation, become wise or foolish in proportion to the capacity and ability of the persons to whom they are entrusted. But with the exception of a few able officers of the ship, the whole management of the undertaking has never yet been in the hands that ought to be entrusted with the arduous duty of getting out of that ship the utmost she is able, with good management in every department to accomplish, and which if she be not destroyed, I am sure she will one day achieve.

The *Great Eastern* was not the only record-holding ship built by John Scott Russell. The *Pacific*, a large passenger vessel built to the order of Australian owners, was launched just as the *Great Eastern* commenced building. She was the first paddle vessel to sail all the way out to Australia under steam and eventually, not being wanted out there, the first to make the round trip out and home under power.

While many paddle steamers had been built in England for delivery to Australian owners, they loaded their paddles in the hold and proceeded to Australia under sail.

Another record breaker, a negative record this time, was the paddle steamer *Lyttelton*, built in the lee of the *Great Eastern* for New Zealand owners. This vessel, with her paddles neatly stowed away in the hold, took 462 days to complete the voyage from London to Lyttleton under sail, and upon arrival her master found that the shipping company had been wound up on the assumption that the ship, their only asset, had been lost at sea.

The idea of a ship's cabin swung on gimbals which would remain level while the rest of the ship stood on her head must have been uppermost in every anguished passenger's mind since very remote times. Several ingenious inventions have been put forward in an attempt to neutralise or at least diminish a ship's movement in a seaway, but before looking into the details of these let us first consider the causes of sea sickness and the mechanics of a ship's motion.

Every one of us has, or should have, inside our ears a minute complex of bone consisting of three semi-circular canals filled with a fluid under pressure and placed in such a way that each canal is sensitive to movement in one dimension of our three-dimensional space. These movements would correspond to rolling, pitching and ascending in a ship, and collectively each little labyrinth will register every movement to which our bodies are subject.

These little computers, in association with our brain, control our physical equilibrium, but they depend for their action on information supplied by sight, hearing, leg muscles and foot position, etc. In a familiar situation, with our leg muscles corroborating the signals supplied by our eyes and other senses, our computers function normally and all is well. In an unaccustomed situation, however, where one or more of our senses is out of harmony with the rest, where, for example, our eyes are desperately searching for a stationary object on a moving horizon and our leg muscles are working overtime merely to keep us standing upright, the information received by our ear labyrinths is conflicting and the signals sent to the brain are confused, resulting in dizziness, faintness and nausea.

As far as a ship's motion is concerned, this can be divided into two separate patterns, oscillation and translation. Oscillation is about an axis through the centre of buoyancy, the axis being athwartships (pitching), longitudinal (rolling), or vertical (yawing); being a function of a ship's geometry, these motions can be calculated and are, in fact, independent of the weather. Translation, on the other hand, is mostly a matter of weather, by which the ship may be moved bodily through the water either forward or aft (surging), sideways (leeway), or just plain up or down, over a wave.

Any one of these six movements would hardly inconvenience the normal person, and if sea travel involved pure rolling only there would be very few sea-sick passengers. Unfortunately pure rolling or pitching are seldom met with, and the normal ship on a normal sea passage is subject to most of the six motions.

As we cannot very well alter our inner ears to suit our comfort at sea we have had to fall back on devising a steadier deck or cabin, and the 1870's were prolific in inventions to this effect.

Bilge keels were introduced in 1870 and they still are the best and cheapest anti-rolling device yet thought of. They should be fitted to the turn of the bilge and should not project beyond the extreme breadth or depth of the hull, to avoid damage when docking. They are more effective when fitted in two lengths, with a short gap between the two, and their width should extend beyond the boundary layer of dead water next to the shell plating, which travels with the ship. Bilge keels are most efficient when the vessel is travelling at speed, as the blades of the bilge keels, roughly at 45° to the horizontal, act as hydrofoils in the water and their steadying effect is then most marked.

Shortly after the introduction of bilge keels Montgomerie Neilson proposed building a cross-channel ferry steamer fitted with drop keels, which would be retracted while in port and lowered when leaving harbour. A large part of the ship would be equipped with a huge centreline trunk into which the sections of plate keel, or centre board, could be housed when not required. The ship would also be propelled by two sets of paddle wheels, one set forward, one aft, of the moveable keels. This idea seemed reasonable, if a shade elaborate, and was based on the same reasoning as that which suggested the bilge keels a few years before. But the design never came to anything, although one feature proposed by Neilson, that of sofas and bunks on swinging chains hung from the deckbeams, strikes one as most sensible and as being the nearest approach to the cabin on gimbals.

A third form of stabiliser, that of anti-rolling tanks, was introduced about 1874 and in its earliest form consisted of large tanks on each side of the tween deck connected to each other at top and bottom to allow free flow of ballast water and displaced air from one side of the deck to the other. The theory was simply to use the rolling of the ship to generate its own dampening effort through the ballast water in the side tanks inevitably lagging behind the ship's movement by reason of the restricted area of the communicating duct. The momentum of this moving mass of ballast was thus made to oppose the inertia of the ship's roll, and its effect was to steady the ship in a seaway. This principle was rather shaky when put into practice and in certain conditions it could get out of hand. A ship's righting moment is a measure of her stability, and in the event of the transfer of the ballast water from port to starboard coinciding and synchronising with the ship's roll from port to starboard a dangerous situation would immediately result.

Present-day vessels often use some form of tank stabilisation in preference to the fin-type stabilisers as being cheaper to instal and run, but in modern steamers the method of operation is by either pumps or compres-

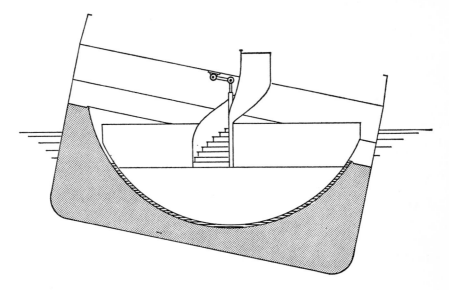

49 Allen's proposal for a floating saloon

sors controlled by a gyroscopic sensing unit. Some large beamy ships, however, notably those huge tankers and bulk-carriers with ample reserves of buoyancy and stability, still use an athwartships tank with a perforated centreline bulkhead to act as a passive stabiliser, with no control machinery whatever.

A more practical approach to the problem was made by Allan in 1873, with his (literally) floating saloon, which was a reversion to the original idea of a ship's cabin swung in gimbals. In this case, however, the cabin would float like a compass card in liquid and be independent of the ship's movement.

To effect this a large hemispherical tank, almost the width of the hull, would be built into the hold. A similar hemispherical shell of approximately the same diameter would float inside this tank, the space between the two shells, some three to four inches, being filled with water. The floating shell would contain a cabin and accommodation on its deck and be ballasted at the bottom, while a central pillar would connect with the ship's deck overhead through a universal joint to prevent the swing getting out of control.

Access to the floating saloon would be by a spiral staircase from the upper deck, and it is concluded that provision would be made at weather-deck level to effectively seal the gap between the rolling deck and the fixed stairhead, which otherwise would act as a pair of enormous shears. This would be a hazard in the best of designs, given the trailing skirts of the 1870's.

One of the drawbacks to this floating saloon would be the difficulty of equating its weight to its buoyancy. Too light and it would tend to float high, and its central pillar would either knock a hole in the deck above or buckle. Too heavy and it would bump against its tank at every roll. In either case this bumping would prove more uncomfortable than an easy roll. Another disadvantage would be its position in the ship. Placed amidships at the centre of gravity, it would occupy the space normally assigned to the machinery, and this would require to be moved either well aft of amidships or split into two units.

One further claim made by its inventor was that, due to the damping effect of the water in which it rested, the floating saloon would be immune to the vibrations set up in the hull by the propelling machinery, although in those days, with modest engine powers, low revolutions, and with no high-speed auxiliary machinery to worry about, this claim seems hardly worthwhile.

True to type the Russians even in those days could not let a British invention remain unchallenged: they claimed a similar arrangement of floating cabin designed by Alexandrovski, of St. Petersburg, a few years previously.

Bessemer

While many anti-rolling devices were suggested in the eighteen seventies it took the mechanical genius and the nervous energy (not to mention the fortune) of a Bessemer to try one out under full-scale conditions. Henry Bessemer, whose business took him all over the Continent, was a very poor sailor, and an idea such as Allan's floating saloon appealed to him as a possible cure for sea sickness.

He constructed a mock-up section of a ship in his garden, which could be rolled by means of a small steam engine to simulate actual sea-going conditions. In the hold of this section he installed a small cabin fitted on a gimbal frame, which could be swung relatively to the ship section; by careful manipulation of the controls he succeeded in maintaining the cabin stationary while the hull of the 'ship' rolled 30° to port and starboard.

Satisfied with his experiments he launched the Bessemer Saloon Ship Company and laid down the prototype for his proposed future channel steamers, a double-ended paddle steamer with the first class passenger accommodation contained in a swinging central saloon which would remain level under all conditions of rolling. This vessel, the *Bessemer*, was built by Earle's Shipbuilding Co. on the Humber in 1875, and he principal dimensions were 350 feet in length, 40 feet beam, or 65 feet over the paddle sponsons, with a draught of 9 feet. Her designer was E. J. Reed, one-time chief naval constructor to the Admiralty and one of the foremost naval architects of the day, but his responsibility was confined to the hull and machinery; the plans of the swinging saloon and its operating mechanism were supplied by Bessemer himself.

As she was built exclusively for the Dover-Calais run, two ports with extremely narrow entrances where it was impossible for a sizeable ship to turn round, she was made double ended and could sail fairly easily in either direction with a rudder fitted fore and aft (as in some modern channel steamers). But, as all steam engines have to obey thermodynamic laws, and as efficiency depends on valve settings which are adjusted to ideal conditions for running ahead, astern running is never efficient, and while a steamer may sail equally well in both directions, her engines will run smoothly and economically in one direction only.

Bessemer's original idea had been to fit his swinging saloon into the ship on a type of gimbal frame along the lines of the wooden model built in his garden, to iron out both rolling and pitching. But the designer very wisely pointed out that the vessel would be confined to narrow, choppy waters where prevailing seas would be on the beam and serious pitching would not be expected, and that the added cost of control gear to swing the cabin along two axes would be enormous. The cabin was accordingly designed to damp out transverse oscillation only.

Pitching was kept to a minimum by reducing the ship's buoyancy at the ends. Instead of the normal raised forecastle and poop structures which provide valuable 'reserve buoyancy' in any ship and which cause her to rise to meet a wave the *Bessemer*'s ends, for some 48 feet, were reduced to a couple of turtle decks with a scant 3 feet of freeboard. Now most shipbuilders will say that, given all the essential requirements of her service, a ship will design herself, and the *Bessemer* was no exception. With a fairly high weather deck dropping down to these low turtle decks, the strength girder formed by the upper-deck stringer plate and the sheer strake on each side was brought down to the lower-deck level and tucked neatly into the round of the bridge front.

The well amidships for the swinging saloon was not so easily disposed of. An open hold, 70 feet long and over 30 feet wide, presented a naval architect's nightmare as the bulk of the saloon prevented any means of tying the sides together in way of the hold, either by decks, beams or transverse bulkheads. To compensate for this gap in the hull girder, which would, moreover, have to support a heavy saloon on point bearings, deep frames were placed at 6 feet pitch and connected by heavy side stringers. Fore and aft bulkheads, shaped to suit the curvature of the saloon sides, were placed to restore longitudinal strength, and extra transverse bulkheads were fitted in the main body of the hull.

The effect of placing the saloon in the middle of the vessel was to drive away the machinery, which is usually located near the centre in this type of vessel. In view of the very high power required it had to be split up into two separate engine rooms, one forward, the other aft of the saloon space. Each machinery space contained four boilers and a pair of oscillating engines working at 30 lb. steam pressure driving a pair of paddle wheels with feathering floats. The total horsepower was about 4,600 and the ship made 16 knots on trials.

There was some doubt in the design stage about fitting two pairs of paddle wheels 100 feet apart, and some experts submitted that the after wheels, working in the wake of the forward wheels, would make no positive contribution to the propulsive power. The argument put forward by the designer, however, placed the problem fairly and squarely in a nutshell.

An ordinary fast paddle steamer, with her engines making probably 35 revolutions and going at some 15 or 16 knots, really has those engines making over 30 revolutions for the one single object of keeping up with the vessel, rather than propelling her: by which I mean that if we were suddenly to remove the engine power and the paddle wheels, the ship would still go for a certain short period of time at nearly the continuous speed which it was maintaining without the application of any power at all. What the engine does from moment to moment is to prevent the degradation of speed, and to keep it up to a uniform amount. It is the few last turns of the wheel which do the propulsive part, by far the larger number of turns being required for the purpose of keeping the wheel at the pace of the vessel without exerting any propelling effect at all; because if the wheel went slower than the vessel it is obvious that it would be a resistance to her progress, and to avoid that we are obliged to turn the wheels at a considerable velocity: the additional revolutions made to keep up the speed are very few. And therefore I thought that if I placed a second wheel at some distance from the first, the disadvantage it would be under would not be great, chiefly having relation to those last few revolutions, and not to all the early number of revolutions required for merely keeping up with the ship; and I went so far as to predict with some confidence that there would not in fact be found a greater difference in the revolutions of the two sets of engines, when both were performing efficient services, than about four or five.

The after engine, on full power trials, made only two revolutions per minute more than the forward set.

(In passing it may be pointed out that Mr. Reed had heard or read of the Danube steamer *Tachtalia*, a river steamer of 150 feet in length by 20 feet in breadth built in 1863, which had two sets of paddle wheels positioned in the same fashion as the *Bessemer*.)

The focal point of Bessemer's ship, the swinging saloon, was placed in that enormous well between the two engines. Together with its framework and operating mechanism it weighed all of 180 tons. The bottom framework consisted of four massive beams placed athwartships and suspended on a longitudinal trunnion forming part of the ship's main structure. The cabin sides were curved in an arc struck from the trunnion centre, and the roof was trunked up to provide a narrow deck, the sides of the trunk taking the casement windows which were, of course, well above passenger eye-level. Movement of the cabin was by means of a hydraulic cylinder attached to each extremity of one of the floor beams, with its piston rod connected to the ship's upper deck in such a fashion that, by altering the hydraulic balance between the port and starboard cylinders, the cabin could be made to move relatively to the ship.

Access to the saloon was from a tween deck alleyway outside the saloon well, and through doorways in the well bulkhead and the saloon bulkhead, which coincided when the vessel was at rest. The gangway between the ship and the saloon consisted of a series of oak beams strung on two iron rails extending through the doorway, one end of which was fixed to the ship structure, the other attached to the swinging saloon deck. The relative movement of the two ends of this cakewalk was lost in its length.

The saloon fitted into its well like the two parts of a matchbox, and the

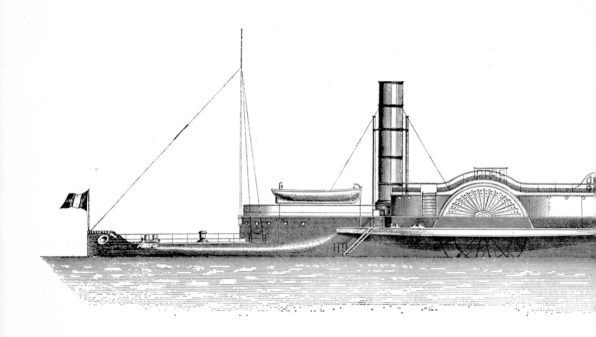

50 *Above* The swinging saloon steamer *Bessemer*

51 *Opposite* Section through the *Bessemer*'s swinging saloon

clearance between saloon end and well bulkhead was only about $1\frac{1}{2}$ inches. To avoid possible accident, the space round the doorway giving access to the saloon was framed with a rubber tube covered in green baize.

Ventilation was from below the saloon and out through the windows in the roof trunk.

Control of the swinging saloon was by means of levers in a console on the floor of the saloon, and the operation was carried out by a quarter-master who gauged the direction and amount of swing required by a spirit level attached to the console. To prevent jarring in the event of excessive rolling causing the saloon to hit the bottom of the well leaf spring buffers were fitted to the cross beams.

The saloon contained one of the first fail-safe devices, in the form of an automatic lock to prevent the saloon getting out of control through a defect in the hydraulic system. The floor of the cabin had a projection, like a keel at the centre, on either side of which was situated a hydraulic ram bolted to the vessel's floor frames. Hydraulic pressure from the

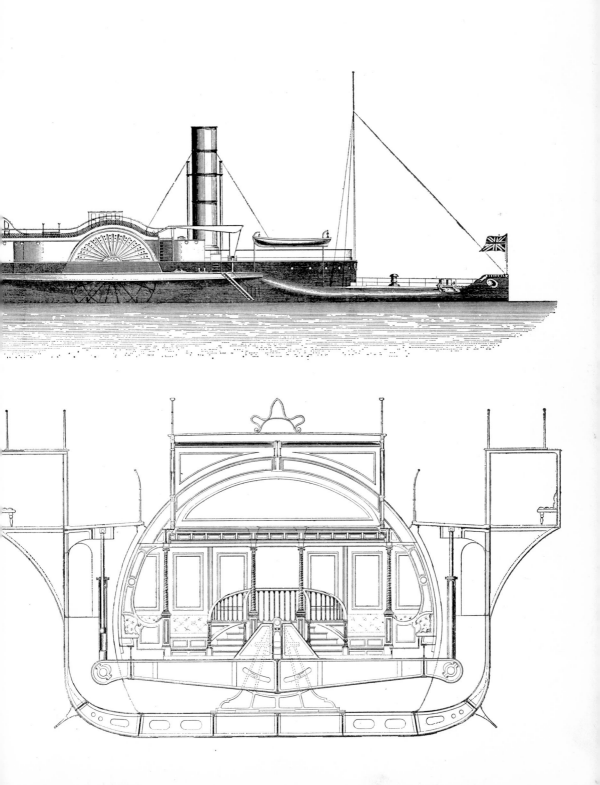

system was applied at the inner end of each cylinder, while water at boiler pressure (feed water) acted upon the other side of the piston. When everything was in order the hydraulic pressure, being so very much greater than the steam pressure, forced the ram pistons outboard well clear of the keel projection. Should the hydraulic pressure fail for any reason at all the pressure at the inner ends of the two cylinders would drop to zero and the boiler pressure would then force the rams in towards the keel projection and clamp it in a central position for as long as pressure was maintained in the boilers.

It would seem that the designers had thought of everything which could possibly affect the swinging saloon. But perhaps their best idea after all was to fit bilge keels 2 feet 6 inches wide—a classic example of belt and braces.

The *Bessemer* depended on hydraulic machinery for the efficient operation not only of the saloon, but of the steering gear, capstans and two cargo cranes, but these refinements brought their own troubles with them to worry the designers. Hydraulic machinery, working at high pressures, requires heavy pumping plant and bulky accumulators, which in turn require a lot of space in the engine rooms, thus detracting from passenger accommodation. This extra weight added considerably to the draught of the vessel, originally estimated at 7 feet 6 inches, and finishing up at 9 feet, and this extra draught caused the paddle wheels to have a greater dip or immersion, with consequent loss of efficiency.

It is a great pity that the Bessemer saloon, by an odd combination of circumstances, was never tried out in practice in spite of the money spent on such a large-scale experiment. The vessel was completed at Hull and sailed down to Dover, but the saloon machinery was not yet in working order and the saloon could not be tested under working conditions. Several trips were made between Dover and Calais, on some of which a select number of personages and members of the Press were invited, but still the cabin was not in operation.

Our old friend Captain Pittock, commander of the *Castalia*, another oddly shaped channel steamer, was placed in charge of the *Bessemer* during her running-in commission, as his experience on a twin-hulled ship was thought to be of use on another freak ship. As things turned out his experience didn't help him overmuch when the steering gear let him down on entering Calais harbour on the maiden voyage and he struck the jetty, doing quite a lot of damage.

Taken by and large the *Bessemer* was not a success, either as a channel steamer pure and simple or as a remedy for *mal-de-mer*. The travelling public in those days had a very definite idea of what a ship should look like and this idea bore no resemblance to the *Bessemer*. They also complained that if the saloon was made to swing why was it not working?

The company shareholders complained about fitting two expensive hydraulic cargo cranes on a ship designed specifically for plying between two ports which had adequate crane facilities on the quay.

The crew objected very strongly to working the hydraulic capstans situated on the low turtle decks, which were awash even in sheltered waters.

The captain is not on record as having made any specific complaint about the hydraulic steering gear. But, after ramming the Calais jetty twice in three trips, news of which of course would be conveyed by galley telegraph to all his junior colleagues, he no doubt gave his opinion of hydraulic machinery with true nautical candour.

Even the owners, optimistic as all owners should be, eventually realised that their ship would never pay. The swinging saloon had failed as a passenger attraction, and the complicated hydraulic machinery throughout the ship and the very powerful propelling machinery were exceedingly costly to install and maintain. She was put up for sale in 1876 but, finding no purchaser, the owners sent her back to the builders to have the swinging saloon removed, a conventional top-gallant poop and forecastle fitted and the ship generally converted into a cargo carrier.

After completion she left Hull for the Thames to load, but unfortunately was overwhelmed in a gale and stranded on the East Coast where she was written off as a constructive total loss, although she was not broken up until about 1880.

Here is a summing up of the *Bessemer* by someone who sailed in her, given at a technical discussion in the steamer:

But, looking now at the vessel as one of the travelling public, what do I see? That a small cabin comparatively, in a large ship, is constructed for the purpose of the rich few who cross the Channel, because I understand there is to be an extra charge for the use of that saloon, and I suppose also the deck above that. Now we have the example of the railways which shows us that the larger number of travellers are third-class passengers, and that the next larger number are second class. Now, will the second- and third-class passengers be in any way interested in the success of this saloon? I think not. Therefore, the great portion of the public, at all events, have not the interest which it is supposed thay have in the success of this invention.

But the notion that this saloon will prevent sea-sickness is, to my mind, utterly ridiculous. I have seen people sea-sick on board an Edinburgh steamer, lying along-side St. Catherine's Wharf, from the upward heave and downward depression of the vessel, and not from the motion which makes them put their best leg forward to prevent their falling. I speak from the experience of eighteen voyages across the Atlantic Ocean, and many hundreds across the English Channel. I have observed many cases of sea-sickness in others, although happily the sea never produced any ill effect upon me. I am satisfied that it will only to a certain extent mitigate the evils of the rough water of the Channel; and therefore, if there is to be an extra charge for the use of the saloon, it does not benefit the great travelling public.

When I look to see what advantage I and others who are not sea-sick would get, I must say that I find the most inconvenient accommodation to my mind in every other part of the ship. The cabins for an ordinary traveller in that ship are inferior in ease and comfort to any of the steamers of the larger class which are now used in the Channel service. I allude more particularly to those between Dover and Calais, and Dover and Ostend. The Belgian mail boats are 225 feet long, while Mr. Reed's boat is only 270. I of course deduct 80 feet for the low freeboard ends, which are not any portion of the ship so far as the passengers are concerned.

It struck me that the comfort of the passengers on the deck of the ship (and that is where I should like to be on a fine day to enjoy the fresh air, and to get a beautiful view of the shipping around) was interfered with. The majority of the passengers are not sea-sick, and they like to get a view of the sea and of the shipping; and the accommodation for passengers at large seems to be inferior to that of the present vessels. And I will give you one particular reason why. If you look at the section you will see that the promenade on the main deck of the ship, between the outer cabins on the one side, and the saloon cabin in the middle, is narrow comparatively (it may be perhaps 10 feet wide), and offers no opportunity to see the sea and the surrounding objects, but as the vessel goes rapidly through the water you will be in a cutting draught which would give everybody cold, and everybody will be dissatisfied, whereas if you mount up to the higher deck above the side cabins, you will find yourself exposed to the whole force of the wind that is blowing, without the slightest protection being afforded by bulwarks: nothing but an iron railing, through which any child would easily tumble. And there is a greater inconvenience than that— because children might be taken care of by their parents—and it is that you cannot take a lady on that deck, for there are no seats there at present, and even if you could take her there, and there was any wind blowing, her dress would be blown over her head. You want protection from the wind as well as from the sea to make the Channel passage agreeable. There must on breezy days—and breezy days are the most enjoyable days—be an amount of spray that will blow up there and make it unpleasant for anybody to sit without the protection of an ordinary bulwark, and there is the absence of a fine wide handsome promenade deck on the ship such as Captain Dicey's steamer has (i.e. Castalia) which probably is the only merit that ship possesses, and which is not the case with this vessel. Therefore, generally speaking, I say that the accommodation in the 'Bessemer' for the public who cannot afford the increased price for the extra comfort of the saloon will be most disappointing to the majority of travellers.

That the 'Bessemer' is a fast ship there can be little doubt. She ought to be, with double the power and double the engines that ordinary ships possess, and in addition to that she has the further element of speed: size. If she does not perform the distance of 21 miles between Dover and Calais in an hour and ten minutes, it will be a great disappointment to everybody.

The above views on sea-sickness, though a shade long-winded, are based on sound common sense and experience; and, speaking as a one-time sailor myself, I agree with the speaker in wondering if Henry Bessemer was working on the right lines to iron out a ship's rolling only. Even had his saloon remained constantly upright with the ship both rolling and pitching it is doubtful if passengers would have felt any happier. The greatest single factor causing sea sickness is, I believe, the sinking of the deck under one's feet to be followed immediately afterwards by a steady upsurge: in short, an alternate decrease and increase in gravity.

Regarding the saloon itself, it is a pity that Bessemer did not consult a professional seaman before installing the stabilising gear, which should have been on deck. In the case of a normal quartermaster in a ship, unless he has his eye on the ship's motion relative to the horizon or to a definite datum line, he cannot steer, and especially is that the case in a heavy sea where he has to watch the run of the seas each way. That is precisely what the operator of the swinging saloon would have to do: to watch the waves and anticipate the roll, not to wait until the roll had started and shown up on a spirit level.

It is fair to say that the distinguished marine engineer MacFarlane-Gray proposed the use of a gyroscopic control as a sensing unit for the swinging saloon, instead of manual operation, but his suggestion came too late; the public had lost interest in the ship by then.

Finally, a word about the fate of the saloon itself. After being dismantled and removed from the ship at Hull it was sent down to Kent and re-erected in the grounds of Mr. Reed's country house as a summer pavilion, where it remained until destroyed in an air raid during the 1939–45 War.

Some of us may have heard the yarn about tailoring a man to fit an expensive suit. In the case of the Obelisk Ship we have one of the very few vessels designed exclusively for one particular cargo, and that for one voyage only.

This ship, the dumb barge *Cleopatra*, was specially built to carry an obelisk from Egypt to London, a monolith weighing 180 tons and measuring 69 feet long, to be erected on the Thames Embankment. Inevitably it was nicknamed Cleopatra's Needle, presumably from the name of the vessel that brought her over as it had no connection with that delightful little hussy who ruled Egypt with a variety of consorts. Neither, for that matter, was it in any way connected with a needle, the obelisk being merely a stylised monument to the Egyptian god Amon-Ra and reproduced in its hundreds throughout the land.

Mehemet Ali, formerly Pasha and later Viceroy of Egypt, was an Albanian national born in Greece, and he ruled the Egyptians on behalf of the Turks. He was a very astute ruler, and having no use for the many ancient monuments which cluttered his land he presented some of these to various western powers in exchange for their non-interference in his many feuds with his African neighbours. Great Britain thus came into possession in 1819 of one of the larger obelisks which had been lying on the seashore at Alexandria for some 3,400-odd years, a present which was graciously acknowledged by our government which, however, absent-mindedly failed to collect it.

The snag, of course, was how to carry 180 tons of stone in one piece from Egypt to England in the sailing ships of the day, either in the hold or on deck, although arm-chair critics maintained that any existing vessel could readily be modified to take the cargo. The trouble was to find a method of lifting the stone out of the sand, transporting it to a vessel either at the quayside or at anchor in the roads, and depositing it safely into the hold without damaging either the obelisk or the ship.

It is not explained why Britain should consider it impossible to transport the Needle on a comparatively short sea passage, when obelisks of generally similar dimensions had been shipped to Paris and New York—and, indeed, one had been brought to Rome from Egypt on the orders of Augustus 1,900 years ago. One can hardly assume that we, a sea-faring nation disposing of the most up-to-date equipment for handling weights, could fail to tackle a cargo of this nature which the Egyptians, a nation of land lubbers, in a remote age floated down stream on a raft as a matter of routine. The answer is probably that we just didn't want an obelisk. We had more to think about in those early years of the nineteenth century and, as the Rosetta Stone was still in the process of being deciphered and had not yet revealed the extent of Egypt's fabulous civilisation, the man in the street was not interested in acquiring a monument which meant nothing to him but might cost him quite a lot in taxes to bring out of the East.

With the advent of more settled and prosperous times, interest in the obelisk was revived and John Dixon, a consulting engineer, was commissioned to bring the stone to England on the usual 'no delivery—no pay' basis. His idea was quite straightforward—he would simply build a cylindrical barge around the obelisk as it lay in the sand, roll it down into the sea and tow it home.

A vessel was accordingly built at the Thames Iron Works in 1877, dismantled and shipped out to Alexandria in pieces. The hull had to be truly circular in cross section, the cylindrical body being flattened out fore and aft in the vertical plane to a chisel edge, the after end being fitted with a rudder.

The specification called for the following particulars:

1 Vessel to be as light as possible but with ample strength to support the obelisk when aground and when rolling over reasonably smooth sand, without risk of damage either to the hull plating or cargo.
2 Vessel must be a good sea boat, capable of being towed easily, without yawing.
3 Vessel must be able to shift for herself in the event of hawser being slipped. For this she would require accommodation for a crew to steer, set sail, drop anchor, pump bilges, man ropes, lights, signals, etc.

When completed, the *Cleopatra* was 92 feet long by 15 feet diameter and was built of $\frac{3}{8}$ inch and $\frac{7}{16}$ inch plating. The hull was sub-divided into 8 compartments by 7 steel strength bulkheads with large openings to allow the obelisk to be supported in the bulkhead openings by spring beams of timber. Her finished weight, light ship, was about 60 tons.

The accommodation, in view of the possible length of time at sea, was not so much plain as downright primitive, and consisted of a single steel cabin about 18 feet long by 8 feet wide set into a shallow well on top of the cylinder, the top of the cabin serving as a bridge and extending forward in a catwalk to a circular structure, like a conning tower, which gave access to the hold. The entrance to the cabin was by a companionway on the deck above.

This cabin contained a very small galley (4 feet × 3 feet), a food locker

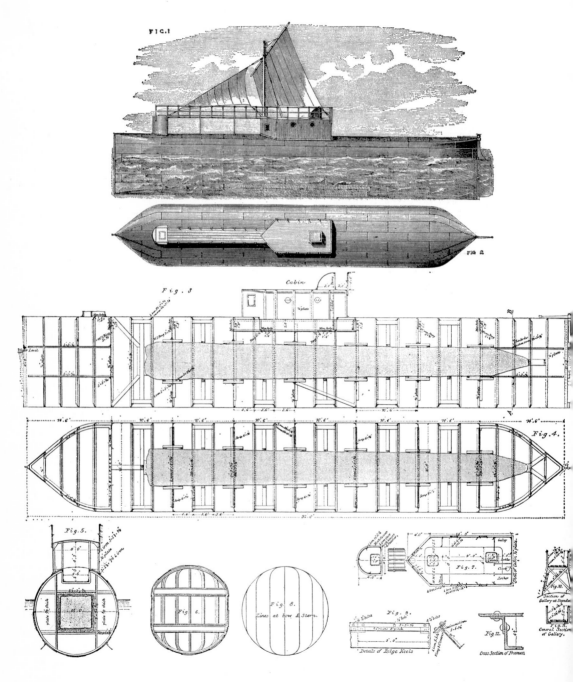

52 The obelisk ship *Cleopatra*, elevation, plan and sections

and a washplace, leaving very little space for the crew. Settee seats round the sides of the well were convertible into bunks but, being part of the hull structure, there was not even the normal space below the bunk for personal gear.

A mast was stepped at the fore end of the cabin and could carry a jib and a lugsail.

While the *Cleopatra* was being built in England an advance party in Egypt had started digging out the obelisk and manhandling it round until it lay parallel with the sea. A trench was then dug all around it and the Needle gradually jacked up and laid on timbers.

With the obelisk thus exposed the various sections of the *Cleopatra* were then rebuilt around it using the stone as a natural centre line. When the hull was completed the obelisk was lowered some $4\frac{1}{2}$ inches below the centre line to ensure that the ship, when afloat, would remain upright. To counteract this eccentricity of the centre of gravity in launching the balance was temporarily restored by lashing some ten tons of old iron rails into the cabin well.

Finally, to protect the hull plating as much as possible, rolling guards were fitted fore and aft. These consisted of two bands of 9-inch baulks of timber 12 feet long, temporarily fixed at each airey point to form wooden wheels. (The airey points in a beam are roughly at a quarter length from each end: a homogeneous bar supported at its two airey points would have minimum deflection of the ends and minimum sag between supports.)

When all these preparations had been completed and checked the ship was rolled down into the water, the motive power being provided by the steam winches on a couple of lighters moored offshore hauling on wires making several turns round the cylindrical hull.

All went well until the vessel was almost afloat, when she suddenly stopped dead and filled with water. In spite of the precautions taken in clearing the beach of stones and debris, and in spite of the clearance given to the hull by the 9-inch rolling bands, the *Cleopatra* had impaled herself upon a rock, and it took several days to drag her clear, turn her over, pump her out and patch her up. All this, naturally, on the beach, and after a temporary repair she was put into dry-dock at Alexandria for a permanent shell repair and general check-up.

She still had to have her cabin, conning tower, catwalk, mast and rigging fitted, and somebody had to find a runner crew to man her on the homeward passage. After that, towing trials suggested a tendency towards tenderness in stability, and an extra thirty tons of ballast had to be found

N

53 The arrival of the *Cleopatra* in the Thames

and cemented into her bottom to prevent too much rolling. As has been pointed out in previous chapters, a vessel of truly cylindrical cross section has no inherent stability, and although the *Cleopatra* was built with bilge keels these were not very effective; they could not extend beyond the midships half length and had to be less than nine inches in width so as to be clear of the ground when the hull was being rolled down to the sea on its bands.

In fact, when the *Cleopatra* was at sea it was found that she hardly rolled at all and that the waves merely slid over her deck, there being very little in the way of superstructure to offer resistance to them.

Towed by the tug *Olga* she eventually left Egypt for London in July 1877. All went well in the Mediterranean, but shortly after passing Gibraltar the weather broke and developed into a full gale off the Portuguese coast. Although the obelisk remained in position the ballast became loose and eventually the towline snapped and left the *Cleopatra* adrift in the Bay. Captain Booth kept the *Olga* standing by in the hope that the weather would moderate and he could resume the tow, but eventually the *Cleopatra*'s crew signalled to inform him that they considered their charge unseaworthy, and that they were prepared to abandon ship. The *Olga* sent a boat across to the *Cleopatra* to pick up her crew but somehow, in the high seas running, the boat missed the tow and was swept away in the dark: the boat and her six crew were never heard of again.

By daybreak the tug *Olga* had lost sight of the *Cleopatra*, which drifted about until sighted by the steamer *Fitzmaurice* and towed into El Ferrol. Here the British vice-consul took charge and arranged for temporary repairs. He also arranged for a tug to be sent out from England to collect the *Cleopatra* and after a couple of weeks she set out from Northern Spain in tow of the tug *Anglia* on her last leg home, arriving in the Thames without undue incident.

Mr. Dixon, the contractor, lost heavily on the venture, for although his estimate had wisely contained certain contingency clauses, as most estimates do, he could not have anticipated the *Cleopatra* sitting on a rock during the launch and the heavy consequential repairs and dry-dock charges—to say nothing of the demurrage costs in having the *Olga* standing by eating her head off.

The salvage claim by the steamer *Fitzmaurice* for towing the *Cleopatra* into a Spanish port, with further repairs and stores, and the double trip out and home for the tug *Anglia* must have cost a fortune, probably as much as the fee for the original assignment.

After the landing and erection of the Needle the *Cleopatra* disappears from nineteenth-century history. However excavations were recently carried out near the Embankment in way of one of the small tributaries to the Thames which had long since been filled in, and in the course of the digging the workmen came across some circular frames and sections which were claimed to correspond with those of the *Cleopatra*. Presumably she had been towed into the tributary when her work had been completed and left to rot away in the mud.

Anybody wanting to start an argument among a group of sailors has only to enquire innocently whether a ship sails *on* or *in* the water. After asking the question he might as well leave the company to it, for he will receive no satisfactory answer. Ernest Bazin, however, transcended the proposition very neatly by building a ship that floated *above* the water.

His idea probably developed from an experiment carried out on a small London tug in the latter half of 1860, using discs for propulsion. This tug, the *Saucy Jack*, had her side paddles removed and replaced by a group of five disc wheels on each side. These steel discs, 14 feet diameter and ⅜ inch thick and spaced about 8 inches apart, were fitted on a hub which itself was bolted on to the paddle-shaft flanges, and the inventor's claim was that the friction between the fairly large wetted surfaces of these discs and the water would be sufficient to absorb the engine power and drive the ship. Another point put forward was that, as this friction would take some time to build up, the slack on a towrope would be taken up gradually and there would be complete absence of shock, inevitable in an orthodox radial paddle wheel where the paddles are constantly hitting the water at an angle. On trials in the Thames the tug made a scant six knots, and many nautical critics voiced the opinion that at least three of these knots were due to the tide. The trial was thereupon abandoned, the 'hamslicers' were removed and the old paddle wheels replaced.

Another idea, more practical this time, was Robert Fryer's buoyant propeller, built in 1882. This craft, called the *Alice*, can best be described as a floating steam roller. The specification reads as follows:

The Alice consists of a triangular framework resting on 3 wheels which are in the same relationship to each other as the wheels of a tricycle. These wheels are spheroidal in shape, six feet in diameter and are fitted with dome-shaped splash guards. Each sphere is a propeller, having flanges or buckets at the sides at right-angles to the vertical diameter and acting upon the water like a paddle wheel. These wheels are driven by a steam engine. At the same time, they serve as floats and are submerged at about one-sixth of their volume. Another odd feature of this vessel is that the propellers, i.e. wheels, have an iron tyre or keel, by means of which they may be made to serve as wheels and carry the vessel along a track on dry land, like a wagon.

An engine rests on the framework between the two after wheels, and this framework forms the deck, being supported on the axles of the wheels. This deck is several feet above water, and carries seats for passengers and space for the crew. Above this deck, there is a steel canopy.

The steam-roller effect was rounded off by a tall stack at the fore end, above the boiler.

While the *Alice* could be considered as a prototype for a Roller Ship she was still a very rudimentary vessel, and should really be classed as a floating steam carriage, equally at home on water as on land, and probably the first truly amphibious vessel. She was very vulnerable to severe, possibly fatal, damage from minor injury. Those three spherical floats, 6 feet in diameter, must have been made of very thin gauge material to float at only one-sixth volume immersion, and the slightest blow to one of them could cause a puncture: then, with one wheel out of three flooded, the vessel would be unstable and capsize immediately.

Another amphibious vessel, the s/s *Svanen*, plied between two adjacent but unconnected lakes near Copenhagen, and apparently made quite a name for herself.

She was built in Sweden by a Swedish enginner called Magrell in 1895, specially to carry passengers between the top end of the one lake to the bottom end of the other lake, crossing the intervening isthmus on about a quarter mile of ordinary Danish gauge railway lines.

The *Svanen* was 46 feet long, 9 feet 6 inches beam, and drew from 3 feet to 3 feet 6 inches water, and was fitted out to carry 70 passengers. In general appearance she looked like an ordinary round-the-lighthouse type of seaside motor-boat, rather beamy and blunt-ended with a striped linen canopy, and she was fitted out with a compound engine driving a propeller in the ordinary way. The hull was fitted with two axles, one forward, one aft, with conventional railway flanged wheels suitable for the local standard gauge. These axles were driven by a lay shaft, which derived its motion, through a clutch, from the main propeller shaft by chain and sprocket gearing.

Apart from the clutch lever to engage the wheels the only additional equipment required for the amphibious operation was a brake lever and a set of brakes on the axles.

The transfer of functions from boat to carriage was very simple. On the shore of each lake, at the terminal of the railway line which ran for a few feet into the water, a funnel-shaped dock was built, the narrow end being very little wider than the overall width of the ferry boat across the fenders. The boat was thus guided into alignment with the railway lines and, by working the propeller slowly ahead, the front wheels were engaged on to the metals, followed by the rear wheels. With the clutch let in the wheels would then take over the drive and run the boat across the dry land, the propeller meanwhile rotating with the engine.

Ernest Bazin must certainly have heard of the *Alice* if not the *Svanen*, as his own vessel, the *Bazin* or Navire Rouleur, was based on a similar principle: a deck supported on revolving floats. His vessel can hardly be described as a ship proper, rather as a compound of locomotive, boat and good old-fashioned seaside pier, and it was with some hesitation that I included her in my list. However she does fulfil our definition of a freak and a description will not be out of place in a review of bizarre ships.

The theory underlying the *Bazin* Roller Ship was that of a hollow wheel floating vertically in the water. If rotated it simply spun idly in the water without forward movement. If stopped spinning and pushed forward through the water, the effect was that of a blunt-ended boat. But, if rotated and simultaneously pushed through the water the wheel moved forward with very little friction. By trial and error the relationship between rotation and translation for minimum effort was established, and this was found to be the same as the rotation and speed of advance of a wheel on solid ground.

This may seem self-evident, but people who build ships know to their cost that there is nothing self-evident in naval architecture, and that designers have lost fortunes in assuming that what is sound common sense on land is necessarily so at sea.

It would seem that Bazin had anticipated Flettner's Rotor Ships *Buckau* and *Barbara* when he constructed his Roller Ship, for although the two types were at opposite extremes of the naval architectural range they both used the same principle for propulsion: the phenomenon of lift stated in Bernouilli's theorem on the flow of water around a rotating cylinder. This lift, the so-called 'Magnus Effect,' helped the *Bazin*'s rotating wheels along over the water just as much as it pushed the Rotor Ships along into the teeth of a strong wind. Incidentally the lift effect can also be used to explain the theory of the ordinary screw propeller.

Ernest Bazin, with the help of his assistant M. Parrot, had a 16-foot working model of his ship built to scale and submitted to exhaustive tank tests, and the results of these tests appear to have been good enough to induce his backers to finance the building of a full-scale experimental vessel. Plans were accordingly drawn up and work commenced in 1896 at the St. Denis works of Cail et Cie.

The vessel consisted of a large steel platform, planked over to form a deck, which was carried high out of the water on a series of hollow circular floats which were caused to revolve by means of steam machinery, while at the same time other motive power imparted suitable forward movement

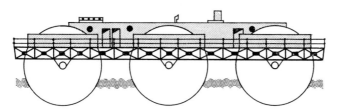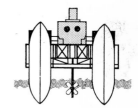

54 Roller ship *Bazin*

to the floating wheels. Under these combined influences the vessel was said to walk over the waters with a speed quite out of proportion to the small amount of energy expended.

Bazin's assistant Parrot, who carried out the investigation on the theory of the Roller Ship, calculated the power required both to rotate the wheels and to propel the vessel, and in his opinion the secret of the design lay in the speed of rotation of the rollers and their rate of translation through the water bearing a certain ratio to each other.

From the 16-foot model tests he found that to propel the vessel at **27·23** knots the rollers would have to revolve at **38·2** revolutions per minute and would require 40 h.p. per shaft. At this speed 440 h.p. would need to be applied to the screw to provide the second part of the ratio. Thus the total power required for both rotation and translation of the six wheels was 560 h.p., and it was estimated that this power would give the vessel a speed of 30 knots.

The platform, 126 feet long and 40 feet wide, was carried on a heavy steel framework with brackets at each corner and at centre, fitted with bushes to take the three driving shafts to each of which was bolted a pair of buoyant wheels. These hollow wheels were 33 feet in diameter and 10 feet wide at the hubs, and each shaft was driven by a separate steam engine. With the wheels immersed to about a third of their diameter the platform would be about 10 feet above water, high enough to be clear of normal Channel waves. Where these rollers extended through the deck splashguards breast high were fitted, the protection round the platform sides consisting of open rails.

This deck formed the ship proper: it contained accommodation for passengers and crew, bridge, boiler house, engine room and bunkers, also a small galley.

Propulsion was, inevitably, a dual arrangement, there being a 50 h.p. engine rotating each axle through transmission gear, and a 550 h.p. engine driving a propeller fitted between the two rows of wheels. This propeller was supported by a type of sternpost which also carried the rudder.

The weight of the ship was distributed as follows:

Deck and castings	130 tons
Boilers and machinery	30 tons
Coal, stores, etc.	30 tons
Six wheels with their shafts	90 tons
TOTAL	280 tons

Bazin's intention was to use his Navire Rouleur on a cross-channel service until she had established a reputation for steadiness and stability, and then to construct a larger, eight-wheeled vessel for the Western Ocean trade, fitted out as a complete passenger steamer. This proposed Atlantic vessel would have rollers 70 feet in diameter and require engines of many thousand horse power to drive her.

However apart from sundry trial trips in the Channel, in which the speed fell considerably short of the promised 30 knots, the *Bazin* does not appear to have made any impact on history.

The Roller Ship could be considered as a sort of nineteenth-century hovercraft. It might appeal to adventurous souls but it would be looked at askance by seasoned travellers, who would probably care more for creature comforts and spaciousness than for speed.

Bazin did have one good point in that it would be difficult to sink his ship other than by direct ramming, as the deck was virtually supported by six separate hulls. In the case of damage to any one roller it would be a simple matter to rotate it until the damaged area was at the top, clear of the sea. The roller could then be pumped dry and patched up or, if this proved to be impracticable, the affected shaft could be stopped and the vessel could proceed on it's sound floats.

On the other hand that wide, rather flimsy deck on the steel platform would stand little chance in a seaway: a short lumpy sea below the platform might either strip the deck planking or simply turn the ship upside down.

The title Marine Engineer covers a variety of professions nowadays: the theoretical designer, the practical engine builder, the meticulous engine tester, the glib salesman, even down to the man who machines components for marine engines. But there is only one true marine engineer— the man who looks after the engine at sea and keeps it running smoothly under all conditions of weather, temperature and loading.

Nowadays, in an era of centralised and automatic controls, the marine engineer keeps watch in an air-conditioned control room somewhere in the engine room and scans the dials and instruments from the comfort of a desk chair, while mechanical, pneumatic or electrical devices, set to predetermined temperatures or pressures, take over the functions previously undertaken by a trained engineer. The modern engineer, without having to move from his desk, is now informed by an alarm if all is not well with the machinery, and it is then his problem to decide whether he must change a valve in the main engine or a module in the data logger. He has the added satisfaction of knowing that if he cannot rectify the fault wireless telegraphy can always put him in touch with the owners or engine builders or, as a last resort, the salvage tug.

In the nineteenth century things were not so easy. The engines themselves were very often poorly designed and built on shoe-string finance without benefit of expert supervision, and engine trials were as often as not carried out on sailing day, leaving no opportunity to adjust any malalignment or correct the inevitable teething troubles. A special type of man was bred to take charge of ships' engines: in the earliest days he was only a stoker, later a mechanic and finally a qualified engineer. Once the ship was over the horizon it was up to him to keep her going without help, with no spare gear and no tools to speak of. He had no air conditioned control room to sit in and no bulkhead full of delicate instrumentation to let him know precisely how every part of the main and auxiliary machinery was behaving; he had no push-button system of starting and manœuvring the engine by relays. The Victorian engineer judged the temperatures of bearings and piston rods by feel or by smell, and manœuvring was an all-hands job, requiring considerable muscle-power and expertise.

Novelists have always had a penchant for the shaggy red-headed Scottish engineer with an affinity for strong language and strong drink, and 'having a way with engines'. In early Victorian times, having a way with engines was a very necessary qualification, and it is doubtful if many present-day engineers could start some hundred tons of paddle engine in motion on steam pressure little higher than a Manchester fog. My brief experience on side-lever and oscillating engines on the Clyde was most instructive, not only in engineering knowledge but also in the finer points of the Saxon vernacular. The drill was to flood the main engine with steam, until it issued from the snifting valves, then quickly open up the sea injection to establish a vacuum in the cylinders, as it was the vacuum which did the work. This simple process involved a lot of jumping about to a running commentary: a gruff 'See's a grup o' thon haun'le,' a querulous 'The auld . . . is no hersel' the day, Sanny,' or a plaintive 'Jest aboot ta'en the fingers aff me.'

In the early days boiler pressures and water levels were decided by intuition. As often as not the steam gauge consisted of a mercury cup: if there was some mercury still to be seen in it you were all right. If the steam pressure was too high the mercury blew out and some obliging fireman shut off the control cock and left it shut. Safe steam pressures were decided by the engineer in charge. There was no such thing as a design pressure, only an absolute maximum when the iron was stressed beyond the yield point and became so much dead material awaiting an opportunity to tear apart.

A few years ago I came across some correspondence sent in the early 1850's from one shipowner to another about a new vessel, in which the boilers were embedded in a seating of cement 'thus ensuring full steaming capacity even when the bottom of the boilers had wasted away'. Truly marine engineers were expendable in those far-off days.

Watchkeeping in a paddle engine room built in the mid-nineteenth century was a unique experience. The control station was usually at crank-shaft level, inside a neat wooden deckhouse with doors and scuttles giving on to the open deck and a nicely shaped skylight or paddle hatch on the deckhead, ensuring plenty of natural light to the running gear. Everything visible from the doorways, copper, brass, steel or mahogany, was beautifully polished and gleamed where it caught the sun. But down below in the engine room proper nothing was to be seen at all, as the daylight never penetrated below the engine entablature and it was considered unnecessary to waste good lamp oil to provide artificial light. The engineer going his rounds carried a ducklamp, which gave just about enough light to enable him to thread his way between the various masses of rotating or reciprocating machinery. None of this was railed off, and most of it was so hot that the attendant, if he valued a full complement of fingers, very soon learnt where not to put his hands.

Manœuvring the old-time paddle engines was probably the most exacting of the engineer's duties, especially as many of the smaller engines had single cranks. In modern marine steam engines each cylinder has its separate ahead and astern valve gear connected to a quadrant, and by simply shutting off the main steam, running over the quadrant to the other position and opening up the steam again, the engine can be reversed with the minimum effort.

In the single-crank paddle engine things were not so easy. There was only one eccentric pulley, set loosely on the crankshaft, which could rotate partially round the shaft and which was driven by one of two stops, the stops corresponding to ahead and astern positions. The eccentric rod driven by this loose pulley worked the main valve spindle through a hook and pin arrangement, whereby it could be lifted clear of the spindle to disconnect the valve. Both the eccentric rod and the valve spindle were provided with hand levers, and when the engine was running these levers were see-sawing up and down to the acute danger of any careless attendant.

To reverse the engine without shutting off the steam, the eccentric rod was disconnected from the valve spindle and the engine soon brought to a halt; then the valve was worked by hand to set the crank moving in the reverse rotation. After a stroke or two in the desired direction the eccentric pulley would then be driven by the opposite stop and the eccentric rod hook allowed to drop on to the valve spindle pin and work the engine automatically, as before. This manœuvre entailed careful co-ordination of both hand levers, with the ever-present possibility of stalling the engine on the bottom dead centre, the natural position for the engine at rest. To obviate this, when the engine was stopped, a small amount of steam had to be constantly blown below the piston to keep it off the bottom.

Another worry during manœuvring was the constant compromise between maintaining the vacuum and flooding the engine with water. These old engines were fitted with jet condensers in which a fine spray of sea water mixed with the exhaust steam, and the injection valve supplying this jet of water had to be under careful control. This mixture of steam and water was then pumped out of the condenser by the engine-driven air pump and discharged to the hot well. When the air pump was stopped this injection valve had to be shut immediately, or something happened.

When the steam was shut off the engine a heavy baulk of timber was placed below the crosshead or the crank at about half stroke and tommed against the base plate. This ensured that the engine would be in a suitable starting position when the engine was restarted from cold.

The above describes the background of a Victorian marine engineer in a conventional ship. If conditions were difficult, they were what the engineer had been brought up to expect and at least he was among familiar surroundings. But, just as shipowners built bizarre ships to try out their theories, so did they build bizarre marine engines to propel them, and, while some oddly shaped ships had conventional engines, many a conventional ship had a very freakish engine, a situation which was by no means peculiar to the nineteenth century. The marine engineer took them all in his stride; if he could not run them economically in the way they were built he worked away at them until they did run economically. Surely it could be said of him in his calling that difficulties were promptly dealt with, but the impossible took a little longer.

On the following pages are some of the more unusual or spectacular types of propelling engines which have at one time or another been built into ships. Most of them are paddle engines, as by the time the screw propeller became popular the marine steam engine had settled down into the conventional vertical inverted type known to engineers the world over.

This is not to say that the day of the old-time beam engine has passed. There are still a few of them scattered about the country. Four of them, all rotative-beam pumping engines, are still working away within a few miles of where these notes were written.

The North American paddle engines

The engines fitted into the North American paddle steamers plying on the Hudson River in the 1850's were every bit as odd, to a British way of thinking, as the ships they propelled, and they could aptly be described as wooden. A prominent contemporary engineer described them in the following terms:

The American steamboat engine has long been a subject of wonder to the English engineer: It is ugly, straggling and inconvenient-looking; its incompactness, want of snugness and economy of room, make it the reverse of everything we think good in a steamboat engine. It certainly made the same impression on me that it has done on all my countrymen, but it was at first sight, and at first sight only. Daily the unfavourable impression became mitigated by familiarity, and after a careful study of its details and qualities, I do not think it possible to design an engine more admirably fit for its use and purpose under the circumstances where it is applied.

In this country there is not a single engine which can be said to be entirely English and pre-eminently suited to any one purpose. The American walking-beam engine on the other hand is universal in the States and acknowledged to be the best suited to their Eastern river navigation. I think it will be admitted therefore, that the permanence of this kind of engine in the American Steamers must be held as prima facie proof of its excellence, and that it is entitled to our respectful consideration, and likely to reward our careful study.

I have examined its structure in the best workshops of America and have watched its practical working in their best steamboats. I have satisfied myself that it is cheaper in construction, lighter in weight, more economical in management, less costly in repair, more durable and better suited for high speed than any of our own engines would be. I think that for the navigation of large rivers, like those of China and India, it might be adopted with great advantage, and many of its details indeed might be adopted with great advantage in any engine.

One great advantage which the walking-beam engine possesses is that of being the only one which imposes no restraint on the engineer with regard to length of stroke or diameter of wheel. The beam engine takes up but little additional room in the ship in proportion to the increase in length of stroke, but only raises the walking beam higher above the vessel.

It will be seen that the shallowness of the water determines one material point in the structure of the engine. It becomes impossible to get a long stroke directly under the shaft, the position in which English engineers have shown themselves so anxious to place it. Driven from below the shaft from want of height, the Americans have placed their cylinder immediately forward of the crank, and with the centre of the cylinder on a level with the shaft. This necessarily throws the walking beam to more than four times the length of the crank above the level of the shaft which, with a 15' stroke, is equal to 30 feet. This also determines four times the length of the connecting rod, and four times its length for that of the walking beam. These parts are therefore in tolerable working proportion, and they necessarily determine the arrangement of the minor parts of the engine.

A major feature of these engines is very remarkable and very un-English. The floor (i.e. bedplate) and framing of the engine are of wood, but it must be remembered that wood is the American staple, as iron is ours—they prefer timber and know how to use it. We have given our preference and study in iron, but there is no doubt that their wooden framing and engine floor are well adapted to their light wooden boats and work well with this kind of engine.

The details of the engine are also throughout remarkably at variance with our improved practice; remarkably like things we have long abandoned, and at the same time well suited to the circumstances. Take for example the framing: we know that timber, weight for weight, on a moderate scale is a better strut than iron; and we know that iron is a better tie than wood. Now the framing on an engine whose work is to be done all round the circle must be prepared to stand both draw and push. The difficulty therefore of choosing between iron and wood is great. The Americans have dodged this very cleverly: they give each wood strut a companion iron tie rod—the two quite independent of each other: the iron to do all the draw and the wood to do all the push. This may seem odd and wasteful, but on consideration it turns out to be economical, purpose-like and convenient.

The struts are made of sound posts of fir unmutilated by fastenings or scarphs, and where the ends support the machinery, the cast iron block resting on the wood has simple bolt holes to receive the tie rods, which are round, and run nearly parallel with their struts. To allow also for the yielding of the wood by force and wear, a coupling is placed conveniently on each rod to be tightened by the engineer and the whole framing is kept at all times a compact and united structure.

The details of the walking beam or great working lever, are quite as interesting a study as the wooden framing. It is quite plain that this lever has exactly the same work to do as the framing on which it rests, and one can quite imagine that at one time it too was a compound trussing of wood and iron. The fault of such an arrangement would be, first, the room it would occupy and next the considerable quantity of complicated fastening required at the working points of the lever. The Americans have, therefore, made the centre portion of cast iron and the four sides of the beam, which is lozenge-shaped, form one continuous bar of wrought iron, the two diagonals of which are the cast-iron frame before-mentioned. There would be no other parts of this lever but for its having to work the air pump, and therefore a small subsidiary truss, similar in principle, is contained within. The whole of this walking beam is a fine piece of workmanship, and nicely fitted and finished.

One of the largest of this type of engine was that fitted into the steamer *New World*, built in 1849. This vessel was 376 feet long, 36 feet moulded breadth and had a depth of hold of 10 feet 6 inches. The engine consisted of a pair of huge trestles mounted on side keelsons set alongside the main keelson, and these wooden structures formed the framework to support the crankshaft on an abutment at the after end, and the walking-beam fulcrum shaft bearings on their apex. This monster engine had a single cylinder fitted between the forward legs of the trestle, 76 inches bore by 15 feet length of stroke, probably the longest marine steam cylinder ever made. Seated on a squat jet condenser, built over the centre keelson, this steam cylinder extended through the main and promenade decks almost up to the bridge deck, for a height of 24 feet. The walking beam was 26

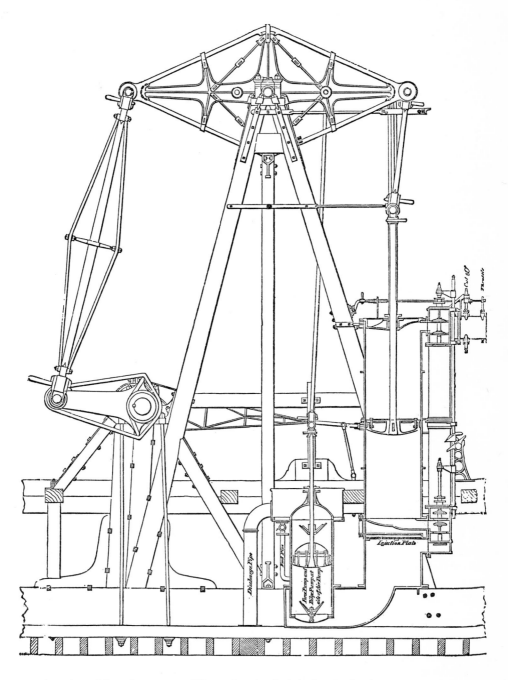

Discharge Pipe

Feed Pipe

Foot Pump and
Bilge Pump or
side of Air Pump

Ejection Plate

55 American River Steamer paddle engine (scale ¼ inch = 1 foot)

feet long and 26 inches broad at the centre bossing, and the depth of the beam at centre was about 12 feet. This engine drove a pair of side wheels 45 feet 3 inches diameter, with radial paddles 12 feet long and 3 feet wide, at 18 r.p.m., giving the ship a speed of 17 knots.

The connecting rod between beam end and crankpin was an exception to the principle regulating the rest of the structure. It consisted of a wrought-iron bar strong enough to withstand both the push and pull of the beam, and looked rather spindly compared with the bulk of the wooden framework. It was trussed against vibration by fore and aft stays on account of its enormous length, and the weight of the stays was possibly compensated by the weight of the piston and rod. In the beam engines of those days the side thrust of the piston-rod crosshead was opposed by Watt's parallel motion, as pretty a piece of mechanism as ever designed by man, but in the American steamers the piston rod carried an extension forming a rather flimsy guide rod in a bushed bracket stayed off from the wooden trestle. A similar arrangement, on a smaller scale, was fitted to the air pump. The crankshaft was an iron forging, with a cast-iron web. This web was reinforced by wrought-iron straps.

The valves were double-beat spindle valves worked by wipers on rocking shafts and appropriate lifters, there being one rocking shaft for the steam valves and one for the exhaust valves. The exhaust valve wipers were so set upon the shaft that the rising of one valve commenced the moment that the other valve closed.

The steam levers or wipers were considerably longer and were placed upon the shaft in an inclined position to each other, so that an interval occurred between the falling of the one valve and the opening of the other; during this time the steam was cut off from the cylinder, the cut-off varying from 50% to 60%.

The valve gear rocking shafts were driven through a pair of eccentrics and rods of light trellis work, working on the Boulton and Watt arrangement of a loose gab on a pin, so that the driving gear could readily be disengaged and the engine backed by hand.

This valve motion was called the 'Stevens cut-off' from the name of its inventor, and had no connection with the almost universal British Stephenson's link motion.

A point worth noting is that the *New World*, built as long ago as 1849, had her boilers supplied with forced draught from two 12 foot diameter fans driven by small steam engines.

The *New World* foundered in a most unusual way. She literally committed suicide. While under way the neck of the main connecting rod happened to snap at the beam bearing, the rod turned down round the crankpin and was driven through the bottom of the ship, and she sank in deep water.

Although this type of paddle engine reached its hey-day in the mid-nineteenth century such was its success that it was still in use in the 1930's on the New York Harbour ferry boats and, I believe, on the ferries connecting Rio de Janeiro and Nichteroy. The atmospheric exhaust and the jerky walking beams were quite a tourist attraction in the two most modern cities of the western hemisphere.

The Western River or Mississippi boatbuilders did not fit this type of engine. It was considered too expensive and heavy to use in their feather-weight paddle steamers with only a few feet depth of hold. These vessels fell into two categories, side-wheelers and sternwheelers, and the engines driving each type were basically the same. Whereas the Eastern steamer had both paddle wheels mounted on the same shaft, and in manœuvring both wheels rotated in the same direction, independent engines were fitted to each side wheel on the Mississippi steamers, so that one wheel could drive ahead with the other stopped or backed. The engine was either a two-cylinder horizontal engine in the case of the sternwheeler, with the paddle shaft supported on long timbers projecting aft from the stern precisely like a wheelbarrow, or a single-cylinder diagonal engine driving a side wheel. The principal object sought in each case was to obtain the greatest possible power out of the cheapest and flimsiest engine, and to economise still more, these engines were made to exhaust to atmosphere.

This type of engine was built and probably designed by a millwright, the engine builder of the 1850's, and reflected his knowledge and use of wood. The bedplate and framework were built up from the side keelson on solid timber supported by wooden cribwork. Where an engineer would have bolted the three separate units of the engine, i.e. cylinder, guide and main bearings, on to a cast-iron bedplate and then bolted that assembly on to the wooden framework, the American millwright simply bolted each unit into its place on the wooden frame by coach screws, trusting to the bulk of the timber bedplate to maintain reasonable alignment and position. The resulting engine was therefore crude in appearance and possibly in action, but it worked, and it was very cheap.

The crankshaft was a simple forged shaft with a cast-iron crank and, as in the Eastern engine, this crank was reinforced by a wrought-iron bar. The cylinder was a simple cast-iron barrel with four cast-iron valve chests, but the dominant feature of the engine was its immense wooden connecting

o

rod, made in three pieces, of cruciform section, reinforced by the inevitable wrought-iron tie bars and with bolted iron strapheads at the bearings. This rod, the 'pitman', could be up to 40 feet long in the larger vessels.

Probably the finest feature of this engine was its spidery valve gear, possibly an invention of the American millwright but one which compared most favourably with the contemporary lumbering valve motion fitted on British-built engines. A pair of cams were mounted on the main shaft, one a full-stroke cam to work the exhaust valves and the other a half-stroke cam (sometimes variable) controlling the steam valves, there being a

56 Mississippi River paddle steamer engine valve gear

separate steam and exhaust valve for each end of the cylinder. The form of these cams was such as to open the valve as quickly as possible, and they worked in a four-foot-square cast-iron frame which answered the purpose of the conventional eccentric strap. It communicated the motion of the cam by means of a long trussed rod to the rocking shaft sited at the centre of the cylinder. This shaft had a double wiper attached to it, and by its alternate motion it lifted in turn the valve lever at each end of the cylinder. Each lever was pivoted at the extreme end of the cylinder, and the valve stem was attached to it near the fulcrum.

Noise was prevented by a piece of leather placed between the wiper and its contact with the end of the lever. The valves themselves were either double-beat valves or what came to be known as 'relief valves', i.e. they were balanced with a small pilot valve let into the main lid, which served to equalise the steam pressure above and below the valve.

Very few of these Mississippi-type steamers had an independent feed pump, or 'doctor', and the only method of pumping up the boilers was by using the main engine-driven feed pump. When lying alongside where the paddles could not be worked, they were disengaged from the shaft by a friction strap and the main engine could then be worked on its own.

The Western steamers had light, horizontal boilers working at high pressure, from 100 lb. to 150 lb., as compared with the larger, heavier boilers in the Eastern steamers, where pressures were more conservative and varied between 20 lb. and 35 lb. These Western River-type boilers were usually a standard size, and to increase the power in a vessel more boilers were added. Furthermore the pressure quoted for a boiler as between 100 lb. and 150 lb. meant exactly what it said: the boiler being designed for 100 lb. it was considered unwise to push it beyond 150 lb. working pressure. To further complicate matters American engineers in those days had no faith in water-level gauge glasses and preferred steam and water test cocks. Taking into account the complication of feeding the boilers, of ascertaining the true water level in them and the condition of the raw river feed water with a large percentage of silt and acids in suspension, one need not be astonished at the high proportion of boiler explosions among the river steamers.

These Western steamers were managed in the most reckless fashion. Here is the description by an English engineer of a paddle steamer leaving her berth:

She was steered close inshore amongst stones and stumps of trees, where she lay for some hours to take in goods; the additional weight increased her draught and caused her to heel a good deal, and when her engines were put in motion, she actually crawled into deep water on her paddle wheels. The steam had been got up to an enormous pressure to enable her to get off, and the volume of steam discharged from the escapement-pipe (i.e., atmospheric exhaust) at every half stroke of the piston made a sharp sound, almost like the discharge of fire arms, while every timber in the vessel seemed to tremble. The numerous explosions of boilers on the Mississippi cannot excite astonishment amid such provocations as that here described.

Harking back for a moment to the Eastern River steamer with its monstrous wooden engine and its single cylinder there is still the question which has aroused endless speculation among marine engineers: how does one start a single-cylinder marine engine when the crank is on dead centre? A marine engine must not only drive a ship ahead, it must also act as a brake when manœuvring into dock or alongside a wharf, and must be capable of responding immediately to an order for ahead or astern. In the case of a horizontal or diagonal engine, as with the Mississippi side-wheelers, there was no problem as the weight of the crankweb and connecting rod brought the shaft to rest with the crank hanging down below the shaft; as in this position the action of the connecting rod made a fairly large angle with the crank there was no difficulty in getting the engine under way. But it was not so in the beam engine or in its associated type, the side-lever engine. Here the thrust of the connecting rod acted in line with the crank, and with the latter on a dead centre, i.e. vertical the resulting effect was a deadlock.

The solution to this problem was given me in the late 1920's by the chief engineer of a small paddle tug driven by a single-cylinder side-lever engine. I was a very junior member of the shipyard party attending sea trials on a motorship in the Firth of Clyde and we were taken off at the Tail o' the Bank by this small tug and conveyed to Greenock. Crowding into the engine room out of interest (and for warmth), we youngsters were intrigued by the manœuvring of the engine and naturally asked the engineer the age-old question. His reply was simple, lucid and unambiguous:

'When yer ingine is stopped, ye must keep her aff the bottom cen're by gie-ing her a wee jag o' steam wi' this haun'le here. But if she does jam on ye, jist go through thon wee door in the paddle boax and pit yer back agin the wheel, but see yer bilersuit disna catch on they paddle links or the auld ————— 'll pu' the claes aff ye. Now gie the spokes a dunt wi' yer shoother and the ingin will come aff cen're, but first make sure ye shut the steam aff her or ye'll go burling roon like a pinwheel.'

It is ironic that, although I am one of the few to whom this priceless information has been given, I still do not know the answer!

The 'Great Eastern's' engines

The main propelling engines in the *Great Eastern* were generally described in the chapter devoted to that vessel, and there is not much to add to the specification for the screw engine: a 4-cylinder horizontal opposed steam engine with 84-inch bore cylinders and a 48-inch stroke, working at 38 r.p.m. Although designed for nearly 6,000 i.h.p. this engine seldom reached 5,000 i.h.p., corresponding to a ship speed of 9 knots on screw alone. Apart from the unusual feature of the heavy slide valves being supported on rollers inside the valve chest, to carry the weight, there was nothing about this engine either in shape or in size to suggest a freak.

The connecting rods, instead of being single forgings as in the modern practice, were each composed of double bars, which also served as bolts for the top and bottom and bearing bushes, and were similar to the normal pump links fitted to the modern tramp engine. This form was common in the engines of the 1860's. The same can be said for the double piston rods

57 *Great Eastern* screw engine room

in each cylinder and the double valve rods for each slide valve. Accordingly we can dismiss the screw engine with this comment: big, yes, but not gigantic.

The screw engine room was exceedingly bare, being merely a square chamber filled by the engine which drove its own air pumps, one for each cylinder. In a modern steamer, even one that is parish rigged with barely the minimum amount of auxiliary gear, the engine room would be reasonably full of steam, exhaust, oil, water, bilge, ballast, etc., pipes, chests, pumps and incidental engines, but in this screw engine room there was nothing that did not belong to the main engine. The illustration gives an idea of the emptiness of this space, and of the size of the immense steam pipe which connected the ten boilers to the main propelling machinery. A modern high-pressure steam turbine rotor, developing the same horsepower as this huge lumbering horizontal engine, could sit quite happily inside this steam pipe.

The *Great Eastern*'s paddle engine, on the other hand, was immense, and the effect of size was possibly heightened because the engine was vertical. When the ship was under way the whole engine from cranks down to cylinders swayed to and fro. The steam oscillating engine patented by Joseph Maudslay in 1827 enabled the piston rod to work directly on to the crankshaft by having the cylinders mounted on trunnions to allow them to adjust themselves to the direction of thrust. This disposition did away with the necessity for connecting rods, crossheads and guides, and the engine was thereby shortened by the length of the connecting rod.

This paddle engine had four steam oscillating cylinders in groups of two forward and two aft, with the two air pump cylinders at the centre. These four cylinders worked two cranks, there being one forward and one aft piston rod laying on to each crank, the crankbearings being forked on one leg embracing the single bearing on the other rod. Each cylinder was 74 inches in diameter with a piston stroke of 14 feet, and this engine, designed to run at 14 r.p.m., developed 3,410 i.h.p. at $10\frac{3}{4}$ r.p.m.

John Scott Russell, the designer and builder of the engine and its four boilers, described it as follows:

It will be observed that these engines rest on four great beams which run the whole length of the 40 feet engine room. These beams rise 14 feet above the floor and are, like the rest of the internal work of the engine room, cellular bulkheads of $\frac{1}{2}$ inch plate and angle iron. These beams are about 10 feet apart, and divide the engine into three portions, viz: a pair of oscillating engines on the left, a pair of oscillating engines on the right, and the air pumps in the centre.

It will be observed that each pair of engines is coupled to a single crankpin, an arrangement in favour of which I have elsewhere avowed my strong partiality. The working of the engines is brought to the centre and they are handled from a platform immediately above the air pumps, which are worked by a crank in the intermediate shaft. The two cranks on the end of the intermediate shaft differ in no respect from the ordinary crank, and carry a crankpin on which the two engines work. It may be noticed that there is no second crank to work the paddle shafts; but instead there is a large wheel of cast iron keyed on the outer shaft, embraced by a friction strap, and into an eye of that friction strap the outer end of the crankpin works and drives the wheels. This friction strap allows the engine to be detached at will from either or both paddles.

In parenthesis it might be pointed out here that in the paddle engines of the nineteenth century the term 'intermediate shaft' was the equivalent of our modern crankshaft, and that the paddle shaft was that section outboard of the crankpin. This was logical, inasmuch as the paddle shafting assembly was composed of three separate sections: port paddle shaft, intermediate shaft and starboard paddle shaft, loosely engaging with each other through their floating crankpins, a normal feature of the paddle engines in those days which served to adjust the alignment of the shaft to the excessive wear of the outer main bearings. It will be appreciated that in the *Great Eastern* the huge cast-iron disc on the paddle shaft with its friction strap took up any malalignment in the line of shafting. Another point to note is that, as all four cylinders were solidly coupled to the intermediate shaft, it was possible to drive both paddle wheels together, or to drive one wheel only, allowing the other to trail, but it was impossible to rotate one wheel ahead and the other astern, contemporary descriptions notwithstanding.

In oscillating cylinders the bottom was cast integral with the barrel and the gudgeons: a difficult casting at any time. When the cylinder is some 16 feet long and over 6 feet in the bore it becomes a very difficult casting indeed, and there were four of them to make. The weight of one cylinder complete with its cover, piston and piston rod, was 38 tons, and this figure alone represents the approximate weight of a modern, medium-speed diesel engine developing the same horsepower as the whole of the *Great Eastern*'s paddle engine.

The two air pumps were worked from a centre crank in the intermediate shaft, as was usual in oscillating engines, and as in the days of jet condensers the volumetric ratio of steam cylinder to air-pump cylinder was about 6, the swept volume of each pump bucket would be about 110 cubic feet, requiring a crank throw of 3 feet.

The paddle wheels originally fitted were 56 feet in diameter, but when these were lost in the storm in the Atlantic they were replaced by ones of 50 feet diameter. Even this seems excessive, if the empirical formula of the day can be relied upon:

$$\frac{\text{Knots} \times 100}{\text{r.p.m.}} = \text{circumference of wheel.}$$

An unusual but practical feature in this immense engine was the toothed rack cut into the wheel circumference which, when engaged by a loose pinion, served as a turning gear. This was possibly a refinement, as the normal turning gear for any paddle engine was a pair of chainblocks on the wheel spokes, one to pull, the other to check.

The lower illustration shows a view of the paddle-engine control platform, looking forward and at about mid height of the engine room, and gives a

58 *Great Eastern* paddle engine intermediate shaft

59 *Great Eastern* paddle engine room

good idea of the spaciousness in the engine design and lack of clutter about the engine. It is unfortunate that as the visual angle of the human eye is relatively small the artist has been obliged to increase this angle by turning round and raising his head to encompass the whole of the picture. The perspective has been lost in consequence.

To emphasise the massive construction, here is how the shafting was built up, with the respective weights:

Two paddle shafts each	30 tons
One intermediate shaft	31 tons
Two cast iron discs, each	9·5 tons
Two crankwebs, each	7·5 tons

The intermediate shaft was forged by Fulton and Neilson of Lancefield Forge, Glasgow, and was satisfactory only at the third attempt. The cost of the three attempts, two of them failures, was extremely heavy, and the price worked out at about £100 per ton as forged, a ruinous figure for those days. This intermediate shaft is shown in the top illustration, set up on keelblocks after machining, and gives an excellent impression of the size and of the air-pump crank throw at the centre.

But a row of dimensions and weights does not necessarily convey an impression of sheer size, and I believe this will best be done by comparing the *Great Eastern*'s paddle engine with one of the wing engines of the *Titanic* or *Olympic*. These two triple-screw ships, built early in the present century, represent the ultimate in steam reciprocating engines, with two 4-cylinder triple expansion reciprocating engines in the wings and a central direct-drive low-pressure turbine driving the centre screw. Each wing engine developed over 15,000 i.h.p., and they were probably the most powerful marine steam reciprocating engines ever built. Developing nearly 4,000 i.h.p. per cylinder, they were indeed monster engines and were massively built, even in their details: it took three men to lift one of the nuts for the connecting rod big-end bolts.

These engines stood nearly 40 feet above the tank top—the *Great Eastern*'s paddle engine stood 52 feet above the tank top.

The outline sketches of the engines for the *Great Eastern* and the *Titanic* are drawn to the same scale for comparison, and in the former the intermediate shaft is picked out in heavy outline. Referring this shaft outline to its actual size in the engraving one can visualise the immense size of the whole engine.

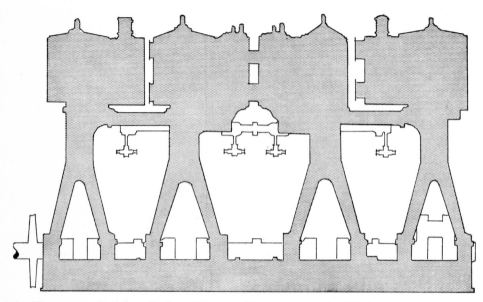

60 *Titanic*—profile of 4-cylinder triple expansion steam engine driving wing propeller, to same scale as profile of paddle engine in *Great Eastern*

The pendulum engine

This engine was the creation of that most versatile of engineers, Ericsson, whose name crops up over and over again in association with the development of the steamship: in the *Monitor*, the screw propeller, the *Ericsson* caloric ship, in addition to improvements in artillery and port installations.

Ericsson's pendulum engine must not be confused with an earlier type of land engine, completely different in every possible way, which was also known as the pendulum engine. This was built by Jabez Hornblower and Maberley in London in 1795 and was a twin-cylinder atmospheric beam engine, and the nickname 'pendulum' was given it simply because the oscillation of the arch-ended beam somewhat resembled the old-fashioned clock escapement.

In Ericsson's pendulum engine the pendulum effect was supplied by the piston itself and was similar in principle to the semi-rotary pump fitted on most pleasure craft, usually referred to as a clock pump.

The engine was constructed in 1841 by Merrick & Towne after Ericsson's designs, and was installed in the American steamer *Princeton*.

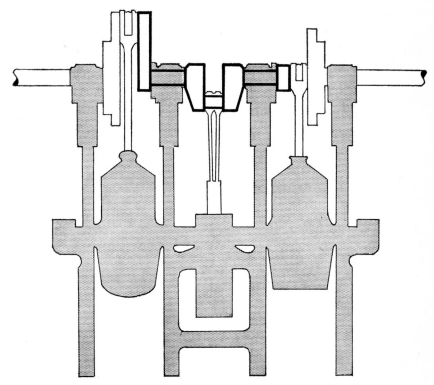

61 *Great Eastern*—profile of paddle engine, to same scale as profile of
Titanic's engine. Compare the intermediate shaft (outlined) with
actual size as illustrated (*page 182*)

Although Watt toyed with the idea in the previous century the *Princeton*'s
engine was the first (and probably the only) one built upon this plan.
Its performance made a very favourable impression on the engineers of
the day, and it is rather interesting to note that when the ship's hull was
worn out, after a modest ten years' service, a new hull was built and the
old pendulum engine installed in it.

This ship was the first ever built with the whole of the engine below
the water line, and this was designed specifically to drive a screw, as
opposed to the other screw steamers whose engines had been converted
from slow-running paddle machinery.

From an examination of the illustration it will be obvious that in the
Princeton's engine the piston moved like a door on its hinges, and that the
piston shaft, which answered to the hinge, by being extended beyond the

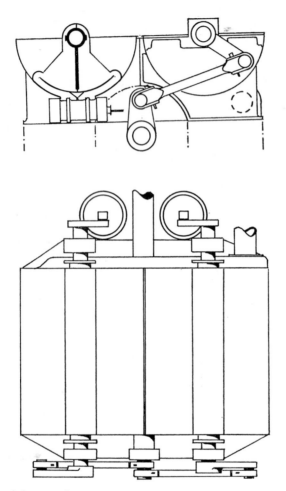

62 Ericsson's pendulum engine

steam chest gave motion by means of a bellcrank and connecting rod to the crank on the screwshaft. The piston was made tight on all sides with metallic packing; it will be noted that the piston shaft was set inside the piston hub, and the small metallic strip projecting above this boss bore lightly on the internal surface of the pipe covering the piston shaft.

There were two 'pistons', each coupled to the same crank on the screwshaft, and the angularity of the connecting rods to each other ensured that the engine could not stall on a dead centre. The valves were placed below the semi-cylinders and were worked from the crankshaft by eccentrics.

At the after end of the engine each piston shaft worked a small crank which in turn gave motion to an airpump and the usual coupled pumps: boiler feed pump, boiler brine pump, bilge pump, etc.

An unusual feature of the ship was its telescopic funnel, which could be lowered into the hull when in action.

The hydraulic jet engine

The notion of propelling a ship by the reaction from a jet of water was fairly general in marine engineering circles of the early nineteenth century, and basically the action of any type of ship's propeller depends on just this principle. The trouble was how to produce the jet, and having done so, how to control it and use it to manœuvre the ship.

The *Enterprise*, a fishing vessel built in Scotland in 1853, was one of the first to use this system of jet propulsion: 95 feet in length and 16 feet in breadth, drawing 4 feet of water, she had a large steam-driven centrifugal pump which discharged into port and starboard nozzles, and we are assured that her speed on full power was about 10 knots.

A later and more authenticated experiment was that carried out on H.M.S. *Waterwitch*, a steam sloop fitted with Ruthven's hydraulic propeller. The vessel was built by the Thames Ironworks and Shipbuilding Company in 1866 and was 162 feet long, 32 feet broad and 13 feet 9 inches depth of hold. Flat bottomed and heavily armour plated, she was double-ended, each end being fitted with a rudder.

As with the *Enterprise* propulsion was by means of a huge centrifugal pump drawing water through gratings in the bottom of the ship and delivering it to two fixed double nozzles on the ship's side.

The pump consisted of a fabricated wrought iron impeller wheel 14 feet in diameter and nearly 5 feet deep, with 12 vanes, the suction diameter being 6 feet. This wheel worked in the horizontal plane close to the ship's bottom and its driving shaft was vertical in line with the keel. In engineering idiom this pump would be referred to as a vertical pump, not a horizontal one as would be expected. The wheel worked inside an iron casing with two tangential passages, diametrically opposite each other, leading to the fixed nozzles fitted outside the ship's hull on the wind-and-water strake, only a few inches above water level. These nozzles, one port, one starboard, were three-ported brass castings protected by armour plating, there being a central port conveying the water discharge from the pump and delivering it to the forward- or aft-facing orifice as required.

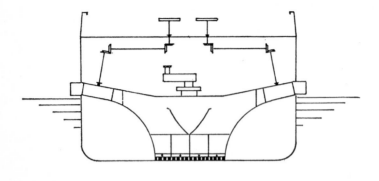

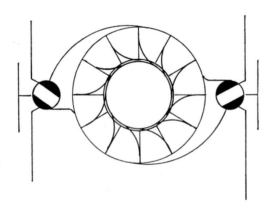

63 Hydraulic jet engine

The directional control of each water jet was through a large parallel plug cock inserted between the pump discharge and the nozzle casting on the shipside. As this passage had an area equivalent to a two-feet bore pipe these plug cocks were huge castings, and were controlled from deck through rod and bevel gear; surely one of the earliest cases of bridge control of the engine.

The water inlet to the pump was along four parallel channels, again fabricated from wrought-iron plating and angles, each inlet having a sluice valve just inside its grating to shut off or control the water inlet. As these passages were roughly 3×2 feet in section the sluice valves were evidently pretty large sliding units. In addition the outboard passages each had a sluice valve communicating with the port and starboard bilges, and it was claimed that, as the main pump could pump out the bilges, no additional bilge pump was necessary.

The pump shaft was turned with thrust collars at both ends to take the weight of the wheel, had a single crankpin, and was driven by a 3-cylinder steam engine with cylinders 38 inches diameter by 3 feet 6 inches stroke, the cylinders being placed at 120° to each other, each driving its own air pump.

As would be expected the efficiency of this hydraulic jet engine was very poor. Records of the ship's speed vary from 6 to 8 knots and, while steamer speeds in the 1860's were low compared with modern standards, an average of 7 knots was not considered suitable for a naval vessel and she came in for a lot of adverse criticism. It was claimed that had she been propelled by conventional paddle wheels the same horsepower would have given the ship a speed of 10 knots.

In passing I would like to comment on the rather sinister observation in the description of the pump: 'the side waterways leading from the ship's bottom to the main pump are furnished with sluices so that they can be made to take their supply from the bilge, and this being the case, other bilge pumps are rendered unnecessary.' In most merchant ships of the world it is a requirement of the Classification Societies for the main condenser circulating water pump (or the main cooling water pump in the case of motorships) to be fitted with an emergency bilge injection valve, i.e. a suction valve situated in the engine-room bilge with a bore at least two-thirds the area of the main sea suction. In the event of heavy leakage in the machinery space the flooding can be kept under control by opening this bilge injection valve, closing the main sea injection, and using the circulating pump as a bilge pump. To enable this operation to be carried out in safety the bilge injection valve is made non-return, i.e. while the bilge water can pass through it into the pump the water in the pump casing cannot flood back into the bilge.

All this is theory: in forty years' experience of ships and their engines I have never heard of a case where this bilge injection valve was ever used, or had occasion to be used. The circulating pumps for main condensers are constructed to move a huge volume of sea water at very little pressure differential, they are not made to suck water from the bilges, and the latter would need to be quite deep before the injection valve opened, by which time the pump engine would be under water and out of action. However in the case of the *Waterwitch*, where sluices were used both to shut off the sea water and open the bilge injections, any attempt to pump the bilges could place the vessel in a very dangerous condition indeed. The four passages leading to the pump suction each had a sluice valve the size of a window. The grooves for these sluices would inevitably fill up with barnacles and marine growth and prevent them from closing efficiently, and when it came to opening up the bilge sluices the sea would simply rush in and flood the ship, pump or no pump.

One can only hope that the ship was equipped with a good general service pump, the donkey pump of Victorian days, which usually did duty as a bilge pump while ostensibly serving as a wash-deck pump, and so kept the Admiralty happy.

The caloric engine

Engineers in the early part of the nineteenth century were very much preoccupied with caloric, a mysterious element obtained from fire, which held the same place in their philosophy as did electricity with a later generation of thinkers. Caloric could be used to drive an engine in much the same way as steam, but no boiler was needed and therefore no water was required.

Caloric was, in fact, nothing other than hot air and it was no substitute for steam, as several inventors found to their cost. But in the early days of steam, before the laws of thermo-dynamics were understood or even formulated, and when the safety not only of the engine house but of a whole factory lay in the hands of an uneducated and untrained stoker, boiler explosions with attendant loss of life were an everyday occurrence. Although the various authorities were concerned at the incidence of explosions nobody knew of a positive way to prevent them, other than by prohibiting the use of steam altogether, putting the clock back, as it were; it therefore became the business of a number of inventors to find some safer type of prime mover.

Sir George Cayley experimented with the caloric engine without getting very far, but the Reverend Dr. Robert Stirling in 1827 designed and patented a hot air engine, using a regenerator, which showed a reasonable promise of success. One of his engines, built in 1845, with a cylinder diameter of 16 inches and a stroke of 4 feet, gave an output of 50 i.h.p. at 80 r.p.m. with a very high thermal efficiency. Poor workmanship considerably reduced this efficiency, and the coal consumption ran out at 2·7 lb. per b.h.p. per hour. This engine suffered the usual fate of hot air engines: the cylinder burnt out after a couple of years.

Several inventors toyed with the idea of a caloric engine: Wilcox, Francis Calvert, Philander Shaw, even the great Dr. Joule himself, but it was Ericsson, that very versatile engineer, who brought the engine before the public in a most spectacular way.

Now the caloric engine bears the same relationship to our sophisticated gas turbine as the steam reciprocating engine does to the steam turbine; our gas turbine is simply a rotary caloric engine working on the constant pressure cycle, the expansion of the air being brought about by the heat from the fuel burnt in a separate chamber. The caloric engine worked on a variant of the Carnot cycle. Its pressure/volume diagram or indicator diagram gave a very narrow area corresponding to a small amount of work done per revolution in relation to the large amount of heat put into the engine.

Assuming the hot air to be introduced into the cylinder at the top of the stroke it would expand isothermally at constant temperature, drawing heat from the cylinder bottom, the supply of heat being shut off at about half-stroke (cut off 50%), the hot air would then expand adiabatically to a larger volume at lower temperature. On the upstroke the piston would compress the air isothermally at constant temperature, giving off heat in a cooler to about half-stroke when it would be compressed adiabatically to the original temperature and volume, thus completing the cycle. It will be noted that the area of the indicator diagram will be contained by the expansion-compression curves for isothermal and adiabatic ranges, and, as the inclination of these two curves is small, the total area per revolution, hence the work done, is small.

Dr. Stirling recognised this aspect of the cycle, and introduced his regenerator to absorb a large amount of the heat given up by the exhaust air and return it to the incoming air, thus widening the area under the indicator curve. Stirling's engine worked on the closed cycle at constant volume, while Ericsson's engine worked at constant pressure, there being little to choose between the two cycles on theoretical grounds.

Ericsson's caloric engine, like all hot air engines, required a working cylinder and a smaller cylinder which served as a compressor or displacer and which constituted a parasite load on the engine similar to the centrifugal air compressor in the modern gas turbine. This displacer compressed the air, forcing it through the regenerator, a fairly large receiver filled with compressed wire mesh, where it absorbed a certain amount of heat before entering the working cylinder, the bottom of which was kept at a dull red heat. Here the already warm air expanded quickly and forced the piston

P

upwards, doing work on the crank. When the piston reached the top of its stroke the slide valve released the hot air back through the regenerator, where some of its heat was given up, and the air continued through a water-cooled coil to give up most of the remaining heat.

Carnot's cycle was thus satisfied in that the difference between the highest and lowest air temperatures was as great as possible inside the engine: $\frac{T_1 - T_2}{T_1}$. As would be expected, the working pressure in a hot air engine could not be very high, and this would result in a large diameter cylinder. Furthermore, owing to the complication of heating the cylinder, it was made single acting, and the added load of a heavy displacer or compressor for each stroke made for a large amount of machinery for very little work done. In one of Stirling's engines the specific weight came out at $7\frac{1}{2}$ tons per b.h.p.

Having experimented with one or two caloric engines Ericsson, in 1853, designed a marine engine on this principle and fitted it in the paddle brig *Ericsson*. This vessel was 250 feet long, 40 feet beam and 26 feet 6 inches depth of hold. She had paddles 32 feet in diameter and was probably the first mechanically propelled vessel ever built without a funnel, there being merely two small stubby vent pipes on deck to carry away the fumes from the furnaces situated below the engine cylinders. This engine had 4 working and 4 displacer cylinders, the working cylinders holding an all-time record for being the largest ever built, being 14 feet diameter with a stroke of 6 feet, while the compressor cylinders measured 11 feet 5 inches bore with the same stroke, the working and compressing pistons being attached to opposite ends of the same piston rod.

Each working cylinder, being open-ended, was single acting only, and the 4 cylinders were coupled to separate cranks, placed at 90° to each other, giving the crankshaft a speed of 9 r.p.m.

These engines were built by Hogg and Delamater of New York, and were designed to give 600 s.h.p. on 8 tons of coal per day. On trials, however, they developed 300 s.h.p. only on 16 tons per day, and the vessel returned to her builders for modifications. A second trial showed no improvement, and the owners thereupon removed the caloric engines and replaced them with conventional steam engines.

I would like to revert to these immense cylinders and to point out that even today, with all our modern and sophisticated techniques, it would be extremely difficult to bore out an open-ended solid-bottomed cylinder 14 feet in diameter. And that is assuming that a sound and homogeneous casting had been produced at the foundry; in 1853 the Americans had no modern machinery at their disposal, and few facilities for pouring such wide and heavy castings. In a boring mill the cylinder has to be well clamped down to the table to prevent movement under the cutting action of the tool, and the clamping and chocking inevitably distort the cylinder, especially at the mouth. Thus, while the bore may be true at the bottom, it will most certainly be oval higher up.

The inside of the cylinder walls in well finished engines were honed smooth by means of lead shoes impregnated with emery and oil, but this operation would only remove the machining marks; it would not correct ovality or barrelling of the cylinder. The fact that these monster engines ever worked at all, with their inherent deficiencies, their large cylinder and valve clearances and their pistons fitting the cylinders only where they touched, has always been a wonder to me.

A last point, and one upon which I must confess failure—I have never been able to find out how one started a caloric marine engine such as the one under review. It took about two hours to get the four cylinders up to working heat, but then it still had to be started to commence the cycle. By definition this cycle started with compressed air at high temperature, but history does not say how this air was first compressed, as the displacers or compressors were themselves worked from the main shaft. The early semi-diesel or hot bulb engines, after having their cylinder covers duly heated by a blow lamp, were started by a quick spin of the flywheel, but what would suffice for an engine with a 6-inch cylinder bore would not necessarily hold for one with 14 feet bore and weighing over a hundred tons. It is possible that being brig-rigged with a full suit of sails the vessel was taken to sea under sail, and that the paddles would be rotated slowly by the action of the moving water, thus starting the compressor pistons pumping.

The ether engine

Early in the nineteenth century Sir Humphry Davy had suggested the use of a volatile liquid which would be boiled off by the low heat of exhaust steam and used expansively in an engine. The idea was to have a two-stage steam engine, with a normal boiler supplying steam to an engine cylinder, exhausting into a tubular condenser. This condenser in turn would contain the volatile liquid, absorbing heat from the waste steam and in its turn supplying a vapour under pressure which would be used in a second cylinder of the engine, finally exhausting to its own condenser.

In 1830, the problem was taken up by Ainger and further developed by du Trembley. The final touches were given by MM. Arnaud and Touache of Marseilles, who fitted out an engine on this dual principle in one of their vessels. This was an iron schooner-rigged vessel with an auxiliary screw driven by a 70 n.h.p. steam engine, of such size that she could carry 100 passengers in addition to 230 tons of cargo. The volatile medium was sulphuric ether, a toxic and inflammable substance.

The engine had two cylinders, only one of which ran on steam. This cylinder took steam from the boiler and exhausted it to the special condenser, the cooling medium for which was the ether circulating in tubes, and a good vacuum was formed below the piston (in the 1850's, the vacuum provided as much power as the steam, i.e. this was still the transition stage of the atmospheric engine). The residual heat from the exhaust steam vaporised the ether which, in its turn, was expanded in the second cylinder, escaping into its own condenser and forming its own type of vacuum.

The steam/ether condenser was unusual inasmuch as the run-of-the-mill steam engine used a jet condenser, a simple closed tank with a jet of water to condense and mix with the steam. The new condenser required both liquids to be kept separate, and the ether was made to flow through a nest of tubes around which circulated the exhaust steam from the first cylinder. This condenser, in fact, formed a tubular flash boiler for the second stage of the engine.

The French government appointed a commission to report on the performance of the ether engine but the findings, although favourable, do not ring true to the practised ear. The engine was first run as a normal two-cylinder steam engine, and the coal consumption noted; it was then run on the dual cycle and the second consumption compared with the first. Coal consumption on steam alone was given as 9·5 to 9·9 lb./h.p./hour, while that on the combined steam/ether cycle showed a figure of 2·5 lb./h.p./hour. In true French *fonctionnaire* style the amount of coal shovelled into the furnaces over a strictly determined period of time was measured in kilogrammes to two places of decimals and equated to the figure for horsepower as supplied by the designers. This figure, incidentally, was given by the following formula for a jet condensing engine:

$$NHP = \frac{D^2 \times \sqrt[3]{S}}{47}$$

This gave a purely nominal horsepower only, and was based on an assumed m.e.p. of 7 lb./square inch. Without the true m.e.p. for both the steam and ether cycles the formula was valueless as a criterion for consumption.

In the event, the marvellous consumption given by the ether/steam cycle of 2·5 lb./h.p./hour was merely an average figure for a normal steam engine of the period.

There were certain disadvantages attendant on the use of ether in a steam engine, the main one being that of keeping the pipe joints absolutely gastight. It was impossible to keep piston and valve glands tight, and even in the present day the only practical way of keeping a sliding joint gas proof is to fit an oil sealed lantern gland under a higher pressure than the gas in question. This method, of course, was not available in the 1850's.

In two vessels built at Nantes for the Atlantic service and fitted out with du Trembley's ether engines the ether was discontinued in the *Jacquard* and never used in the *Arago*. It was found impossible to keep the gas joints tight, as the common jointing medium of the day, red lead putty and wire gauze, was not suitable for such a subtle gas. The *Jacquard* lost between 100 and 150 litres of ether a day, and the engineers had to use Davy safety lamps in the engine room. Another ether engined vessel, *La France*, caught fire at Bahia and became a total loss, it being impossible to approach her on account of the danger from exploding gas bottles.

The hydrocarbon vapour engine

This was an engine developed by Yarrow in 1887–8 to propel river launches and light craft generally, and it consisted essentially of a steam engine driven by the pressure of gas given off by a petroleum distillate.

The propelling machinery, placed in the stern, consisted of an ordinary direct acting inverted steam engine with the usual link motion, feed and bilge pumps. The vapour generator, or boiler, was situated immediately behind the engine and consisted of a copper coil contained within a sheet-iron dome, below which was placed a perforated iron ring to serve as a Bunsen-type burner.

The fuel was kept in a 40-gallon tank in a bow compartment, with a gas-tight bulkhead. This tank communicated with the engine feed pump by means of a pipe outside the hull placed alongside the keel, and the pump delivered to the bottom of the generator coil; the vapour, after passing through the engine, was condensed in a return pipe, also alongside the keel, back into the fuel tank. The generator copper coil was heated by by-passing some of the vapour in it to the Bunsen-type burner below it and igniting it. The hydrocarbon vapour therefore served both as fuel and as working medium in the engine.

To start up from cold was a matter of a few minutes. Two hand-pumps were fitted alongside the engine, the one on the port side having its suction at the tank with its delivery to the feed pump discharge: by working this hand pump fuel could be pumped into the bottom of the coil. The hand pump on the starboard side forced air into the top of the tank which became charged with fuel and passed back through a small pipe to a pilot jet in the main burner.

To start the launch the pilot jet was first supplied with fuel-enriched air and ignited, gradually heating the copper coil. When this was judged hot enough a few strokes of the fuel hand pump forced fuel into the coil from the tank, which in turn flashed into vapour ready to drive the engine. By opening the by-pass valve, part of this vapour was led into the burner and started a continuous cycle, which was automatic in action. As soon as the main burner was lit and the engine started the main feed pump took over the fuel supply and the hand pumping could be stopped.

This engine, fitted in a launch 36 feet long by 6 feet beam, gave a speed of 7 to 8 miles per hour and, together with its generator, weighed only 650 lb.

The claims made by the promoter were, apart from its light weight, that it required no boiler or coal bunkers, that the engine and fuel tank occupied those parts of a vessel which were of least use for passengers or cargo and were very much cleaner, and that the working costs were no higher than those of a coal burning steam plant. Also that, as the boiling point of petroleum spirit was considerably lower than that of water, the amount of heat lost by radiation would be less; finally that the engine could be got under way in five minutes.

What was not mentioned in the claim was the very great danger of explosion and fire from leaky joints or from vapour escaping from piston and valve glands, and it is doubtful if this hazard was fully realised in those days.

The hydrocarbon engine

The steam engine of the 1860's was suitable only for medium-sized and large passenger ships, or possibly for tugs. Even after several decades of research and development it was still far too heavy for small craft. The massive engine and boiler, with their voluminous bunkers and stokehold, occupied the best part of a small vessel, leaving little space for passengers and none for cargo.

In desperation the Victorians cast about for some means of utilising the power latent in all fuels other than by burning them in a boiler: such as internal combustion instead of external combustion, and by a lucky chance this fuel was just coming on to the market.

Petroleum had been known for hundreds of years as a sort of natural curiosity, like geysers, lava, marsh gas, etc., which happened in a fortuitous manner in places remote from civilisation, and it was not until the first oil tube-well was sunk at Titusville, Pennsylvania, in 1859 that 'rock oil' became a commercial commodity, and could be used like coal or gas.

This petroleum produced a large number of distillates and in the early years the terms petrol, paraffin and petroleum were used indiscriminately for the same liquid. On the Continent petrol was sometimes used to describe lamp oil, while the paraffin as sold contained a certain amount of volatile hydrocarbons and could therefore cause an explosion. Even today the harassed motorist crossing Europe will need to juggle with variations of the words for essence, naphtha, benzine and gasoline when he stops for petrol, but in Victorian times the design engineers neatly side-stepped the difficulty and called it hydrocarbon.

Otto and Langen in 1867 and Hock in 1873 developed a low-power gas engine working on a mixture of petrol and air drawn into the cylinder and ignited by a constant flame burning outside the cylinder. As a prime mover, this engine was most inefficient, the power derived from the gas explosions being hardly sufficient to turn the flywheel; it was the Brayton petrol engine which started the motor industry in America in 1876, not only for land machinery but also for river launches.

In the reckless years of the early steam engines, when appalling risks were taken by engineers and their attendants through sheer ignorance of the basic principles, death from explosion was an occupational hazard for all those in charge of engines, and when these men took over the working of gas and petrol engines using highly volatile fuel this risk was considerably increased. The Brayton engine, however, by forming and igniting its petrol-air mixture inside the cylinder was inherently less dangerous than its predecessors, and may be considered as the prototype of the petrol engine.

The early Otto and Langen engines worked on the Lenoir cycle, in which the air-petrol mixture was drawn into the cylinder at atmospheric pressure on the beginning of the downward stroke, the inlet valve closing

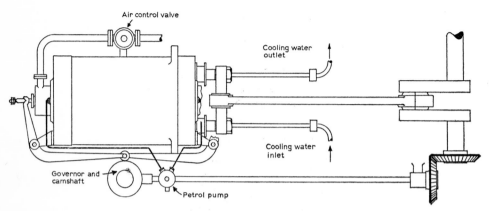

64 Hydrocarbon engine, section through cylinder

at about 30° after top centre. The mixture was then ignited by a small flame blown into the cylinder from an outside source through a small non-return valve in the head, a very hit-and-miss arrangement indeed. This cycle made for a very inefficient engine because only a small quantity of fuel could be burnt per stroke, no matter how rich the mixture.

The Brayton engine worked on a modified cycle, the air being forced into the cylinder by a compressor, but its principal interest from the historical point of view is that it contained a number of features which were thought to have been 'invented' in our modern diesel engines some 50 years later. It was a two-stroke engine (the Lenoir cycle would not operate on a four-stroke engine), it was also double acting in that the piston was powered from both sides, and it had a water-cooled piston, with telescopic supply and return pipes through its piston rods. It also had the novel arrangement of its valves being worked by cams on a rotating camshaft instead of by eccentrics on the crankshaft.

The engine itself was built on the lines of a steam engine so far as the running gear was concerned, there being a layshaft driving the governor and camshaft through bevel gearing; this layshaft also drove a small petrol supply pump, with discharge to the inlet valve casing at each end of the cylinder.

The cylinder itself had water-cooled heads into which fitted separate inlet and exhaust valves, the lower cover also having a pair of stuffing boxes and glands for the double piston rods which were themselves water cooled, and which connected to a bridle contianing a crosshead for the connecting rod top-end.

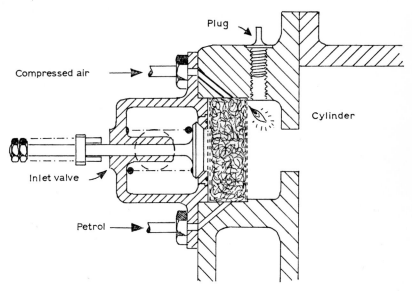

65 Hydrocarbon engine combustion chamber

The shaft drove a double-acting air pump or compressor which discharged into a receiver built around the working cylinder, the compressed air from the receiver being delivered to each inlet valve as required.

The cylinder head was constructed with a vaporiser or mixing chamber with a full opening on the outside into which fitted the inlet valve, and a restricted opening into the cylinder. This vaporiser was half-filled with teased asbestos compressed between two perforated steel plates and several layers of wire gauze as a prevention against a back-flash from the cylinder into the mixing chamber. A connection from the fuel pump discharged a steady quantity of petrol into the vaporiser, which saturated the wad of asbestos, forming with the compressed air flowing through it into the cylinder a highly combustible mixture.

Ignition was by a pilot petrol vapour flame inside the vaporiser, which was kept alight at all times. A small bore pipe from the compressed air receiver led to one side of the asbestos wad and formed a pilot jet of petrol-air mixture into the pre-combustion space. By removing a plug leading into this space the pilot jet could be ignited by a taper.

The running of this engine was very similar to that of the steam engine: the closing of the inlet valve corresponded to the cut-off, the exhaust being expelled on the return stroke, and the governor controlling the inlet valve

Q

cam to modify the speed. The speed itself was only about 200 r.p.m., with a consumption of ·7–·8 lb./h.p./hour, and these conditions were not materially improved until 1886 when Daimler brought out his high-speed, low-consumption petrol engine using the Otto cycle with high compression and a hot tube in a pre-combustion chamber.

Direct acting steam engines

The original marine steam engine, developing as it did from the old atmospheric engine, was essentially a beam engine and, in association with its boiler(s), required more than its fair share of space and weight in the early steamers. This simple beam engine, with its variants of the grass-hopper and the side-lever engines, eventually gave way to the direct acting engine which was applied to a slow-running paddle shaft. To provide the required power at very low steam pressures (15–25 pounds per square inch) the working parts had to be made very large and heavy. The original concept of working a rotating crank by a reciprocating piston had been developed along different lines by many inventors and engine-builders. The 1850's, when steam was getting into its stride, were the Golden Age of engineering, when inventors were ten a penny and there was plenty of capital to finance the most outrageous schemes.

There were five main types of direct acting paddle steam engines: the gorgon, oscillating, double-crosshead, steeple and siamese. Gorgon engines were those which had the connecting rod between the piston rod and the crank, and as such have persisted in a refined form up to the present; they are, in fact, the only type of steam reciprocating marine engine in use today. The gorgon engine, however, was not at all popular in the 1850's, for in those days it was still considered necessary to have the engine sited directly below the paddle shaft, in a vertical position. This entailed a very short stroke with a correspondingly larger diameter of cylinder to obtain the power, and with a greater loss of steam in the clearance spaces. The alternative, to keep the stroke longer, meant having the paddle shaft situated high on the deck, with large diameter paddle wheels. Here again in the days of radial paddles, i.e. with fixed wooden floats, these had an excessive velocity in entering and leaving the water, with consequential waste of energy in throwing the water astern instead of driving the ship forward. In fact in one Australian paddle steamer the wheels were of such extraordinary size that the paddle shaft was placed on what would then be described as the awning deck, and the passengers walking along the main deck had to duck underneath the shaft.

The neatest solution to this problem of the long connecting rod was the oscillating engine, first brought into favour by Penn. This engine

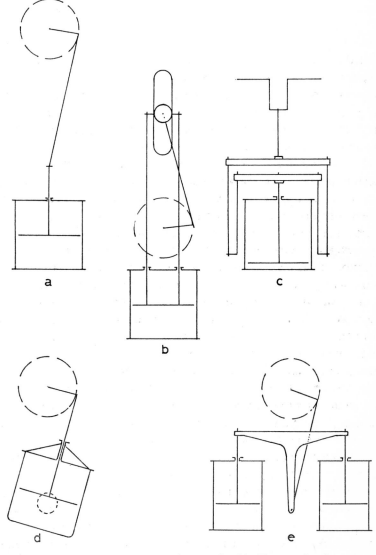

66 Paddle engine basic types: (a) gorgon, (b) steeple, (c) side crosshead,
(d) oscillating, (e) siamese

dispensed completely with the connecting rod and had its piston rod coupled direct to the crank, the cylinder rocking back and forth on a pair of trunnions which also acted as steam inlet and exhaust pipes. The alignment of the moving parts in the cylinder was maintained by having a deep piston and a conical cover with a heavy gland bush. (The oscillating engine had one cover only, the cylinder being bottomed, i.e. cast in one piece.)

This engine was immensely popular in paddle steamers and was still evident on the Clyde in the 1930's, as smooth-running as the proverbial sewing machine.

Another type of short engine was the double-crosshead design, produced by the firms of Bury and Fawcett. This engine stemmed directly from the side-lever design. The vertical piston rod drove a yoke with side rods depending from its ends, each side rod engaging in a guide and crosshead alongside the cylinder. The connecting rod was forked, the single end being coupled to the crank, and each forked end coupled to a side crosshead. This engine was never very popular as the complicated linkage made for added expense and maintenance.

A fourth type of direct acting engine was the steeple engine, or in a modified form, the table engine. In this type the connecting rod was fitted above the crank. In general the steeple engine piston had a pair of long piston rods which extended one on each side of the crankshaft to a crosshead high above the engine, from which depended the connecting rod, coupled to the crank. The crosshead guide usually consisted of a roller running in a cast-iron track, rather in the shape of a steeple top, and the similarity was enhanced by the sloping framework of the engine about this track. If the crankshaft, instead of being *above* the cylinder had been fitted *below* it, the engine would have become a table engine.

The steeple engine, in spite of its height above the shaft, was fairly popular for river steamers but not, apparently, for deep sea vessels. A variant of this engine was extensively used in the old donkey pump, as it had the advantage of both reciprocating motion and circular motion. The donkey pump, as originally fitted and still evident in some very old tramps, had a single steam cylinder wherein the piston rod worked a 'banjo' which encircled the crankshaft, and extended into a pump rod beneath the engine. The reciprocating motion of the banjo worked the pump bucket and, through a short connecting rod, drove the crankshaft to provide power to turn the main engine during overhaul.

The last type of direct acting engine was Maudslay's siamese or double-

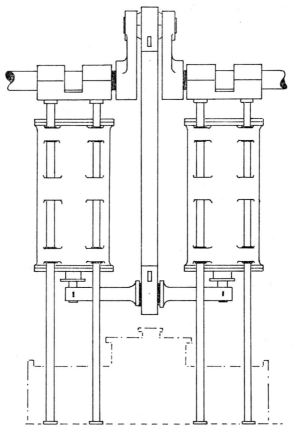

67 The inverted-siamese-table engine (valve and pump gear omitted)

cylinder engine, not to be confused with the compound engine, as steam had not yet attained sufficient pressure to be used in compound expansion. Instead of using one large steam cylinder the siamese engine used two smaller ones, with the pistons in each working together on a common T-shaped frame. Each piston rod was coupled to one end of the T crossbar, and the common crosshead and guide was at the bottom of the T vertical bar, between the two cylinders. From this crosshead the connecting rod extended to the crank in the usual way. This arrangement involved the use of a low condenser which the air pump could not always drain, and the pitching and rolling of the vessel, by causing the water to run from end to end, sometimes caused the air pump to choke with water, resulting in fracture.

While the siamese engine was unusual, even for those early days, a still more unusual engine developed from it and was fitted in the steamer *Helen MacGregor*, built by Forrester for the Hull and Hamburg Line. This engine had two cylinders 42 inches in diameter by 4 feet 6 inches stroke, and developed 220 i.h.p. at $23\frac{1}{2}$ r.p.m. The engine specification reads as follows:

The engine consists of two inverted cylinders standing each upon four strong wrought-iron columns which rest on and are secured to the foundation plate, and which, passing through suitable bosses on the sides of the cylinders, support the entablature plate and crank pedestals above. The cylinders are placed athwartships, with their stuffing boxes below them, and at a sufficient height from the bottom of the vessel to allow of the main crossbar, which connects together the two piston rods, working the full length of its stroke below them. The power is transmitted directly from the main crossbar below to the crank above the cylinders, by the connecting rod. The two piston rods and the connecting crossbar are further secured and made to work uniformly together by means of a strong vibrating frame of cast iron, forming part of the parallel motion, and which, with side levers, serves also to work the air pump as well as the feed, bilge and brine pumps.

The cylinders have loose covers at each end, and from the upper ends the pistons are accessible without the intervention of the piston rods, so that there is double space for examining and adjusting them without disturbing the lower covers or disconnecting any of the working parts of the engine.

All the above direct acting engines, having their cylinders on or near to the bottom of the ship, suffered from a common defect: the danger of flooding back from the condenser. In those days of jet condensers, where the circulating water mixed with the exhaust steam, it was only too easy for the water to wash back into the cylinder and either stop or damage the engine, either by cracking the steam cylinder or the air-pump barrel.

These, then, were the bizarre ships and marine engines of the nineteenth century; not all of them, of course, but most of them. In general they were costly failures and they ruined designers, builders and owners alike, and yet . . . they all had something, a germ of an idea which with a little more luck and a lot more capital, or possibly in a different setting or another age, might have blossomed into an accepted type of ship. After all, hovercraft and hydrofoils did not evolve naturally from the main stem of merchant shipbuilding, they were created on the drawing board. Nevertheless, successful or no, these bizarre ships by their sheer audacity have woven some welcome coloured patterns into the drab material of conventional naval architecture.

Unusual ships were not necessarily confined to the nineteenth century; our present century had its share: the wood and canvas conversions of cargo vessels into 'men of war' in the 1914–18 war and again in 1939–45; Flettner's rotor ships *Buckau* and *Barbara*, the latter still sailing the high seas with her towers removed; the arc-form vessels, the corrugated ships, the concrete barges, the off-shore oil rigs, *et al*. But these were not freaks from our point of view, these modern oddities were designed by professionals for hard-eyed shipowners to fulfil a special purpose and they had none of the naive charm of their ancestors of the previous century.

Earlier in the book I had speculated on the possibility of some of the ideas put forward by the amateur ship designers being adopted by professional shipbuilders in subsequent ships and it might now be pertinent to subject our list of bizarre vessels to a quick re-appraisal of their salient features. The argument holds good even if these innovations had lapsed and been re-invented and re-introduced into modern steamers and motorships. The North American river steamers cannot be questioned, their number, ubiquity and above all the romance surrounding them tell of their success. A ship type that has run to three generations without basic change just cannot be written off as an experiment.

Ericsson's awkward and uncouth Monitors justified their existence and developed into the battleships of the Twentieth Century simply because they were designed on sound principles, offering minimum target area with maximum firing angle to the existing warships of the 1860's. The cigar ships failed as merchant vessels, in spite of their ideal shape for sailing on, through or below the sea, and the Winans brothers just had to accept the incontrovertible fact that a vessel that cannot carry freight or passengers at competitive rates is of no earthly use to a shipowner. Circular ships, as might have been expected, came to naught simply because, considered as sea-going vessels and not just as stationary gun platforms, they were too slow and unmanageable.

The twin hulled ships had a mixed reception, even among professional shipbuilders and designers, and after a hundred years it is difficult to determine the travelling public's reactions to them or obtain any idea of their running costs as compared with those of the conventional Channel packets of similar size. The fact is, the design was not continued, and present-day catamarans in our yacht clubs stem directly from their prototypes in the South Seas.

While the true jointed ships died in infancy, the idea of a hinged vessel lingered on into the middle of the twentieth century when it was revived as an articulated ship, in two sections permanently joined together by a hinge mechanism. However, here the similarity ends: the jointed ship undulated over the waves because she was hinged, while the twentieth century model was hinged to allow her to undulate over the waves and so avoid excessive strains in her hull members.

The submarines need no mention here. With their sinister connotations they have justified only too well the hard work and grave risks incurred by Garrett, Nordenfelt and the early pioneers, and one may well wonder if the world is, in fact, the better off for their invention.

Bessemer missed the bus with his swinging saloon ship through a combination of bad luck and bad management. Less ballyhoo and softening up of the travelling public while the ship was fitting out, and more hard work put into the saloon mechanism before she was commissioned and we might have had swinging saloons in our present day Channel steamers. As it is, the experiment was still-born, the saloon never swung. But Bessemer's fortune was not spent in vain; if it achieved nothing else, it brought home to shipowners and designers alike the salutary fact that their passengers expected a higher standard of comfort than that hitherto provided. Until then the travelling public had meekly accepted what the shipowner offered in way of food and accommodation, and in bad weather sea-sick passengers were confined to a stuffy, smelly cabin below deck. As W. S. Gilbert put it:

> *crossing the Channel and*
> *tossing about in a steamer from Harwich—*
> *Which is something between a large bathing machine*
> *and a very small second class carriage.*

The swinging saloon was an attempt to alleviate the worst of the discomforts attendant on sea travel, and it pointed the way to the stabiliser fins and tanks in our modern steamers. In an indirect way it also hinted at the sun deck, the Lido bar and the swimming pool, with the suggestion that the passenger might possibly wish to enjoy the voyage instead of merely enduring it.

The fact that very few of the vessels described in the book made any impact on the general public is evidence enough of their failure; to have one's achievements condemned by history is bad enough, to be ignored is positively fatal to the inventor. Ships must be designed and built by professionals, the traditionalists, if they are to earn their keep, and this was more so even in the nineteenth century with its sharper distinctions between profession and trade. But one likes to think that in an age when the amateur boat builder was dismissed with a sniff, some of his ideas rubbed off on to the professionals. After all, it is the spectator who sees most of the game.

Index